WITHDRAWN

HARVARD LIBRARY

WITHDRAWN

# Views from a Hermitage

# Views from a Hermitage

## *Reflections on Religion in Today's World*

RICHARD W. KROPF

LEXINGTON BOOKS

A division of
ROWMAN & LITTLEFIELD PUBLISHERS, INC.
*Lanham • Boulder • New York • Toronto • Plymouth, UK*

LEXINGTON BOOKS

A division of Rowman & Littlefield Publishers, Inc.
A wholly owned subsidiary of The Rowman & Littlefield Publishing Group, Inc.
4501 Forbes Boulevard, Suite 200
Lanham, MD 20706

Estover Road
Plymouth PL6 7PY
United Kingdom

Copyright © 2008 by Lexington Books

*All rights reserved.* No part of this publication may be reproduced,
stored in a retrieval system, or transmitted in any form or by any
means, electronic, mechanical, photocopying, recording, or otherwise,
without the prior permission of the publisher.

British Library Cataloguing in Publication Information Available

**Library of Congress Cataloging-in-Publication Data**

Kropf, Richard W., 1932-
  Views from a hermitage : reflections on religion in today's world / Richard W. Kropf.
    p. cm.
  Includes index.
  ISBN-13: 978-0-7391-2549-6 (cloth : alk. paper)
  ISBN-10: 0-7391-2549-4 (cloth : alk. paper)
 1. Religion and civilization. 2. Civilization, Modern. I. Title.
BL55.K76 2008
202--dc22
                                  2008010155

Printed in the United States of America

♾™ The paper used in this publication meets the minimum requirements of American National Standard for Information Sciences—Permanence of Paper for Printed Library Materials, ANSI/NISO Z39.48–1992.

# Contents

**Foreword by A. J. Morse** ix

**Introduction** xi

**Part 1: Thoughts on Faith**
Faith and Religion 1
Faith and Belief 3
Faith and Doubt 4
Mature Faith 5
Rousseau's Vicar: Hero or Hypocrite? 6
C. S. Lewis and Make Believe 8
Pascal's Wager Revisited 9
Atheism on the Rebound? 10
Gnostics and Gnosticism 12
In Search of a Logical Faith 13
The Creeds as Symbols of Faith 15

**Part 2: Science and Religion**
God and/or the Big Bang? 17
Evolution and the Problem of Evil 19
Creationism and Evolution 20
Astrotheology 22
Religion versus Science 23
Darwin and the Demotion of Humanity 24
Is There a "God Gene"? 26
The Cardinal, the Pope and Intelligent Design 27

**Part 3: War and Peace**
Kosovo and a New Moral Order 29
September 11, 2001 31
The U.S. and the UN 33
America's "Superiority Complex" 34
Preventive War? 35
World Peace: The Papal Prescription 36
The Global Test 37
Darfur 39
World War III? 40

|  |  |
|---|---|
| War Crimes | 41 |
| Five Years After | 43 |

### Part 4: Religion, Ethics, and Politics

|  |  |
|---|---|
| The Death Penalty | 45 |
| New Year—New Era? | 46 |
| The U.S.A. "Under God" | 48 |
| On Church and State | 49 |
| AIDS and Genocide | 51 |
| Public Morality and the Ten Commandments | 52 |
| Reflections on Hurricane Katrina | 54 |
| The Relatively Poor and Absolute Poverty | 55 |
| Religion and Society | 56 |
| Abortion and Embryonic Stem Cell Research | 57 |
| Capital Punishment | 59 |
| Universal Health Care: A Basic Human Right? | 60 |

### Part 5: Jesus and Christianity

|  |  |
|---|---|
| A Gift from the East | 63 |
| Has Christianity Made Any Difference? | 65 |
| Atonement | 66 |
| James, the Brother of Jesus | 68 |
| The Incarnation | 69 |
| Thoughts on the Interpretation of Scripture | 71 |
| Dogma | 73 |
| Cooked Books? | 75 |
| Schweitzer's Radical Christianity | 76 |
| Did Jesus Have Faith? | 78 |
| The Gospel of Judas | 79 |
| Essential Christianity | 80 |
| Inventing Christ | 82 |
| End Time | 83 |
| The Knowledge of Jesus | 84 |
| The Tomb of Jesus and the Body of Christ | 86 |
| Buddhism and Christianity | 87 |
| The Incarnation Revisited | 89 |

## Part 6: The Church and the Churches
| | |
|---|---:|
| Women in the Church | 91 |
| The Rapture Craze | 92 |
| Clerical Celibacy? | 94 |
| Systemic Failure | 96 |
| Christian Unity | 97 |
| Pope John Paul II | 99 |
| Catholicism or Papalism? | 100 |
| Divisions | 102 |
| Catholic Disbelief | 104 |
| The Original Mistake? | 105 |
| Pope Benedict and the True Church | 107 |
| The Church and Change | 108 |

## Part 7: Islam and the Middle East
| | |
|---|---:|
| Islam | 111 |
| The Holy Land | 112 |
| Christians in the Middle East | 114 |
| The Religious Roots of Conflict in the Middle East | 115 |
| Abu Ghraib and Moral Bankruptcy | 116 |
| Iraq's Christians | 118 |
| Muslim Outrage | 119 |
| The Sunni vs. Shiite Division | 121 |
| Can Islam Change? | 122 |
| Apocalypse Now? | 123 |
| Regensburg: Did the Pope Misspeak? | 125 |
| The Annapolis Initiative | 126 |

## Part 8: Spirituality
| | |
|---|---:|
| Spirituality and Therapeutic Religion | 129 |
| Commitment | 130 |
| Hypocrisy | 132 |
| The Devil You Say? | 133 |
| Religious Extremism | 135 |
| Prayer | 136 |
| Solitude | 137 |
| Seeing | 138 |
| *Shabbat Shalom* | 140 |

What Does It Mean To Be Christian? 141
All Souls 143
Spiritual Blindness 144
Confession 146
Holy Indifference 147
The Secret of Sanctity 149

**Part 9: Philosophical Musings**
Arguments for an Afterlife 151
Ends and Means 153
The Trinity for Monotheists 154
Coping with Tragedy 155
Tradition and Change 157
Sexual Evolution? 158
The Five Loves 160
The Quest for Meaning 161
Instinct and Reason 162
Oneness, or a Theory of Everything 164
Time, Memory, and Meaning 165
Spinning Our Own Cocoons 166

**Part 10: The Environment**
Fishing, Hunting, and the Appreciation of Life 169
Of Mounds and Men 172
God and Nature 174
Environmental Concern as a Moral Imperative 176
Christians and Global Warming 178
Population and Pollution 179
Facing the Future 181
Environmental Escapism 182
The Earth and Humanity: Further Thoughts 184

**A Final Word** 187

**Index of Proper Names** 191

**About the Author** 199

# Foreword

In the woods of northern Michigan, a group of friends get together occasionally during warm summer evenings for stimulating discussions. This "Gaylord Group" includes a professor of mathematics from the City University New York, a former editor of the *Philadelphia Inquirer,* a philosopher and former head of the philosophy department at Vanderbilt University, a writer out of the University of Michigan, and a Catholic theologian with doctorates from the University of Ottawa and Université St-Paul, Ottawa.

That theologian is Richard Kropf, whose essays are presented in this book. Kropf's history is an interesting one. Under the influence and personal advice of the spiritual writer Thomas Merton, Kropf moved from the life of a parish priest into academia, earning his two doctorates. After about ten years of teaching, Kropf eventually left the classroom and retired to live a more strictly contemplative life. Kropf's voice and views were more impressive at the Gaylord Group discussions. John Compton, the philosopher of the group, told me that Kropf "leads the most authentic and envied life of a real philosopher."

Many of Kropf's essays were first published in a local newspaper, the *Gaylord Herald Times.* Composed with the goal of exploring the influence of religious thought, for better or worse, on many aspects of contemporary life in this world, the essays address real problems that any concerned person must confront if he or she is to honestly lead a conscious and intelligent life. They are written within the context of if not strict Catholic doctrine then a more general Christianity. Kropf's strength is humanistic, ecumenical, liberal, and catholic—in the broadest and original sense of that word.

Kropf cuts through all pious rhetoric, jargon, evasiveness, and incurious certainty. His primary aim in writing these essays, as he explained to me, was not to serve as a spokesman for Christianity but, rather, in drawing from his Catholic tradition, to make people think.

And these essays certainly did make me think. Kropf asked me, the writer of the Gaylord Group, to help him select the essays that would be included in this book. My selections, which comprise about half the essays in the book, were chosen based on my own secular approach, first as a student of intellectual history and second as a student of the Bible, the oldest literary effort and the most inspiring course for capturing the drama and dilemmas of life. Kropf has shown me time and again a life-supporting awareness making his essays, even those couched in learned orthodoxy (and unorthodoxy), a joyful personal yet universal fund of truth-bearing insights and inspired revelations.

Anthony Jenckes Morse<br>
Gaylord, Michigan<br>
August 14, 2007

# Introduction

Many years ago, while still a young man, I was drawn to reading, at the suggestion of my English teacher at St. Xavier High School in Cincinnati, the autobiography of a young monk named Thomas Merton. Born in 1915 in France of an American mother and an artist father from New Zealand, Merton had spent most of his early years in England before moving to the United States where he graduated from Columbia University in New York. It was also during this time, after a somewhat dissolute youth, that he also became a Roman Catholic. After a few years of college teaching in upstate New York, and on the eve of America's entrance into World War II, Merton, a pacifist, also ended up joining the strictest monastic order that then existed in the church. This was the Order of Cistercians of the Strict Observance, commonly known as the "Trappists"—after LaTrappe, the name of the town near which their original foundation was situated in rural Normandy. One of their oldest foundations in the United States is located near Bardstown, Kentucky.

It was this monastery that Merton had joined, and within a year or so after reading his autobiography, titled *The Seven Storey Mountain* (it was printed under various other titles in many other languages), I traveled down to Gethsemani Abbey while still a college freshman to see the place (if not Merton—at that time few outsiders knew his face) for myself.

I did not stay there for long, but I came home with an indelible impression, as well as the determination to somehow give my life to God in whatever capacity the Lord might indicate was his will for me. So at the urging of the college chaplain I entered the local diocesan seminary shortly thereafter, and was eventually ordained, in 1958, as a priest for the Diocese of Lansing, Michigan. I chose that diocese (where I had once lived for a short while in years past) cognizant of my situation as an only child, mostly because my parents planned to return to my mother's home state.

However, my decision to become a parish priest turned out to be, at least for me, a poor one. It seems that I had made it as a kind of temporary measure, while actually being drawn almost equally between what seemed to me to be two opposite directions, these being seminary teaching on the one hand and, on the other, monastic life. I was repeatedly refused permission to do the first by the bishop who had ordained me, so after his death I eventually went back down to Gethsemani (by then I had been back down there once or twice previously), this time to try to decisively determine my future course.

The retreat master there at that time, Fr. John Vianney, had himself once been a seminary teacher, and when I explained my dilemma to him, he asked me to speak with the Master of Novices, "Fr. Louis"—who was, of course, no one else but the by-now-famous author, Thomas Merton.

Merton patiently heard my story, and then very incisively said that he was convinced that I was called to the contemplative life, but that he felt that I should try to acquire a more advanced degree in theology or philosophy, and then maybe teach a few years before taking the final step. He also recommended that I visit a small community of Camaldolese Hermits that had recently emigrated from Italy to southeastern Ohio—which I promptly did. Later on, after his premature death in December 1968, I was to learn that Merton himself had almost left the Trappists to join the Camaldolese, but changed his plans when his religious superiors finally gave him permission to become a hermit while remaining attached to the Trappist community.

By then, Merton's many books, not just on spirituality and monastic reform but also on such divisive issues as war and peace and racial justice, had caught the attention of many others, not the least being Pope John XXIII. The pope was especially impressed with Merton's pleas that the life of true contemplative solitude be restored within the Church.

Merton's efforts were posthumously rewarded when the 1983 Code of Canon Law, commissioned by the Second Vatican Council, recognized such a state of life under the direction of a local bishop when duly solemnized by the taking of the usual religious vows of poverty, chastity, and obedience. So after I had finished grad school and been teaching for most of a decade in various local colleges and seminaries in southern Michigan, Bishop Kenneth J. Povish blessed my formal entry into this state of life on October 3, 1984. On that occasion I also made a vow of "stability," that is, a promise to stay put and not wander around looking to get back into the classroom—much less back into a parish—or even for a more scenic place to live in my solitude.

Raised as an "only-lonely," living alone has never been a trial for me. Yet that does not mean that a hermit's life is one of uninterrupted bliss. In his "Notes on a Philosophy of Solitude," Merton wrote that it is the particular trial of a hermit to feel utterly useless. As he described it: "Utter poverty. Often an incapacity to pray, to see, to hope. Not the sweet passivity which the books extol, but a bitter, arid struggle to press forward in a blinding sandstorm. The solitary may well beat his head against a wall of doubt."[1]

However, back then before Vatican II, and most likely mindful of his ecclesiastical censors, Merton went on to explain that he spoke of doubt not so much in a theological or philosophical sense but more in regard to one's vocation. Yet, as we have seen in the recent revelations of the long struggle endured by Mother Teresa of Calcutta, the doubts, even in the case of a person who lived her whole life in the service of others, can reach to the very heart of the life of faith itself. So if my retreat into the north woods of Michigan was inspired in part by Merton's example, it was his advice that I first pursue further studies in philosophy and theology and, like him, to teach a few years before I entered solitude that I believe have better prepared me to grapple with the crucial philosophical and religious issues confronting humanity today.

Indeed, the ominous events that have marked these first seven years of the twenty-first century—in contrast to the euphoric feelings in the last years of the preceding century, especially after the virtual collapse of the totalitarian threat posed by the Soviet Union—has made it practically impossible for me to remain silent. After nearly twenty years of writing letters for Amnesty International and letters to editors, congress members and an occasional article for other publications (in addition to a few short books) I decided in late 1999 to begin speaking out to the general public. My model in this was not so much Merton (whose literary talents I could never hope to match) but the late theologian Karl Barth, who is said to have written his sermons at a kitchen table with a Bible at one hand and a newspaper by the other. That my commentaries were published only in a small town biweekly may testify to my relative unimportance. However, my insistence that these articles, often appearing under the heading of "Religion in Today's World," *not* be relegated to the weekly "Church News" page but be published on the regular editorial page, nevertheless testified to my determination to try to reach out to the general public instead of only, as the old saying has it, "preaching to the choir."

The extent to which I succeeded in my aim, both locally and on a broader scale (via the Internet) rather surprised me. After about five years of publishing in the *Gaylord Herald Times*, people began to ask me if I would consider assembling these articles into a book, so I began trying to recover old computer files and in some cases scanning old printouts. It seems that by early 2007 I had written at least two hundred such short pieces, with about eighty-five of them having been published, while many others—and this may have been just as well, considering what I sometimes wrote—sent to friends but not actually sent to the local paper. Yet all this presented me with a problem. The job of putting these essays together and having them printed into a single volume propelled me into persuading one of my oldest and best-educated friends to help me make a selection. For that purpose I gave him, in the fall of 2005, about one hundred and fifty printouts with the request that he choose about a third of them for possible publication. Then, using his choices as something of a guide, I chose about thirty-five more, mostly from others that had been actually published and from the fifty or so more pieces I had written while my friend was making the first selection.

At this point my idea was still to simply have the selection published at my own expense, in hopes that I might recover my costs by sale in the local market. Still, it occurred to me that perhaps a regular publisher might be interested, so I took my collection, arranged in chronological order in a loose leaf binder to show to a couple of publisher's representatives at the 2007 meeting of the Catholic Theological Society of America. I was somewhat, and most pleasantly, surprised when the first one I showed it to showed great interest and suggested that I submit it, after a partial rearrangement of the essays by topics, to his firm.

However, once this rearrangement had been made, it became obvious to me that to achieve a more *balanced* view, at least on some subjects, some additional essays needed to be added. This concern for balance or completeness, difficult to achieve in individual essays limited by newspaper standards to five or six hundred words (though I seem to have occasionally gotten away with submitting a bit more) in turn reflects a second aim or concern in my writing, which is *reconciliation*. In a world torn apart by political as well as religious strife, I have repeatedly tried to further this aim by looking at both (or all) sides when it comes to any particular question. Hence the addition, just before this collection went to press, of several more essays on some particular subjects. Nor should it be assumed that I my thinking on many of these topics will not continue to be modified as time passes.

Nevertheless, to achieve these goals, still another aim—or perhaps it would be better to call it a technique or approach—has been used, and that is to try to get to the *roots* or *origins* of any issue or subject. In other words, although some might consider this a kind of an obsession with the past, it is really an attempt to be faithful to the sources. I think this is particularly necessary when dealing with religious matters; otherwise, one is all too apt to lose sight of what is really important or essential. The results may appear to be excessively liberal to some, but I tend to believe that when the real reasons behind the origins and purpose of any tradition are understood, what appears to be "liberal" turns out to be, on a deeper level, as I see it, radically conservative.

Perhaps another way of saying all of this is to simply say that I have tried to remain faithful to what I believe is, in the broadest or most inclusive sense of the term, *catholic*. For far too many, this word has become a sectarian label. If so, then both for those who accept it and those who reject it, it becomes the antithesis of what was originally intended. In this matter, especially as a theologian, I have attempted to speak frankly. Nor should my statements be taken, unless they are direct quotations from official Church documents, as being necessarily representative of the Catholic Church. Indeed, on some issues, I realize that my opinions may be quite to the contrary. If so, I offer them as a possible corrective.

No doubt, some may complain that my comments, written from my observation post far removed from the fray, may seem unrealistic. Perhaps so, but in the long run, or taking the long view of things, I don't think so. In the traditional and somewhat romantic ideal of the contemplative life, the hermit, precisely because he lives in a state as far as possible removed from ordinary life, is assumed to have a more comprehensive or total view of what is actually going on in the world around him. He is supposed to be like a sentinel stationed on a mountaintop or a forest fire ranger placed in a watchtower. Other than pray he may be able to do little but sound an alarm or warning. Yet it is his job, indeed I think it is his duty, to do so. Without that little, often seemingly futile gesture, precious little more can be done, and what might be done by those on the ground or closer to the danger points can end up making things worse, turning a danger into a disaster.

My mountaintop may only be a bluff overlooking a trout stream in northern Michigan, and my watchtower a small log cabin. A phone line gives me a very slow connection to the outside world via the Internet, and a small radio and a rabbit-eared TV set brings in all I care to see or hear of the wider world via a nearby Public Broadcasting Service relay tower—with the added advantage of no commercials. Although what I see or hear often drives me to prayer in a chapel in my cabin's loft, a reflecting telescope out back under a roll-away roof, affording me views millions of light years into deep space, helps me keep all human foibles in perspective. When I do travel the twenty-some miles to town to pick up mail, buy groceries, or talk with a few friends, I'm amazed to see how often people have read my column and, even more, in a rather conservative area of our state, that they actually agree with many, if not all, of my opinions.

Accordingly, I want to thank them all, especially those who asked for this collection to be made, and especially Tony Morse, to whom I gave the task of making the initial selection of essays. I wish to also thank Mark Midbon over across the big lake at the University of Wisconsin. Although we've never met face to face, he faithfully attempts to untangle my too often convoluted sentences. My thanks to Glen Shepherd, the publisher of the *North Woods Call*, for his initial encouragement.

I also want to thank Pat Collins, Bob Francoeur, Don Huntimer, Denise Russell, and Dick von Korff, who have told me that they have often passed these essays on to their friends via the Internet. Thanks also to Tom Friere, Daymon Hartley, and Rich Sayre, who have been sometimes sharply critical of what I have to say or have taught me to be a bit more sensitive as to how I say it. I also want to thank Chris Grosser, editor of the *Gaylord Herald Times*, who although she may not have always been able to find space on the editorial page for all my offerings, nevertheless found enough to keep me writing. Finally, I wish to thank the senior acquisitions editor for Sheed & Ward, Ross Miller, and his colleagues at Rowman & Littlefield Publishers, especially Julie Kirsch, who did her best to streamline my often still-tortured prose and ultimately Jessica Bradfield and Kia Westwood who oversaw the book's production. Special thanks are also due to my keen-eyed astronomer friend, Patrick Stonehouse, who could not only discover a very faint comet (Comet 1989 B) out of a dazzling background of stars, but also graciously agreed to look for typos in my nearly finished manuscript. I hope he caught nearly all of them. Any that remain have been most likely reintroduced by me, the author.

1. Thomas Merton, *Disputed Questions* (New York: Farrar, Strauss, Cudahy, 1960), 202.

# Part 1
# Thoughts on Faith

Among the earliest, as well as the latest, reflections composing this collection, the subject of faith, particularly the distinction between faith and particular beliefs, is crucial. Otherwise great confusion is apt to ensue. While the foremost modern exponent of the distinction, the late theologian Wilfred Cantwell Smith, had the advantage of having two different English words to work with, the distinction between at least two distinct meanings of the single Greek New Testament word *pistis* is hardly new. St. Cyril of Jerusalem, back in the fourth century, spoke of the difference between "the faith that can move mountains" and the faith by which Christians adhered to the articles of the Creeds. In fact, the medieval scholastics even spoke of three different kinds of faith: faith in the sense of believing that something is so; believing or trusting God; and finally, the faith or confidence by which something can be accomplished. Most of the following essays, to one degree or another, reflect these fundamental differences as well as the thought of theologian Paul Tillich, psychiatrist Viktor Frankl, and theologian-psychologist James W. Fowler. Taken together, the essays in this section either foreshadow or sum up some of the themes that were developed at more length in several books, especially my 1990 study *Faith, Security and Risk: The Dynamics of Spiritual Growth* and its long delayed (for lack of a willing publisher) 2006 sequel, *The Faith of Jesus: The Jesus of History and the Stages of Faith.*

## Faith and Religion
(March 15, 2000)

A look at Webster's reveals up to seven meanings each for both the words "faith" and "religion." But not only that, both words are often used in place of each other. So obviously, there is not only a close connection between the two, but also not a little bit of confusion on the subject.

Many who like to delve back into the origin of words seem to think that the term *religion* comes from the Latin *ligare* meaning "to tie" or "to bind" or to hold oneself obligated in some way—in this case to the ultimate origin of our existence or, in another word, to God.

Accordingly, for many people, this means church-going at special times set aside for formal worship. Yet there are religious people for whom the whole world is sacred, and their devotion is simply part of their daily life. Perhaps this is why the word "spirituality" has become a popular substitute for "religion" today. A lot of people don't want their religion to be organized.

For others, religion means primarily doing good to or for others. In fact, in the New Testament, we are even told that "Religion that is pure and undefiled before God is taking care of widows and orphans in their needs" (James 1:27). It's obvious that James had little regard for those who considered themselves religious just because they claimed to believe or have faith.

Nevertheless, for most people, religion has something to do with belief in God, especially one who rewards or punishes—otherwise many of them wouldn't do the things listed above. Yet this is not always so. Most everyone, for example, considers Buddhism to be one of the world's major religions, yet most Buddhists claim not to believe in God—at least not in a personal one. For them, religion is living completely in tune with ultimate reality, but the ultimate reality itself defies definition of any sort. In a sense, Buddhism preaches a kind of "reverent agnosticism" and holds that reward or punishment comes simply from whether or not one lives in harmony with the way things really are.

Obviously, then, "religion" can mean a lot of different things to different people. In view of all this variety of ways of being religious, probably one of the best definitions of religion is that given by the late Viktor Frankl, a psychiatrist and Nazi concentration camp survivor. "Religion," Frankl wrote, "is the search for ultimate meaning." So too, according to Frankl, "Faith is trust in ultimate meaning"—which is to say that such a meaning exists. Frankl learned this the hard way. Many people he knew in the camps died without the Nazis having to gas them. They simply gave up on life because it no longer held any meaning for them. For them, God was indeed dead.

Approached this way, we might be able to say that whether we love it or hate it, religion is one of those things that we can't escape taking seriously. Without it—or at least without the search for ultimate meaning, our lives will be at best superficial. With it, or more exactly, when religion includes faith, everything, even the very worst, still may have meaning.

## Faith and Belief
(May 9, 2000)

Many of the problems associated with religion nowadays, be it religious strife in the Middle East or sectarian rivalry in Northern Ireland, or even just the competition between various churches here in America, can be traced back to confusion between faith and belief.

*Faith*, in the gospel sense of the word, means a loving trust in God. *Belief*, or more exactly religious beliefs, are ideas that we have about God. Granted that the two are closely related—one can hardly have faith in God without believing that God exists—but still, they are not the same. To some extent, they are even opposed, because even though beliefs attempt to explain the reasons we have faith, it seems that the more certain we become about our beliefs, and the more we become convinced they are true, the less real faith is involved. Why is this so often the case?

Perhaps it is because faith is concerned with a person—a *who*. Belief is concerned with things associated with that person—a matter of *what*. Faith is an affair of the heart. Belief is more of a head-trip. Much as in love and marriage, faith must be placed in another as a person in a covenant-relationship. If that is not the case, and the emphasis is placed on what qualities or assets the other brings to the relationship, then a marriage is turned from a covenant into a mere contract.

In the same way, when religion is reduced to the acceptance of a list of propositions about God, then whatever loving trust we may have had in God "for better or for worse" is turned instead into a kind of business deal in which God is expected to conform or even perform according to our expectations. This is not to say that beliefs are not important. Some beliefs are liberating and life-giving. Yet others can have disastrous consequences. Often the reason these beliefs, whether good or bad, can become so disruptive is that the risk of making a real commitment to God in faith has been replaced by a security blanket—often consisting of an effort to eliminate all other beliefs but one's own.

One thing more. If people really trust (have faith) in God, could they really believe that God will reject others who don't happen to agree with their particular definition of God or the way that they think God expects us to act? Could it be that God is really that narrow-minded? Instead, genuine faith in God (who is infinite or without limit) would be able to accept or even expect differences in belief—which are, after all, the product of our limited intelligence. In a word, faith unites, while belief divides. I hardly expect everyone will agree with me, especially on this last point. However, would not that disagreement in itself go a long way toward proving it is indeed so?

## Faith and Doubt
(May 31, 2000)

The great Cardinal Newman once made the claim that "ten thousand difficulties do not make one doubt."

This may very well be true, especially if we make a clear distinction between faith as an act of the will, on the one hand, and belief as an exercise of the mind or intellect, on the other. In that case, to have difficulties with various articles of belief—like how God could be both three (a "Trinity") and still one—is not the same as withholding our willingness to trust God or to hesitate to commit our life to him.

Unfortunately, the life of faith is not always that simple. People, often very good religious people, still often wrestle with real doubts, worried that the commitment they have made to God or the trust they have placed in divine providence may be nothing but an illusion. They sense that faith, in a way, is a gamble. It is something like a marriage, in which we place all our trust in another person, and such trust, to be untroubled by doubt, must assume that the other partner is equally trustworthy and devoted to our well-being. And as sad experience too often proves, such human trust and faith can be misplaced.

However, should not faith in God be different? One might hope so, but it is not always that easy. Elie Wiesel, like Viktor Frankl, another survivor of the Nazi death camps, said he never once ceased to believe in the existence of God in the midst of all the horrors he witnessed, but he did continue to doubt for a long time the goodness of God, even for years after the horrors had ended: otherwise, how could God have allowed such terrible things to happen?

So too, quite aside from the many difficulties people may have, real doubt about the God we cannot fully comprehend struggles with our need to trust in God and make sense out of this often senseless universe. Yet should this not be? If we could fully understand God, would God be God any longer?

In fact, we might even go so far as to say, as did the theologian Paul Tillich, that faith that is untroubled by doubt is suspect. For while it is possible that some persons may be blessed with a simple, or even naive, faith, one that suffers from no disturbing doubts, it is more likely that such faith is the result of belief in a God who has been reduced to an idol of our own imagination. Like "cheap grace"—a blessing that demands nothing in return—a faith that is without doubt may involve no real faith at all! After all, when something is a sure thing, what need is there to make a commitment to a foregone conclusion?

## Mature Faith
(February 24, 2001)

Following in the footsteps of the pioneers of developmental psychology such as Erik Erikson, Jean Piaget, and Lawrence Kohlberg, contemporary theologians and spiritual guides have begun to see that a mature faith shows characteristics that are quite distinct. Such a faith stands out clearly from the more conventional forms of faith and belief that the majority of people—even those who have undergone a religious conversion—cling to throughout most of their lives.

A mature faith, to begin with, is one that no longer sees the world in black and white, either/or terms. It is able to discriminate shades of meaning, and because it does, it is able to tolerate ambiguity and uncertainty. It no longer needs to believe that in order to be right either everyone else must agree with you, or else everyone else must be wrong!

A mature faith is continually able to learn and to realize that other peoples, other cultures may have better insights into certain aspects of the truth—that the collective wisdom and experience of the whole human race (as well as the truths of science) are themselves a form of revelation along with the written word of God.

Thus a mature faith learns to appreciate (often after once having rejected it as childish) the depth of meaning contained in religious symbolism, ritual, and myth. It also is able to distinguish between faith (as a loving trust in God) and beliefs as expressions or formulations of the convictions by which we attempt, often so inadequately, to explain why we have such faith.

A mature faith no longer needs to base its moral standards simply on a list of written commandments or merely on what is legal, or even less on simply what feels right, but rather on the basis of a divine logic or Wisdom (*Logos, Tao*) that is built into the very structure of the universe.

Finally, a mature faith is one that is able to face the truth about oneself and that learns to live with, and to some extent even forgive, the imperfections in one's own self. This does not mean that one ever gives up on trying to be better, but simply that one realizes that only God's grace can complete the task. So at best, a mature faith is really always in a state of maturing, remaining in a constant process of growth.

In consequence of all of this, the hallmark of a mature or maturing faith is its being "ecumenical" in the broadest sense of that term. It sees the purpose of all religion as the unification of the human spirit with God and knows that this cannot be accomplished without striving mightily for the unity and harmony of the human race.

Yet a mature faith also knows that this task cannot be accomplished without commitment, without putting the whole meaning of one's life on the line. While the seemingly cool rationality of a truly mature faith may sometimes cause it to be mistaken for rationalism (and vice versa—as typically, rationalization serves as an escape from commitment) yet nothing could be further from the truth. For while a mature faith is one that is lived in a state of constant hope against hope, it is most of all a faith that expresses itself in a love so lavish that our lives would make no sense at all unless God exists.

## Rousseau's Vicar: Hero or Hypocrite?
(September 9, 2006)

In his 1782 novel *Émile*, the philosopher Jean-Jacques Rousseau aired his thoughts about religion in the form of "a profession of faith" by a nameless clergyman whom he called "a Savoyard Vicar" who seems to have been modeled on two Catholic priests who favorably impressed Rousseau in his youth. Rousseau, raised as a Protestant in Geneva, professed a thorough-going rationalistic natural theology—what might be termed "deism" today. This was much in keeping with his times, as well as with Rousseau's own naturalistic philosophy, which held that primitive man, uncorrupted by civilization and its prejudices, would naturally arrive at a reasonable and happy mode of existence.

Rousseau's religion, as expressed by his vicar, follows suit. After a rather lengthy discussion of various points of philosophy, he lists the basic articles of his faith. They are the existence of a supreme "Will" that in its workings in nature displays intelligence, power, and goodness—in short the attributes we generally ascribe to God. Next, he holds that Man, as the highest being within the order of nature is "a free agent and as such is animated by an immaterial substance" that he later on calls "soul." Finally, he says that there can be discovered within nature itself an innate order of things that can function as a sure moral or ethical guide as to how we should act to guarantee the good order of society and through it our own happiness. From these three rational principles can be deduced everything else that follows, including a more or less complete repudiation of the necessity of Revelation or a supernatural foundation to religion backed by miracles, prophecies, and many of the other claims that Rousseau (or his vicar) finds often to be as much a hindrance as a help.

As for the Christian religion in particular, Rousseau's vicar says that while the majesty of the Scriptures fill him with admiration, it is the purity of the gospel that most influences his heart. Though he finds the "life and death of Jesus" (but mentions no resurrection) "that of a God," it is obvious that Rousseau's view of Jesus is of one more sublime than divine. In other words, his good vicar is not even a believer according to the official definitions of practically every Christian church.

Yet despite his repudiation of all dogma and his opinion that one religion, provided it truly lead people to God, is probably as good as another, given the various circumstances under which people live, Rousseau's free-thinking cleric remains in his post, scrupulously observing every rubric of the prescribed rituals of his office, believing "all that are established to be good when God is served in sincerity of heart." As for any doubts he may have about his own integrity, the vicar endeavors "to silence on this occasion the voice of reason before the Supreme Intelligence."

What are we to make of such an attitude today? If our own pastor were to confess that he really didn't believe most of what he preaches but only that the observance of religious customs is probably good for most people, would we not deem him a hypocrite—especially if his position guaranteed him a good living and public respect? On the other hand, knowing how much people need a sense of meaning or purpose in their lives, would it not be a special form of heroism for a person to dedicate his or her life to helping people find the sense of security that faith alone affords, even while he or she secretly believes very little of it or even suffers agonies of doubt?

What do you think? Was Rousseau's vicar a hero or a hypocrite?

## C. S. Lewis and Make Believe
(September 12, 2006)

In his ever-popular 1948 book *Mere Christianity*, C. S. Lewis, the Oxford professor and writer of imaginative fiction such as the *Chronicles of Narnia*, makes a surprising comparison. A couple of chapters before the end of the book Lewis asks the reader to recall how, as a child, he or she may have imagined himself or herself as a grown up perhaps taking charge of something or of others—whether it be a boy pretending that the inside of a large packing case is a ship or an airplane, or a girl lining up her dolls and pretending she is a schoolmarm. Such play, said Lewis, is a necessary part of growing up. In it we try out roles that we might think about pursuing later. And the role that we eventually settle on may very well turn out to be our call or vocation in life.

In the same way, Lewis suggests, the Christian creeds function not so much as a mere list of beliefs to be memorized or adhered to but, rather, as a guide or role model to be, as much as possible, imitated in our life. For example, in relating the basic doctrines about Jesus, how he lived and died "for us and our salvation" and especially how was he raised again to live a new kind of life with God, we are being told about not just something he did for us but are being bidden to do the same for each other. In other words, being a Christian is not so much believing a list of doctrines but rather living in the footsteps of Jesus.

No doubt some will suspect some kind of evasion in this. Might it not be a sly way of suggesting that it really isn't very important whether Jesus actually rose from the dead as long as we try to live our lives *as if* he did? However, this is not what Lewis is saying. If, in fact, Jesus was not really raised, then we are all fools to try to walk in his footsteps. The reason is that being a Christian is not a call to be a nice or decent person, or even just to be a generous one. Anyone of good will and determination can probably do that—and in doing so, leave good memories behind. What Lewis is talking about is something much more radical. It is matter of human *evolution*, of developing a whole new species of human being.

Though Lewis resisted using a pun, I can't. We've all probably heard of *homo erectus*, believed to be the earliest form of humanoid that habitually walked around on just two legs. Then there was *homo habilis* (the first primitive tool maker) and later the Neanderthals, the first to move into Europe after the ice age. And of course the scientific name for us modern humans is *homo sapiens*, which is supposed to mean that we are fundamentally intelligent or wise.

All this is fine of course, except for one thing. All these early forms of human life are now long extinct. And science tells us that sooner or later—probably sooner if we keep inventing weapons of mass destruction or polluting and mismanaging the environment on which our life depends—we'll join our more primitive ancestors in extinction. Hopefully, we will be *sapiens* or wise enough to prevent this from happening before our allotted time as a species on planet earth runs out.

Instead, what Lewis was talking about is a whole new kind of human; *homo resurrectus* if you will. Jesus is, according to the creeds, this sort of human. Yet it is not something he could do on his own. It was only in giving himself up totally to God, his heavenly Father—as well as ours—that he was able to rise again to this new kind of divinely human life. And this is why knowing our creeds and pretending we are Jesus is so important; for it is, as St. Paul tells us, only if we imitate him in dying to our selfishness, that we can rise into this new resurrected and eternal life. And of course, the bottom line is, as St. Paul also told us, that if Jesus really didn't rise, then we are all self-deluded fools.

Some may ask why it wouldn't be enough to live one's life for others, even if one does not know Jesus or consciously imitate him. Wouldn't this be enough? In fact, the Catholic Church's Second Vatican Council, which was held some years after Lewis's death, did recognize this possibility. Still the question remains: what surer way is there except in following Christ's example by imagining we are him and doing, as much as possible, what he would have us do?

---

# Pascal's Wager Revisited
(October 20, 2006)

In his *Pensées* or "Thoughts," the seventeenth-century French mathematician and philosopher Blaise Pascal pondered what he called his "wager" regarding the existence of God and the fate of the soul. Suppose, he wrote, that God really does exist and will hold us accountable for the way we live our lives: in that case we'd better behave or we'll surely end up the losers. On the other hand, suppose such a belief is an illusion: still, when we die, what really will we have lost? Perhaps an excuse to have lived however we pleased—the rest of the world be damned? Yet, on the other hand, if we have lived as if God exists and holds us accountable, we will have, if nothing else, at least earned a reputation as a basically decent person.

Today, such a gamble is apt to be perceived as insincere or as a very shallow form of faith at most. Would God really reward us for simply playing it safe? Might we not say that what we have here is not faith at all, but at best a vague hope, or at worst venal self-promotion?

Others, however, have raised questions about Pascal's logical consistency. What if, for example, God—if he exists—rewards people not for their goodness but for cleverness? After all, did not Pascal himself famously say that "the God of the prophets is not the God of the philosophers"?

Nevertheless, I think these critics are missing the real point, which is not so much a question of proving the existence of God but, as Pascal says, a question of whether or not the human soul is immortal. If it isn't, then all talk of a wager seems pointless. After all, did not the Hebrew prophets—who certainly believed in God but had no clear idea of an afterlife—wrestle continually with the problem of sinners sinning with seeming impunity?

Yet what if we do not have immortal souls, but, instead, only the potential of making ourselves immortal? Suppose the condition of such an advance is not simply our own willpower but instead our conscious alignment with that creative energy that lies at the heart of the evolution or future of the universe. In other words, suppose that what we call "ethics" or "morality" is not just a question of behavior (and its social consequences) but is instead the very essence of what we have generally called "religion." In that case, at least it seems to me, Pascal was essentially right. Either we cooperate with this great creative force—which we have hitherto called "God"—according to its rules, or else we go off by ourselves to play our own little game.

In the first case, our immortality is ensured by becoming part of the larger game of life. And the price that we have to pay in order to play is, to a certain extent, to risk ourselves and the meaning of our own short lives with the goal of achieving something much greater. Either that or the alternative is to relegate ourselves to the sidelines of evolution.

---

## Atheism on the Rebound?
### (May 25, 2007)

Recently, after a long period of dormancy, militant atheism seems to be trying hard to make a comeback. Evidence for this can be found in such popular diatribes as *The End of Religion* by Sam Harris, the recently published *God Is Not Great* by *Vanity Fair* editor Christopher Hitchens, and *Breaking the Spell* by philosopher Daniel Dennett. Then there is *The God Delusion* by the most widely read spokesman of contemporary atheism, the biologist Richard Dawkins, whose wholesale attacks on religion are so impassioned that the British scientist Jonathan Miller, who is the producer of a new PBS television series on the history of atheism, calls Dawkins "a born-again atheist." How to explain this phenomenon?

I think there are three possible answers, any one of which or in one combination or another might be correct.

First of all, we have the understandable reaction to 9/11 and all the other apparently religion-inspired terrorism around the world. If anything could give religious belief a bad name, this kind of fanaticism could hardly be surpassed. Yet curiously, those who point to religion in general as being the cause of all this mayhem seem to conveniently forget that most of the millions of violent deaths in the twentieth century were caused by political regimes that were avowedly atheist (Marxist communism) or (like Nazism and Fascism) were contemptuous of religion except where it could be manipulated for their own use.

Second, we have the equally understandable reaction to the kind of religious and political conservatism that seems unable to face or offer realistic solutions to other current problems such as skyrocketing population increases, the spread of diseases like AIDS, and widespread poverty, which are affecting the future of the world. All of this seems to give the impression that while belief in God may give many people some consolation (belief that there is a better life beyond) or may even inspire some to try to alleviate the suffering, in the long run religions tend to prolong the conditions that cause so much misery in the world.

However, I suspect there is a third factor at work, one that those who place their faith in science instead of religion are rather reluctant to admit. It has to do with cosmology, the branch of science that deals with the nature, origins, and future of the universe. The big bang theory raises a very unsettling question: what was there before the big bang began some 13-14 billion years ago? Some (mostly mathematicians who like to play with numbers) can hypothesize about the existence of other "universes" or even a "multiverse" of which our universe is only a temporary phase. Yet, as astrophysicist Eric Chaisson points out, without observational or experimental data to support it, such speculation is more in the category of science fiction than real science. The result is that, unable to otherwise explain how something (the whole universe) has apparently come from nothing, some (like Dawkins) are trying to redefine science as being purely descriptive—something like an examination of effects without a cause.

All this would seem to suggest that atheists sense that they are being backed into a corner and are forced to turn to denouncing the misuses of religion—of which there are certainly many—or else substitute theories that, unsupported by any hard evidence, require just about as much faith to accept as any religious belief. However, instead of reacting the way they are, would it not be more wise, at the very least, to adopt an attitude of reverent agnosticism before the mystery of Being that believers have been too ready, and no doubt all too quickly, to call "God"?

---

## Gnostics and Gnosticism
(August 3, 2007)

Gnostics and Gnosticism have been, as of late, popular topics in religious writing. Any search on the Internet for books on the subject will turn up page after page of references ranging from scholarly treatises to sensationalized discoveries of lost manuscripts like *The Gospel of Judas* to popular novels like *The DaVinci Code*.

Why all this interest in the esoteric and what seems to border on, at times, the occult? It seems to me that it has a quite obvious cause, which is the discontent with what is taken to be "dumbed down" religion and the quest for deeper, more satisfying truth.

The word *gnosis* is simply Greek for "knowledge" and the term *gnosticism* is used to describe the search for the deeper understanding of religious truth. Gnostics like to think of themselves as those who are "in the know" as distinct from those who are content with the usual understanding or, as the Gnostics see it, the misunderstanding of common beliefs. And because this tendency is nothing new, it is no surprise that the deeper we dig the more we turn up evidence that this sort of division goes far back human history. In fact, one might even say it was even present in Christianity from the beginning, since according to Luke's Gospel (8:10) Jesus himself explained to his disciples that he spoke to the common people in stories and parables "but to you it is given to know (*gnonai*) the mysteries of the kingdom of God."

So why this seeming double standard when it comes to the imparting of spiritual truths? As the early Christian scripture scholar and theologian Origen of Alexandria (185-254) explained it, while a deeper and more spiritual understanding of the scriptures must be given to those who are more educated, the pastors of the common people were constrained to preach mostly in terms of what we now call "hellfire and damnation" in order to keep their flocks of followers in line.

The problem today, however, has become immensely more complicated. The printing press, widespread literacy, and now the Internet and other forms of popular media have blurred the distinction between the educated and those incapable of understanding things except in crudest terms. Religious leaders today have to be capable of conveying the central truths found in religion and at the same time translating or separating them from the various layers or coverings that at one time or another served as a means of communicating but now may serve only to obscure the truth. Otherwise, due to vastly increased knowledge of how the world works and increased levels of education, religious leaders will end up only misleading their followers or driving them to seek other less reliable ways to fulfill their spiritual needs.

The upsurge of what is called "New Age" spirituality is a good example of what happens when religious leaders fail in this task. Nearly a century ago, the Catholic writer G. K. Chesterton saw this coming when he wryly commented that the great tragedy in people losing their faith is not that they will so much turn into atheists but instead end up believing almost anything, no matter how far fetched it may be. If so, we must blame, at least in part, the failure of the leaders to truly lead their people into a deeper understanding of the truths that lie beneath the old stories and symbols.

---

## In Search of a Logical Faith
(September 29, 2007)

For many, the idea of a "logical faith" sounds like a contradiction in terms. In fact, perhaps even for most people, faith seems like in irrational thing, a kind of blind leap in the dark against all odds, prompted by some kind of vague or even desperate hope that things can or must be different.

One reason for this situation is a widespread confusion between faith and belief. We have in faith, on the one hand, a deep sense of trust or conviction that the universe or life somehow makes sense. And then we have, on the other hand, the particular set of beliefs or mental attempts to make sense of this basic trust or conviction. In fact, so stubborn is this conviction that many people are convinced that religion should make no sense, and are in fact quite happy to leave it that way—maybe because they are too insecure to examine their beliefs. Or else they may be delighted to be freed from the burden of thinking deeply about life's meaning and its responsibilities.

Neither of these escapes, whether it is into *fideism* (readiness to believe anything) or complete *skepticism* (refusal to believe anything at all) is worthy, I think, of human beings. Instead, if we are, as the philosopher Aristotle said, "rational animals," then, if we are to act as humans, the motives for our actions, including our deepest held beliefs, must be subjected to reason. In fact, even the Scriptures tell us this, when we are told that we must be ready to give an account for the hope that is within us (1 Peter 3:15). So what are we to do?

Some, no doubt even many, are reluctant to take up the challenge. They seem quite content to live their life in a kind of state of mental schizophrenia, their faith more or less totally cut off from world of mundane and everyday reality. Or as one modern author (Theodore Rubin) has put it, "There are two ways to slide easily through life; to believe everything or to doubt everything; both ways save us from thinking." Perhaps such an attitude is often motivated by nostalgia for the past, when life seemed simple. Perhaps it was, but they should not be surprised when others, their own children, for example, look elsewhere for solutions to life's dilemmas.

This is not to deny that, as Cardinal Newman said, "The heart has reasons of its own." Certainly this is true, at least if we are not completely self-absorbed, in terms of the human drive toward self-transcendence. Yet it is equally true that many of these more emotional needs or drives have become, in the course of human evolution, counterproductive. Thus, it is my conviction—or "belief" if you will—that Christians are obliged to submit all their beliefs to the test of reason, and if necessary, to change or at least adjust those beliefs in a way that seems to make sense in light of our contemporary understanding of reality.

For example, back in the days before modern medicine and deeper understanding of how the human mind works, it made sense to think of illness and mental problems in terms of evil spirits or demonic possession. If the gospel writers had used today's explanations, who back then would have understood them? However, today such explanations, rather than being a rational, appear to be utter nonsense. Not only that, such ideas also provide too ready of an excuse for human irresponsibility and bad behavior. In fact, if one were to be completely logical about it, could not such a belief itself be used as a kind of biblical alibi for a loss of faith? After all, what better excuse could be cooked up for rejecting faith than "The devil made me do it"?

Accordingly, reason leads us to the conclusion that faith itself must transcend belief or particular beliefs that may seem, at least at times, self-contradictory. Nevertheless, logic itself should lead us to the conclusion that any God who could be totally comprehended would not be truly God, but more likely an idol of our own making.

---

## The Creeds as Symbols of Faith
(December 8, 2007)

Recently, a retired Roman Catholic bishop in Australia, the Most Reverend Geoffrey Robinson, has been causing quite a stir. This has been not just "down-under" but also in quite a few other places around the world where he has called for a thorough-going church reform from top to bottom, from the operations of the papacy to even a rephrasing of our basic profession or official statement of faith.

However, I think that is important to note that these latter, commonly called "creeds" in English (from the Latin word *credere* meaning "to believe") are officially called "symbols" (*symbolum* in Latin). This word itself is rather curious, being a combination of the preposition *sym* (Greek for "with" or "together") with the verb *ballo* (which means to "throw," to "fall," to "place") suggesting that a symbol is a means of bringing various ideas together—apparently in a way that is meant to remind us of something, which in this case, are the reasons that we have faith or can have faith. But these reasons cannot substitute for faith, at least in the gospel sense of the word, which means absolute trust in and reliance on God.

However, even when that symbolic function is understood, it is equally important that we be aware that these ancient symbols or expressions of belief are in some ways dated, that is, very much marked or conditioned by the way that people thought back at the time in which they were first composed. For example, back when the first baptismal creeds, similar to what is now known as The Apostles' Creed, were composed, most people still believed that heaven was a place located somewhere out in space. Or else they believed that "the resurrection of the body" meant that our dead bodies would be literally raised out of the grave, thoroughly remodeled and set free to wander about in a reconditioned or renovated (and one presumes, considering the number of people who have lived) greatly enlarged, planet Earth. But by the time the Nicean Creed was written, about two and half centuries later, the language had become a bit less graphic, content to speak of hope for "the resurrection of the dead and the life of the world to come."

As a consequence of this shifting historical perspective, we have to also realize that these creeds or symbols are provisional or relative to the needs of the time. This is especially important when we consider the Nicean Creed. At the time it was first composed, a theologian by the name of Arius had raised doubts about the divinity of Christ. He believed Jesus was truly divine, but not of the same "substance" (*ousia* in Greek)—by which Arius seems to have meant "nature." Accordingly, although many of the bishops at Nicea disliked using that word (it wasn't in the Bible and it almost sounded like you could slice God up into pieces like pie) the council felt compelled to state in turn that Christ is *homoousios* or of the same substance as (or "consubstantial" with) the Father, and consequently we are still stuck with the tricky issue as to how to translate this strange word.

However, almost immediately, the doctrinal turmoil that followed Nicea's soon proved to need its own counter corrective, which finally came at the Council of Chalcedon in 451. This council added to the *homoousios* of Nicea another *homoousios*, asserting that Jesus is also "consubstantial" or of the same nature as us in our humanity. Yet unfortunately, this correction was never added to the Nicean Creed, probably because it raises too many questions in peoples' minds as to how Jesus could possibly be both at once. But as result of this omission there has been a long-standing tendency (officially condemned as "monophysitism") for Christians to think of Jesus as God parading around in a human skin, much as we might wear a suit of clothes. And so it goes.

All this tends to confirm, in my mind, that our beliefs cannot be considered to be unalterable absolutes, but have to be seen, at their best, as playing a supporting role for faith, yet, at their worst, sometimes getting in the way of real faith. It also reminds me of two passages in Paul's epistles: one (1 Corinthians 13:12) where he spoke of our faith in terms of seeing dimly as in a mirror and the other (2 Corinthians 3:18) where we see God's glory slowly or gradually revealed in our own reflection.

Perhaps the same must be said of the Creeds, and even more, of our theologizing.

# Part 2
# Science and Religion

The presumed conflict between science and religion and, all too often, the actual friction between scientists and believers is, without a doubt, one of the most critical issues in today's world. This conflict also occasioned some of my first attempts, back in my undergraduate days, at theological writing and determined the specific direction of my postgraduate studies in philosophical and systematic theology. At that time I specialized in the pioneering thought of Pierre Teilhard de Chardin (1881-1955), the French Jesuit paleontologist whose attempts to reconcile evolutionary theory with Christian doctrine attracted worldwide interest but also (as he predicted) raised suspicions and resentments in both camps.

Accordingly, the second part of this book is given over to various aspects of this conflict, particularly as it is reflected in the popular press. While the second topic that is treated in this section—the problem of evil—has long remained the most serious challenge to belief in God, I have argued (at some length in my book *Evil and Evolution: A Theodicy*) that evolution, rather than further complicating things, is seen as providing the best possible solution to the issue.

In more recent years, however, my interest, first occasioned by my newfound interest in astronomy and telescope making, has turned especially to cosmology. Instead of the theological issues raised by biological evolution, it is the sheer immensity of the universe that is seen, in these essays, as now bringing the biggest challenge to Christian theology.

---

## God and/or the Big Bang?
(June 27, 2000)

Not too long ago I heard someone on the radio come out with an either/or statement that went: "Some say God created the universe, while others say it all came from a big bang—but I don't know which." But need it be an either/or proposition? Why not both?

In fact, much of the big bang theory of the origins of the universe had its beginning in the speculations of the Belgian Catholic priest and mathematical physicist Georges Lemaître (1894-1966). Back in 1927, after studying math and physics at Cambridge University, Lemaître first published his idea of the universe expanding from a "primeval atom," showing how Einstein's general theory of relativity contradicted the then current belief (including Einstein's own convictions) in a stable, unchanging universe. Einstein told Lemaître that his math was correct but that his grasp of physics was "abominable." In the meantime, in Russia, Aleksandr Friedmann came to much the same conclusions as Lemaître, but Einstein ignored him as well.

Then, in 1929, the American astronomer Edwin Hubble began to publish his own observations that not only proved the existence of other galaxies than our own Milky Way but also indicated, through measurement of the "redshift" in the light from these other galaxies, that we live in an expanding universe. In 1933 both Einstein and Lemaître met with Hubble in California where Einstein admitted to Hubble that in fudging some of his equations (namely, holding for a "cosmological constant" to allow for a steady-state, nonexpanding universe) he'd made "the biggest blunder" of his career. Next, after hearing Lemaître explain his own theory further, Einstein is said to have admitted that Lemaître's presentation was the most beautiful and satisfactory explanation of creation that he had ever heard!

Yet much of the scientific world remained unconvinced. Sir Arthur Eddington (one of Lemaître's mentors at Cambridge) thought that the idea that the universe actually had a beginning was "repugnant." Another Cambridge astrophysicist, Fred Hoyle, has spent most of his scientific career trying to prove that Lemaître was wrong. In fact, it was Hoyle who derisively dubbed Lemaître's idea "the Big Bang"—admitting that he found its religious overtones rather unsettling. That Pope Pius XII eventually appointed Lemaître to the Pontifical Academy of Sciences probably didn't help.

Since then, however, almost every new astronomical discovery has continued to confirm as well as refine Lemaître's original ideas. George Gamow and Ralph Alpher, in particular, developed the current "inflationary" version of the theory, which has been further confirmed in recent years by the detection of background radiation left over from the initial stages of the big bang. So too, astronomers have just about given up the intense search for enough "dark matter" to reverse the big bang or even to cause it to repeat itself, and even more lately they have come close to concluding that the expansion rate of the universe, which they generally thought had to be slowing down, may actually be speeding up, apparently due to the effects of what cosmologists call "dark energy."

If these latest estimates turn out to be accurate, then not only they vindicate Lemaître's idea that the universe began with a "primeval atom," but also his description of the universe as being like a burst of celestial fireworks—but now, it seems, with the dying embers of creation growing dimmer as they expand into the nothingness of empty space. So too, perhaps, we might hope that long before then much of the long-standing tension between modern science and religion will evaporate.

## Evolution and the Problem of Evil
(July 20, 2000)

As a theologian, I have long been puzzled by the problem of evil in the world. *"When Bad Things Happen to Good People"*—as Rabbi Harold Kuschner put it—we also cannot but wonder *why*. Must it be that maybe God isn't as good as we think? Or might it be that God is not as all-powerful as we once thought?

After I began reading, back in the late 1950s, the works of the French Jesuit paleontologist, Pierre Teilhard de Chardin, who devoted his life to reconciling evolution with Christian beliefs, one of the things that struck me most about the theory of evolution is that it gives us an "out" that takes God "off the hook," so to speak, when it comes to the dilemma stated above. How can this be?

Consider this: if humans have evolved from lower forms of life, then it must be that the same laws of nature that produced these other forms are also at work in us. Now we know that evolution works on the basis of two principles: first, random mutation, and second, the principle of natural selection or "survival of the fittest." While lately most of the argument has been over the latter principle (fittest individuals, fittest species, or fittest genes?) it is the first principle that is most important in regard to the thesis I would advance. Although it has been our large brains and capacity for reasoning that has enabled the human species to survive and to advance beyond other animals, it has been the randomness, the "chanciness" that is built into the process that seems to be the key to our capacity for free will. Without the working of chance producing endless variety in the universe, what would be left to choose?

Still, there is a lot more to it than that. Just as our distinct ability to engage in reflective awareness (to not only know but "to know that we know" as Teilhard often put it) depends on the sensory awareness that we share with the animal world, so too our ability to make firm decisions (free will properly speaking) depends on our ability to be reflectively aware of all the implications of what would be otherwise simply instinctive choice. In other words, unless the Creator had given chance a role in creation, we would have all turned out to be robots!

Does this mean that God couldn't have created things differently—another possible world with purely angelic beings also capable of free will? Perhaps; but we are talking about the real world as we experience it, "the only possible world" as C. S. Lewis called it, a world where earthquakes and floods, plagues and famines, failures and tragedies have all occurred and are likely to continue to occur. All these possibilities are the prerequisites for the emergence of truly free creatures that cannot only know but also "know that they know," and in so doing, not only choose whatever attracts them but also rising above mere instinct, truly exercise free will and consciously love.

## Creationism and Evolution
(August 1, 2000)

A recent poll taken by "Citizens for the American Way" has apparently established that a large majority of Americans think that the theory of evolution rather than "creationism" should be taught in the public schools. This was despite a minority who were unfamiliar with the term "creationism"—which means taking more or less literally the stories told in the Book of Genesis as an explanation of the origin of the world or of the human species. There are others, however, who believe that *both* approaches should be taught; allowing the students to decide which explanation makes more sense to them, or whether or not to take the Bible as their ultimate authority.

The major flaw in such reasoning, which is also sometimes misnamed "Creation Science," is to mistake the Bible for a book on science. As one wise churchman pointed out around the time of Galileo (too bad they didn't listen to him) the Bible is a book about salvation—"going to heaven"—not about science or "how the heavens go." As such, its human authors took for granted certain ideas about nature (for example, that the earth is flat, or that the sun circles the earth) that were part of the "science" of the time, but which we now know are incorrect. But we readily excuse such errors as being "a manner of speaking" to which God had to adapt to get the main ideas across.

Yet if we admit that much, then why not admit that the persons whom God inspired to write these books also used various sacred stories ("myth" in the original sense of that often misused word), legends, poems, and so on, to help communicate these same basic ideas? If we deny these writers these basic means of communication, then must we not throw out large portions of the Bible, like the Psalms (poetry) or even the parables (very short stories of an obviously fictional nature) that run through the gospel accounts of the preaching of Jesus? Really, when you get down to it, there seems to be something rather arrogant—like telling God what He can or can't do—in insisting on the idea that the Bible should be as literally factual as the local newspaper or telephone book!

Another major flaw in the "creationism" approach is that it fundamentally misunderstands the nature of science. Although creationists often trumpet the fact that evolution is "only a theory" (as no one has ever seen an ape turn into a human being, or even a fish turn into a bird) what they fail to realize is that all science rests on theories (such as the law of gravity) that seek to explain how it is that what we see happens or appears to have happened has come about. If I observe, for example, the fossils of salt-water sea creatures in stones that turn up in my yard, then, I am tempted to "theorize" that what is now my yard must have been not too far from what at one time was part of a tropical sea. Or if scientists discover that 98.4 percent of human DNA is identical to that found in chimpanzees, then they are apt to theorize that the human species is, biologically speaking, a rather close cousin of this species of ape. True, God could have created "Petoskey Stones" (fossilized coral from the Devonian period of the Paleozoic Era) in my backyard just to fool me or given humans much the same DNA as chimps just as a kind of practical joke. But logic would dictate otherwise.

Some sixteen hundred years ago St. Augustine suggested that if the scriptures seemed to clash with "clear, consistent reasoning" then it must be that we are interpreting the scriptures wrongly. All this scientific evidence, I would submit, is the kind of clear and consistent reasoning that shows that so-called "Creation Science" is neither scientific nor even profoundly biblical.

---

## Astrotheology
(February 11, 2002)

By now we've all heard the term astrophysics and about scientists who are described as astrophysicists—specialists in the composition and characteristics of stars and other objects in outer space. More recently, there is even an emerging field of astrobiology as astronomers become more and more convinced that there are other planetary systems orbiting other stars, planets that may provide the conditions for the appearance of life. If this keeps up, could we end up having "astrophilosophers" and "astrotheologians" as well?

It may come as a surprise to some, but there have long been such thinkers, long before the term astrophysics, much less astrobiology, was ever thought of. Cardinal Nicolas von Kues (Nicolas of Cusa) was writing about the possibility of other inhabited worlds around 1440, as was the Franciscan theologian William of Vaurouillon (1392-1463). This was nearly a century before Copernicus. Then closer to the time of Galileo, the Dominican scholars Thomas of Campanella and Giordano Bruno both held for a plurality of inhabited worlds. In fact, it is often believed, especially by those who like to highlight the conflict between religion and science, that it was this particular belief of Bruno's that got him burned at the stake by the Roman Inquisition in the year 1600. But if so, then why wasn't Campanella also torched?

The likelihood was that it was a combination of Bruno's vitriolic personality and his denial of the doctrine of the Trinity, a heresy that got Spanish theologian Michael Servetius burned at the stake by the Calvinists in Geneva in 1553, that was the major cause of Bruno's demise. Fact is, that despite Luther's condemnation of Galileo (for once Luther thought the pope was right) there have been quite a few Protestants—particularly those along more liberal American lines—who have seen no conflict between the Bible and belief in extraterrestrial life.

Closer to our own time, the German theologian Joseph Pohle, who once taught at Catholic University in Washington, D.C., even wrote a book titled *On the Starworlds and Their Inhabitants* that went through seven editions (in German) by the time of his death in 1922. So while the term "astrotheologian" may not have surfaced up to now, it is obvious that such thought is hardly new.

As for my own thinking on the subject, we know that there are over a billion galaxies in the visible universe, with hundreds of billions of stars in each, most of them probably, as it now appears, with planetary systems of their own, with the odds that at least some of them (about one in ten in the case of our own solar system) are capable of being the home of intelligent life. Although we may never come in contact with any life outside of that on our own planet because of the vast distances involved, to suppose that such life isn't out there would mean that the human race is either entirely an accident of nature or that God, as a creator, is rather incompetent.

This obviously poses problems for Christian theology and its claims of a universal redemption through Christ. Would such extra-terrestrial creatures even need redemption? How could an original sin of Adam have affected them? Or even if we are talking not about an inherited sin but simply a creaturely condition, how could any of the gospel "good news" ever reach them? Long before the people like von Kues, Campanella, or Bruno began to wonder about such things, the biblical scholar and teacher, Origen of Alexandria (185-254) had speculated about successive creations and hence, multiple worlds. Maybe it was in light of Origen's thinking that the assembled bishops in the year 325 carefully penned the famous phrase "for *us* men (i.e., humanity) and *our* salvation" (emphasis mine) into the Nicean Creed. If so, "astrotheology" has been around for a very long time.

## Religion versus Science
(December 5, 2003)

In a recent "Focal Point" guest editorial titled "Science and Religion; Can We Talk?" in the December 2003 issue of *Sky & Telescope* magazine, Jesuit astronomer (and head of the Vatican Observatory) Rev. George V. Coyne, S.J., took issue with a statement by the Harvard-Smithsonian historian of science Owen Gingerich. Coyne disapproves Gingerich's opinion, based on the fact that just a slight difference in "any physical constant" in the makeup of the universe would have made the emergence of human life impossible, and that "a common-sense and satisfying interpretation of our world suggests the designing hand of a super-intelligence." In other words, as it becomes clearer in Coyne's article, he strongly disapproves of anyone, even a scientist, trying to use scientific arguments to prove the existence of God.

I also think we have to be very careful about such attempts. Too often, the "gaps" in the scientific account of the origin of life that seemed to require God's intervention to remedy turn out to be bridged as science has advanced. But in defense of Gingerich, I would point out that he only used the word "suggests" not "proves," and add that while people may argue about whatever "commonsense" is (some of Einstein's theories may defy what we once took it to be), still, whatever is "satisfying," like beauty, is largely in the eye of the beholder.

However, what I have noticed, ever since my own exposure to contemporary thinking on the subject, is that cosmologists are more and more asking questions that seem to be outright theological. And when they try to answer them, they are coming up with theories that seem to me to fall more into the realm of speculative philosophy than what I understand to be empirical science. I think this is particularly evident when some cosmologists start resorting to appeals to "other universes" or other dimensions of reality (I think "string theory" proposes eleven of them—seven of them completely undetectable by us!) to try to explain away the kind of cosmic "coincidences" that Gingerich is talking about. I wouldn't want to see scientists forbidden to engage in such flights of mathematical imagination—certainly real breakthroughs resulted from Einstein's "thought experiments." Still, such theorizing needs to be constantly weighed against established scientific evidence, much the same way as the speculations of theologians need to be grounded not just on "the data of revelation" (Sacred Scripture) but also in touch with the realities life and the world.

So while I'm all for the kind of "respectful dialogue" that Coyne encourages in his article, I think the discussion has to go far beyond "the respective roles of science and religion in our lives." I think it must also include serious interaction between the disciplines of science and theology as we address the ultimate questions. More and more the natural sciences and religion appear to me (as it would to someone looking down a railroad track) like two different rails that are nevertheless "tied" together. While they must remain distinct and parallel to function correctly, they appear to converge as we gaze toward the horizon, and, we might hope, lead to the same destination.

---

# Darwin and the Demotion of Humanity
(February 12, 2003)

The shock produced by the publication of Darwin's *The Origin of Species* in 1859 was not so much the theory of evolution itself, which had been around in one form or another for many ages, but, rather, it was the implications of this view for human origins, something that Darwin himself hesitated to openly present until the publication of his second great work, *The Descent of Man*, a dozen years later in 1871. The reason for this shock was, of course, the apparent demotion of the human species implied by the word "descent." One can only wonder if the shocked reaction might not have been lessened if Darwin had used the word "ascent" instead.

Either way, however, the implications were clear. There is not all that much that separates us, physiologically speaking, from the ape. Instead of being seen as altogether special, created in God's "image and likeness," humanity was now reduced to being one rather curious species within the family of primates. This is somewhat the reverse of the view long taken by humans, who once saw these other creatures as strange and amusing mirrors of ourselves. Where one comedian used to say "monkeys are the funniest people," now people were seen as the strangest variety of monkeys!

Even today this residue of shock remains. Although the Catholic Church finally admitted in 1950 that evolution could account for the physical origins of the human race, it still stubbornly holds on to the ideal that human "souls," each and every one of them, are a special creation of God—even though the present pope admits that the exact moment at which this event takes place cannot be established either from philosophical argument or from divine revelation. And if that ignorance is admitted, then how do we know for sure? Perhaps we might say that we feel it "in our guts." But is that really a valid argument or is it simply a futile effort to save face?

On the other hand, if we compare the accomplishments of the human race to those of the rest of the primates, the differences, for good or bad, are obvious enough. Apes, like many other animals, may display a certain "language," but none of them, to our knowledge, have produced a Shakespeare. They may even fashion primitive tools, but again, none, as far as we know, have ever discovered how to use, much less make, a fire. Nor do they, except in some rare cases, seem to have any reflective awareness of themselves as individuals, even when they see themselves in a mirror—a beginning, but perhaps only the feeblest sign of what we humans are capable of. This is not only to know things but even more to "know that we know" and to make decisions according to that knowledge.

Some will say that all this is only to point out differences in quantity but not in quality—for example, in the amount of "gray matter" in the brain. But even so, as the philosopher Engels pointed out, does not a significant increase in quantity sometimes effect a change in quality as well? Accumulate sufficient amounts of gas, and the force of gravity alone produces stars. Assemble increasingly complex molecules and eventually life is born. Bring together millions upon millions of neurons and human thought occurs. In other words, while evolutionary "leaps" may indeed take place, they are more like steps over certain "thresholds." But the significance of each step may be more apparent to us as we experience the differences than it really is, at least in terms of the whole evolutionary direction taken by nature.

Yet if this is so, why should we assume that all thresholds have been crossed? For if science has long pictured evolution as a tree ascending upward, then logically, the next great step forward may be not just more life, or even more intelligence (quantitative advances), but an even greater qualitative leap forward—the eternal life that all along religion has promised.

# Is There a "God Gene"?
(November 15, 2004)

Last month a featured article appeared in *Time* magazine regarding the existence of a "God gene"—which is another way of asking whether or not there is an inherited attraction to religion. It is a very interesting article, even if not especially surprising for anyone who has kept up with the field of sociobiology or what's called "the new Darwinism."

However, the initial summary question—"Did God exist first or did the human need for God come first?"—also underlies most of the ambiguities or confusions of the article. The first question is a philosophical issue. The second is more strictly a psychological matter. As a result, the answer can be—although it doesn't necessarily have to be—"yes" to both. Or as a biologist friend of mine recently said, *what* one thinks is largely a matter of environment (which includes education or lack of it), but *how* one thinks is largely a matter of heredity or genetics—which translates into psychology.

So Freud could be, and probably was, correct when he saw God, or our ideas of God, as a projection in terms of the superego, of our father figure. The biblical statement about God making man in his own image can be seen in reverse—which is the origin of idolatry. It also explains the findings of a study done years ago at the University of Michigan that discovered that many self-declared atheists seem to have had somewhat troubled relationships with their fathers.

But none of this psychological theorizing has anything to do with the philosophical logic involved in deciding whether or not God exists. As I see it, the main point of contention is whether are not the universe is self-sustaining. Did it have a beginning or not? The present cosmological evidence all points to the contingency of the universe, that is, its dependence on something else. Whether one wants to call it (in astrophysical terms) a "horizon event" like the big bang, or (in philosophical terms) a "prime mover," an "uncaused cause," or "a ground of being," or simply "God," may be simply a matter of preference.

However, if the *Time* article is correct from the sociobiological perspective, then I would also find it no surprise if evolution has also selected in favor of belief, especially if that belief has helped our species to survive. But I would suggest that something else may be going on here as well—namely an evolutionary instinct not just to survive but also to advance. What I'm talking about is an inborn drive toward *self-transcendence*. We see it all around us in various forms: the quest for wealth, power, success, fame, and so on. That many seek something (or Someone) transcendent or beyond us is not surprising, especially when worldly wealth, power, and the rest prove unreachable (hence the popularity of religion among the poor) or, at the opposite end of the spectrum, when one has experienced all the goodies the world can offer and found them wanting.

Of course, nothing here is really all that new. St. Augustine wrote some sixteen centuries ago, after experiencing most of what life had to offer: "Our hearts were made for you, O Lord, and they will not rest until they rest in you." So at most, it seems that the *Time* article and the book it features possibly give new evidence for what we already knew—and maybe a new twist on why it turned out that way.

---

# The Cardinal, the Pope, and Intelligent Design
(July 11, 2005)

The current flap within the Catholic Church triggered by Vienna's Cardinal Christoph Schönborn, chief architect of the official *Catechism of the Catholic Church*, has all the hallmarks of an attempt at a "course correction," but one that has resulted in a bit of "over-steer."

What the cardinal was apparently attempting to do, with the new pope's approval, was to counteract some overly permissive interpretations of the previous pope's 1996 admission that "evolution is more than a hypothesis." It seems that some people took that remark to mean that the church had gone over to a full-scale endorsement of the current neo-Darwinian interpretation of evolution—which of course it cannot. If most Catholics are generally accepting of evolutionary science as the only logical explanation of the workings of nature, they still see it as part of God's ongoing creative activity. In other words, they hold to a Christian form of what philosophers of science call "theistic evolution." Thus they see God as both the origin of the universe and the goal of its existence. And they would also like to believe that they see divine Providence or God's wisdom at work throughout the whole evolutionary process.

But it is this latter point that is the especially tricky one. Does this mean that nothing happens by chance? To those who advocate an "intelligent design" version of evolution (among whom are a few Catholic scientists) it seems that every critical turn in the evolutionary process—for example, the appearance of the flagellum as a propulsive appendage on simple cells or, to take a more basic example, the occurrence of life in the first place—is caused by some kind of divine intervention rather than simply the result of an "algorithmic" process of long-term trial and error.

Some of these attempts to explain what seem to be highly implausible events in the evolutionary process are rather impressive. Yet, on the other hand, if the interplay of chance or indeterminacy with the determinism imposed by biological necessity is not given its full role, then the whole structure of the evolutionary theory seems to be undermined.

More serious yet, I believe, is the effect on what is probably the strongest asset that the evolutionary explanation of nature can bring to religious belief and to theology, which is a logical explanation for the immense amount of evil and suffering in the world. It is only when the evolutionary origins of human freedom are recognized that the amount of evil that we are capable of begins to make sense and that a greater purpose that God seems to have had in mind in leaving so much to chance emerges. To paraphrase Pierre Teilhard de Chardin (1881-1955), the Jesuit scientist who was Catholicism's foremost theorist of evolution, God, by "playing creatively with chance," has not so much made mankind but "made man to make himself."

# Part 3
# War and Peace

The essays in this section proved to be among the most controversial when originally published, generating some angry letters to the editor of the newspaper in which they appeared. However, time has proved at least some of them to have been right on target and perhaps, in a few cases, even prophetic, although, based on the continuing tension in the Balkans and turmoil in the Middle East, no one should take comfort in that fact.

While much of the material commented upon in this section involves matters that are also treated in Part 7 of this book, the reflections contained here attempt to concentrate more on issues of general ethical principle, international law, and the Christian tradition of "just war" theory or thinking.

## Kosovo and a New Moral Order
(July 3, 1999)

As NATO troops flood the Yugoslavian province of Kosovo, the world stands horrified as they find, in mass gravesites or even, in places, without even the benefit of a grave, the remains of hundreds, perhaps even thousands, of Kosovar men slaughtered by Serbian police and military during the past few months. Clearly, this is evidence not just of a campaign of terror intended to put down the guerrilla forces of the Kosovo Liberation Army but also of a policy calculated to empty the whole province of some 90 percent of its inhabitants—so as to "ethnically cleanse" the area of its non-Slavic Albanian majority to reclaim it for the Serbs who some six centuries ago lost the area to the Turks. It seems that the Albanian people (known as "Illyrians" back then) had made the mistake of supporting the Turkish invasion as way of regaining the territory taken away from them by the invading Serbian Slavs many centuries before that.

And so it goes precedent before precedent without end! Someone once described the Balkans as a part of the world with too much history for too little space. No doubt this is true. Yet, is this not also true of almost every other place on the face of the earth if we insist on using the crimes of the past as justification for retaliation by way of new crimes?

Even the Bible can supply us with such precedents. Have you ever taken a good look at the story of the fall of Jericho in the Book of Joshua? There we are told that the Israelites (after the walls miraculously fell down) slaughtered not only the men of Jericho but also all the women and children (save Rahab and her family) as well. Whether or not this actually happened—some archaeologists have long claimed the site of Jericho, one of the oldest cities on earth, was actually deserted at the time of the Israelite invasion of Canaan—is largely beside the point. The lessons of the story were clear, and one of those lessons was that the Canaanite peoples had better clear out or else! The Jews were to later claim that God told them to do this—supposedly because the Canaanites were idolaters. But that lesson seems to have stuck enough to impress modern Serbs who, as they themselves are quick to claim, consider Kosovo as their "Holy Land," with the mostly Muslim Albanians no doubt playing the role of the "pagan" Canaanites. If so, considering the present wrangling over Jerusalem, such a comparison bodes ill for any chances of future world peace.

How long will it be before the world wakes up to the fact that the past—especially what someone else's ancestors did to one's own ancestors years or even centuries back—can never be a justification or standard of conduct for the present? Yes, people have done terrible things to each other, but both the victims and the perpetrators of these crimes are, for the most part, long dead. Human rights belong to all living persons regardless of their race, their religion, or what their father or grandfathers may have done.

We have to recognize that along with the rise of civilizations, human morals or ethical standards must evolve as well. Years back, Raïssa Maritain, the artist wife of the great French philosopher Jacques Maritain and no mean philosopher in her own right, wrote a provocative essay on the evolution of moral consciousness in the history of her own Jewish forebears, from the near stone-age "eye-for-an-eye, tooth-for-a-tooth" mentality of ancient times to the "new commandment" proclaimed by Jesus—to love one another as our brothers and sisters without regard for the kind of distinctions that divided the ancient world. Instead of retaliation for past wrongs, the new standard must be "to forgive one another" and to disarm the forces of evil not by returning evil for evil but by "turning the other cheek."

No doubt such an evolution of morality is seen by many as impractical, even as too "revolutionary" to ever be tried. But is it? Was not the Marshall Plan following World War II such a gesture—one that turned our former enemies into friends and allies? Might not such a plan, had it been tried after World War I rather than the vindictive Versailles Treaty, have prevented the reoccurrence of war in 1939 in the first place?

This is not to say that justice must not also prevail. Major war criminals must be singled out, tried, and punished. But unlike the convicted war criminals of World War II, they should not be put to death—even if they deserve it. After all, more deaths (even judicially sanctioned ones) will not advance the cause of world peace. If this century of disasters has taught us anything, it should be that either we rise above the limitations of our past history or else, as the American philosopher George Santayana observed, we will be doomed to repeat it. Considering the slaughter of one group by another—there have been some 137 million such casualties during this past century alone—can the human race afford to continue this way? Anything we can do to break this vicious cycle of death and destruction must be done. And while we finally brought the killing in Kosovo to an end by means of a superior technology, we must remember that this same technology could be turned against us, and probably will be, unless a new moral order is brought to bear on the face of the earth.

# September 11, 2001
(September 12, 2001)

The horrors of September 11, 2001, have already provoked an almost unprecedented amount of blame laying and calls for retaliation, revenge, and punishment. Americans are understandably outraged and angry, unable to understand how it is that the greatest economic and military power in the world could become the victim of a handful of fanatical terrorists. The national intelligence community and airline security systems, in particular, are being subjected to intense criticism. But hardly anyone, at this point, seems to be questioning America's foreign policy or stance before the world.

This could be seen as a fundamental and eventually fatal mistake. Fifty-some years ago, the renowned British historian Arnold Toynbee warned the West that the peoples of the once-powerful Muslim world would try to reassert themselves after centuries of invasion by the European powers that had carved up the Middle East for their own convenience and economic profits, particularly after the collapse of the Ottoman Turkish empire at the end of World War I. As these European powers relinquished their colonies in the aftermath of World War II, Arab and various other ethnic national movements took their place. But while many of their politicians, much like Ataturk already had in Turkey, embraced modernity, Islam itself struggled to revive the religious and cultural values of the past. The stage was being set for an epic struggle between the secular West and the religious East.

The entry of the United States in this region of the world was first dictated by our need for oil. But stricken by guilt over what had happened to the Jews under Hitler, we were soon to become embroiled in the controversial and highly disruptive creation of the modern state of Israel, carved out of the then former British-ruled "mandate" territory of Palestine. When the surrounding Arab states, led by Jordan, resisted, the newly created United Nations stepped in to try to keep the peace. Instead, a series of short spectacularly successful wars were fought by Israel largely with American money and materiel, each of which expanded the territory occupied by Israel with the resulting displacement of at least half of the native Palestinians. These people, now grown to a population of about seven million, continue to exist, either as second-class citizens in Israel, as residents of an Israeli-ruled "West Bank," or as refugees in Jordan, Lebanon, Syria, or elsewhere around the world. The Palestinians are demanding their country back, or at least a fair portion of it.

As I quickly learned as a resident scholar there in 1981, Palestinians, almost to a man, hold the United States responsible for their plight. Attempts to explain America's position (to see peace and justice for all) are impossible when the Israeli occupation forces wield U.S.-made and U.S.-supplied M-16 assault rifles, when air strikes into Lebanon (which I witnessed while visiting in Galilee) are carried out by U.S.-supplied F-16s, and when Israeli "settlements" are built on West Bank land confiscated from Palestinians whose land deeds were lost when the Turkish empire collapsed. As I was told over and over again by Palestinians, "the Israelis could not treat us like this except for U.S. aid." Or when I asked another scholar, an Egyptian Christian, what he thought of Israel, he told me bluntly, "it is an American colony—the latest inflicted by the West on the Middle East."

The only way for the United States to stop terrorism against it will be to broker a real peace by demanding justice for Palestinians—even while we attempt to ensure a safe place for Israel. Short of that (as the Israelis should have learned by now) there can be neither security nor peace. Desperate people will continue to do desperate and horrific things.

## The U.S. and the UN
(September 8, 2002)

From its very beginning, the United Nations has been supported and encouraged by the vast majority of Christian churches of the world. It was strongly endorsed by Pope Pius XII (and every pope since him) who saw it as the world's last best hope in preventing catastrophes like World War II, which had just ended, as well as by the World Council of Churches, representing nearly three hundred different Christian denominations, and which was founded almost simultaneously to the UN as its religious counterpart.

The U.S. administration has done well in heeding the voices of so many of its critics in approaching the UN with its case against the government of Iraq. Indeed, as President Bush's address to the General Assembly put it, of what real use is the UN if it cannot effectively address and remedy the dangers to world peace presented by dictators like Saddam Hussein? If it fails to do so, the UN will have failed miserably to fulfill the very function for which it was created.

That being said, however, what are we to do if the UN fails to respond to this clear challenge? President Bush and several of his spokesmen have more than hinted that if the UN fails in its job, then the United States must do what it must (to put it into their own words) "for its own national interests." Perhaps this is rhetoric designed to frighten the rest of the world. If so, it seems to be working, but in a way that will eventually turn most of the nations of the world against us.

No one doubts that U.S. armed forces are capable of blasting Iraq, the site of one of the oldest known civilizations on earth, back into the Stone Age. But in doing so, would not the United States be "winning the battle only to lose the war?" Are we not engaged in a greater "War on Terrorism?" Yet if we go off on this tangent alone, without the support of the rest of the world, we will end up being regarded as the world's biggest terrorist ourselves, and we will be the perpetual target of the rest of the world's terrorists. We shall be judged as hypocrites, preaching democracy to the rest of the world but acting like the whole world's self-appointed dictator.

It is only when we realize that our own long-term national interest is served by acting in unison with the rest of the world that we can expect anything but eventual disaster.

## America's "Superiority Complex"
(December 22, 2002)

Recently, a friend of mine, reacting to my suggestion that there are certain moral or ethical norms that need to be met before we invade Iraq, answered to the effect that since we are morally superior to our intended target there really is no ethical problem to be faced. I would say quite the contrary.

First there is the mistake of trying to assert one's own righteousness—which I believe the Bible reminds us is gone the moment we think we are better than others. But even given that common human failing, I think we need to be reminded that, even aside from the folly of judging our own perfection, how we judge another culture's moral standards is not necessarily the standard (correct or not) by which they judge us. For example, for Muslims, a single glance at our movie posters, as seen in the streets of Cairo or Beirut, convinces them that we are a corrupt and licentious society.

Yet it goes a lot deeper than that. We in the West tend to rank our individual rights and privileges (our "freedoms") above everything else. To a Muslim, this sounds like idolatry, the worship of self in the place of God, much the same as it would have to a Jew in ancient times. To them, the highest value (even as reflected in our own Lord's Prayer) is the realization of God's will or kingdom on earth. In fact, the Muslim code of conduct is remarkably close to the Ten Commandments as they were originally understood (including not forbidding polygamy) by the Jews, and even include some of the other Jewish ritual commands (like circumcision) and prohibitions (against eating pork or taking interest on loans) as well. Many, perhaps even most, Muslims look at the Jewish and Christian failure to keep these commandments and the kind of society this failure has produced as a prime sign of our infidelity to God.

Add to this our readiness to assert our debased (as perceived by them) society on them, either by proxy (Israel) or directly by our own force of arms. All this makes American talk about preemptive strikes against their countries particularly threatening. As Osama bin Laden put it succinctly in an interview some years ago, "If we punch you in the nose, you Christians are supposed to turn the other cheek. But if you punch us in the nose, we will punch right back." In other words, it is not our ideals that Muslims object to, it is our hypocrisy in failing to live up to them and yet claiming we are superior at the same time.

So, granted that people like Saddam Hussein also are hypocrites (bin Laden has had Saddam, as well as the high-living Saudi royalty, on his enemies list as well), the problem still remains. Once we claim a moral superiority yet try to justify preemptive strikes as "self-defense," we proclaim our own double standards to the world and invite them, who still believe in an "eye-for-eye" and a "tooth-for-tooth," to do the same. And while we worry that Saddam just might be able to do this someday, in Pakistan, a country that is a real hotbed of Islamicist fundamentalism compared to Iraq, we have a country that already can.

## Preventive War?
(December 23, 2002)

On Dec. 20, 2002, PBS's *Now with Bill Moyers* featured an interview of Robert Kaplan, author of *Warrior Politics: Why Leadership Demands a Pagan Ethos* (Random House, 2001). In it, Kaplan argued that no matter how reluctant we may be to engage in "preemptive war" against Iraq, we must in order to prevent even greater catastrophe for the human race. Over Moyers' Christian objections, Kaplan, a self-avowed atheist, insisted that the traditional "just war" reasoning as to whether or not a war could be considered permissible or not is simply irrelevant—that in a world full of nuclear bombs and other weapons of mass destruction, such ethical or moral reasoning no longer applies.

If this is true, I wondered, where does this put anyone who seriously claims to follow Christ? Most Christians, to begin with, felt morally obliged to avoid any involvement with the military might of pagan Rome. Many refused to take up arms, sometimes even to the point of sacrificing their own lives. Those who converted to Christianity while in service often resigned—giving up the generous pensions afforded to army veterans as well.

All this changed when Constantine became emperor in 312 AD. While not yet officially proclaimed "Christian," the empire itself became the great defender of Christianity's right to exist, and Christians, in turn, felt obliged to defend the empire. Within a century, St. Augustine formulated his famous principles governing what he considered to be just causes for declaring a war (the most well known of these being that it must be purely defensive in nature) and that when such a war cannot be avoided that harm to civilians must be, as much as possible, ruled out.

Of course, everyone knows that these principles have rarely been followed perfectly. Invasions of other lands were even blessed to promote the spread of the Christian faith. Innocents starved to death in the sieges of towns occupied by armies and in World War II whole cities were attacked, even entirely incinerated, as in the cases of Dresden and Tokyo. Atomic bombs were dropped on Hiroshima and Nagasaki, both cities without any significant military installations yet picked out to be "examples" of what could be done to the rest of Japan.

So is Kaplan correct? Has everything changed with the advent of modern weapons of mass destruction, or is it that we have finally realized that the neat distinctions in St. Augustine's theory were really never worth much? And in either case, what must a Christian decide to do?

Do we naively go back to the early Christian practice of avoiding all violence, even in self-defense and even when it might mean our own death and the deaths of those we love? Or do we drop all pretense of Christian rules of war and simply return to a carefully calculated policy (very carefully, lest it end in our own self-destruction) of "might makes right"? And if this latter is the only practical choice left us, on what basis can we claim that our civilization is morally superior to that of anyone else?

---

## World Peace: The Papal Prescription
(December 28, 2003)

In his World Day of Peace message scheduled for release on New Year's Day, Pope John Paul II seems to have taken direct aim at U.S. foreign policy—in regard both to its invasion of Iraq as well as its general approach to combating terror. Not that the pope named names; popes generally leave that to their lieutenants. But the target of his criticism was unmistakable. What other country, except possibly Britain, could currently be charged with violating international standards the way the United States has in launching its preemptive attack on Iraq?

No doubt this message will not be well received by many American Catholics, especially by those whose moral sense was formed back in the cold war days when stanch adherence to Christianity got much too easily confused with unquestioning patriotism. Bombarded by the pro-war propaganda doled out from Washington, and traumatized like other Americans by the events of September 11, 2001, Catholics, just like many of their fellow citizens, were all too ready to believe anything their government told them—despite the warnings of their bishops, who like many other church leaders in the United States, tried to advise the public that things were not all that simple.

This warning in particular seems to have been lost on the majority of Americans, who still seem to be convinced that there was some kind of direct connection between Saddam Hussein and the 9/11 attack. Not that there couldn't have been, despite the lack of any convincing evidence so far to prove it. But even if there existed the remote possibility that al Qaeda could have gotten its hands on some Iraqi-produced "weapons of mass destruction" (something that is far more likely to occur in Pakistan) would stopping that possibility have been the "end" that, contrary to all accepted rules of morality, justifies the "means"?

It is on this point in particular that the pope's message bears on the future. Terrorism in the world cannot be successfully controlled by the use of brute force. Armies can never successfully defeat people or groups of people who are willing to use any means possible to strike back at what they see to be oppression, particularly the kind of oppression that occupying armies represent. This has been the lesson of history again and again. The tactics of terrorism represent the last line of defense of people who believe they have been denied fundamental freedoms or lack any other means of having their voices heard. America will remain the main target of terrorists until it is seen to be the major promoter of, rather than the major obstacle to, a fair sharing of the world's wealth and resources.

What this pope—whose own "Solidarity" movement, perhaps more than anything else, defeated Communism in his native Poland without firing a shot—is urging here is not some kind of ideal of Christian "turn-the-other-cheek" pacifism. What he is telling the world is that there can be no peace in this world unless there is first of all that for which Solidarity stood, and all Christians must stand for—fundamental justice.

---

# The Global Test
(October 6, 2004)

According to the United Nations Charter (Chapter VII, Article 51), a nation has the right to act in legitimate self-defense, even without UN permission, when seriously threatened. In the opinion of international legal experts, a country only needs to prove that what has now become known as a "preemptive strike" was intended to eliminate a danger or threat that was truly *grave*, *certain*, and *imminent*.

Unfortunately for the United States, we seem to have failed the test when it comes to Iraq. As subsequent investigations have proved, the danger, even if certain (certainly Saddam wanted to have his WMDs—just like the rest of us have), was, due to continuing UN sanctions, hardly imminent. Instead, what is becoming increasingly clear is that American public opinion was deliberately manipulated by the use of highly questionable intelligence in order to justify not just a "preemptive strike" but a "preventive war" or invasion of Iraq that had long been advocated by such groups as "The Project for the New American Century." Whether the president was equally a partner in this plan or simply duped still remains to be seen. In any case, the issue is extremely serious and something that far transcends politics or even international law. It is, instead, a matter of fundamental ethics or morality.

How so? In a sense, it goes back to the "Golden Rule" of Jesus to "do to others what you would have done to you." Another way of stating it, this time attributed to Confucius, is "not to treat others the way you would not want to be treated." And still another way, as articulated by the great philosopher Immanuel Kant, is that to judge the morality of any act one must first be able to answer the basic question of what would be the likely result on society in general if everyone acted the way that is being considered?

Failing this test, Saddam Hussein (if he had known what we now know) would have been fully justified in hitting us first—if he could have gotten away with it. The Soviet Union might have also during the long cold war, absent any U.S. guarantee that we would not use nuclear weapons in a preemptive first strike, something the Soviets vowed they'd never do and (thank God!) didn't.

The invasion and occupation of Iraq has already cost between 10,000 to 30,000 Iraqi lives—depending on who is doing the counting. The U.S. government only counts its own dead, something that, along with the flagrant violation of the Geneva Conventions at Abu Ghraib and elsewhere, raises the question as to whether or not America can be trusted any longer. If America is not to be considered "a rogue nation"—which most of the world seems to have concluded that we already are—we have to win back the world's confidence.

It would be nice to believe that this test could be met in this year's presidential election. Yet it is evident that both major parties are unwilling to effectively lead when it comes to settling what has been called "the Mother of All Conflicts" in the Middle East—the Palestinian-Israeli (the latter with its own hidden nuclear arsenal) situation. If we fail to pass this "global test" to the rest of the world's satisfaction, then I'm afraid we should not be surprised if some day we find ourselves preempted by any nation that feels that it too, because it is a "super power" (like China, with a billion more people than the United States), is somehow exempted from the rules that govern other nations. Meanwhile, it should be no surprise if smaller countries, like North Korea or Iran, are in a haste to get themselves a few nukes of their own before they find themselves preempted.

## Darfur
### (March 24, 2005)

As diplomats debate whether or not the atrocities being committed every day in the Darfur region of western Sudan officially rate the designation of "genocide," people around the world wonder why it is that something more effective can't be done to stop the killing, raping, starvation, and disease that has already begun to follow. While the Sudanese government claims to be reining in the violence, its military not only seems to be unable stop the aggression but is even deeply involved in it. Meanwhile, due to restrictions placed in their way by the Sudanese government, various international aid agencies have only been able to reach some of the refugee camps, while a small number of African Union troops are for the most part unable to do much more than stand by to make sure the refugees in some of the largest camps are not attacked again.

In the face of all this, what have we done, we who claim to be the leading country in the world when it comes to championing freedom and human rights? So far the United States has argued for economic sanctions against Sudan, but this has been blocked by four out of five of the major veto-holding members of the UN Security Council. Meanwhile, efforts to indict the leaders of the Sudanese government before the International Criminal Court have been stymied by the U.S. government's refusal to recognize the court. So while economic sanctions might help some (they did to some extent cause the Sudanese to become more cooperative in the U.S. war against terror), so far the renewed threat of sanctions seems to have done nothing to curb Sudanese terrorism against their own citizens in Darfur—no more than a decade of sanctions against Iraq prevented Saddam Hussein and his cronies from abusing the Iraqi people.

What then is to be done? Experts who have studied the situation say that two things are necessary. One is that an effective protective force has to be deployed immediately to prevent further bloodshed. The African Union forces are willing to do what they can, but without more international help and logistical support, little more can be accomplished.

The second thing that could help the situation in Darfur, and probably the most necessary in the long run, is to put some teeth into international law. If we were living in a country where the rulers considered themselves to be above the law, wouldn't we be doing everything we could, even to the point of revolt, to remedy the situation? Yet this is similar to the situation that still exists on the international scene, largely due to a few countries such as our own, who (like the Sudanese) continue to plead immunity from any world court on the basis of "national sovereignty."

If we really believe that our Judeo-Christian ethical system, even without an international court system, somehow guarantees our moral superiority, how do we explain, after nearly a quarter million deaths in Darfur, our failure to do anything effective? The same Bible that forbids murder also commands us to "judge your fellow men justly" and demands that "you shall not stand by idly when your neighbor's life is at stake" (Leviticus 19:16-17, *New American Bible* translation). And after what Jesus taught us, who can claim that the people of Darfur, or any other people in today's world, are not our "fellow men" and neighbors?"

## World War III?
(July 28, 2006)

Viewing the violence in Lebanon, which those on the scene tell us is much worse than the sanitized clips shown on U.S. television, we may well ask if World War III has already started. Although it could be so—indeed, some say September 11, 2001, was the real beginning—I don't think we have quite reached that point. What I see happening now is a final "choosing up sides" before the global mayhem begins in earnest.

So just what are those sides? Many, especially the radical Islamicists, see it as a clash of civilizations: Islam versus the Jewish-Christian cabal that has invaded their territory. Certainly it must look like that to them. The recent call by Dr. Zawahiri—Osama bin Laden's strategy theorist—to kill the infidel "crusaders" everywhere and to restore the Muslim empire from Iraq to Spain is a clear reference to long-past Islamic glory. However, that Zawahiri curiously left Indonesia—today the world's largest and most liberal Muslim nation—out of his vision of a worldwide caliphate is telling. What it tells me is that this is not so much a clash of civilizations as it is of eras in time or psychological mind-sets.

Granted—all of us are "conservative" when it comes to protecting our own skins or pet interests. But what most characterizes modern Western civilization is its liberal secularity. We see individual freedom—*libertas* in Latin—as the paramount value, and in one nation after another we have repudiated the once close ties between church and state that once characterized medieval civilization. No doubt we have overdone it at times, confusing the institution of an official church with religion in general.

Yet, within the Islamic world, the ideal is completely different. The ideal Islamic nation is one where there really should be no distinction between church and state, even if there is such, to some extent, in practice. We see this particularly in Wahabist (Sunni) Saudi Arabia and in Shiite-dominated Iran. For these two radical sects, the "Crusader" West is not the only enemy; the more or less liberal or secular governments of Turkey, Egypt, Syria, and, yes, Saddam's Iraq, are seen as traitors to true Islam. If there is any alliance between the Iranian-backed Hezbollah Shiites and Baathist Syria, it is only because, as they say in the Middle East, "the enemy of my enemy is my friend"—at least for the time being.

However, the fact that it really all boils down to a war between modern secular liberalism versus a radicalized religious conservatism should make us think twice before we launch any new "crusades" in defense of "Christian" civilization. While there are some religious nuts, especially in the United States, who believe in bringing on an "Armageddon" is just what the world needs (so that Christ can come a second time), such thinking, like Zawahiri's call for a restoration of medieval Islam, especially in this nuclear age, is a sure road to disaster.

## War Crimes
(August 15, 2006)

While no one expects terrorists to follow international conventions regarding warfare, nevertheless, no one can dispute the fact that Hezbollah, led by the Shiite Imam Hassan Nazrallah, is guilty of the indiscriminate killing of civilians through repeated rocket attacks in northern Israel, as well as using the Lebanese civilian population as a cover or shield. These tactics constitute war crimes prosecutable by the International Criminal Court, which after many years of preparation, was definitively established by the Treaty of Rome in 2002.

Still, what about the Israeli Prime Minister Olmert and his generals who in their claims to Israel's right to "self-defense"—which few would dispute—nevertheless have killed approximately ten times as many Lebanese civilians? While the Israelis claim to be trying to avoid killing civilians in their attempts to eliminate the Hezbollah fighters, the means being used, primarily bombing and artillery is grossly disproportionate, and, without follow-up with ground troops, ineffective. But even if it was effective, the lack of proportion—which is one of the requirements for waging a just war, even in self-defense, is also a war crime.

So what are the chances that Nazrallah or Olmert, or any of the Israeli generals, will eventually stand trial? The Lebanese government is probably too weak to ever lay hands on Nazrallah without plunging the country into civil war. Nor is it likely that Israel which, along with the United States and Communist China, has the distinction of being among the few nations which have either failed to sign or ratify the Treaty of Rome, is going to indict its own politicians and generals. All this gives the distinct impression that for some, who like to think of themselves as military "superpowers," might alone makes right.

Unfortunately, the history of past war crimes trials so far has given us only mixed results. No one disputes that the Nuremburg trials, at which the Nazis were condemned for their crimes, were justified. But the 1946-1948 Tokyo war crime trials, which indicted the Japanese militarists, inexplicably let Emperor Hirohito, who gave them the green light to begin the war, off the hook. Yet as General Curtis LeMay, who ordered the massive incendiary bombing of Japanese cities which killed far more civilians than the two atomic bombs, admitted, had the allies lost, "we would be the ones on trial." So let's face it: the real court is the world's opinion and the jury is highly unpredictable. Otherwise, how is it that Yasser Arafat, repeatedly denounced for his long association with PLO terrorism, and Menachim Begin, whom Israeli premier Golda Meir refused to allow in her cabinet because of his reputation as a terrorist, both ended up, after apparently mending their ways, winning the Nobel Peace Prize?

For the time being it seems that Israel, once considered the underdog, through its excessive use of force, no matter how successful its Lebanon operation might be, has lost whatever moral high ground it once had. And its main backer, the United States, in failing to rein its client in or, from the start, to join the world in calling for an immediate cease fire in Lebanon, has up-to-now largely discredited itself as an even-handed broker for peace.

Compared to the tens of thousands of civilians killed in Iraq during the past three years, so far the toll in Lebanon and Israel has been much less. But unfortunately, it is America, rightly or wrongly, that has been already blamed for either not preventing or for prolonging most of this violence. And no doubt it will be America that will end up paying for most of the damage that has been done.

## Five Years After
(September 11, 2006)

Five years after the September 11th attack by terrorists on America, perhaps it is time once again to try to access what this traumatic event and all that has followed means for both the U.S.A. and the world.

For one, the perpetrator of that attack, Osama bin Laden, remains alive, and his al Qaeda network, while having suffered great setbacks, is still alive and even growing, while the Taliban, which once gave it refuge, appears to be regaining ground in Afghanistan. Meanwhile, the U.S. invasion of Iraq, which largely diverted our troops from finishing the job in Afghanistan, has succeeded in tying up American military resources in what appears to be a thankless and interminable occupation that has so far cost us just about as many American lives as did 9/11—not to mention the deaths of about 130,000 Iraqis. And if we are to finish the nation building there that we vowed to do, we'll be there for who knows how many years to come. Indeed, a united and democratic Iraq may well be a lost cause already, with Shiites and Sunnis at each others throats, and Kurds well on their way to declaring themselves a separate nation. In that case, the major bonus that the U.S. occupation has given to al Qaeda recruitment will come back to further haunt us, while our use of torture, abduction, and secret detention centers has lost us the respect of our allies. What is widely perceived as America's one-sided support of Israel almost guarantees that the U.S.A. and American interests will be the targets of choice for Islamic terrorists for many years to come.

In the face of all of this, more than ever before we see some politicians succumbing to the temptation to see the whole situation as a "war of civilizations" on an epic scale—even likening it to the World War II era battle against fascism or the Cold War struggle against communism. Perhaps, but it is doubtful that it could turn out that way unless we really want it to. That there are fanatics on the other side who relish such rhetoric, there is no doubt. But we must recognize that extremists exist on our side as well, and that if we allow ourselves to be talked into the same kind of "crusade" versus "jihad" mentality, it only increases the chances we will end up with what we fear most.

Instead, I suggest that what we are seeing is a struggle not between civilizations or even between major religions, but between modernity and a past era that is only slowly losing its grip on the Muslim world. That there are likely to be spasms of resistance to changing times is only to be expected—certainly we have seen them here in the West as well. That modernity, with its secular values, is especially threatening to Muslim sensibilities, with its ideal of a unified religious-political order, there can be no doubt. Yet we forget that such was once also the ideal of the Christian world. Years of bitter rivalry and bloodshed between Catholics and Protestants—not unlike that between Sunnis and Shiites today in Iraq—taught us, the hard way, that something less ideal from a religious perspective, but more practical and more respectful of human rights and freedom, is the only sane way to go.

So instead of threatening either military or cultural annihilation, America and the rest of the Western world must employ its hard won patience and painfully acquired tolerance to help Muslims, both Sunni and Shiite, come to peaceful terms with each other, with the modern world, and with others, be they of other religions or even none at all.

# Part 4
# Religion, Ethics, and Politics

An old proverb has it—no doubt due to the close proximity of straight razors—that neither religion nor politics should ever be discussed in a barbershop. However, considering that in public life religious convictions generally translate into ethical and political issues, the topics that follow in this section have generated (even among friends) the most heat next to the shooting wars discussed in Part 3. While many of my friends, who think of themselves as conservatives (don't most of us become more so as we age?) consider me to be a "liberal," yet, as I see it, this liberalism is, in many cases a more radical form of conservatism, if by radicalism meant going to the roots (*radices* in Latin) of any issue or question. When that happens, as in the application of the gospel of Jesus in human life and relationships, the result could turn out to be quite revolutionary. Thus the aristocratic Pope Leo XIII was accused of being a "Communist" by wealthy Europeans when he, in 1891, issued the first in a line of what is by now a more than century-old Catholic tradition of social teaching. Perhaps what follows should be viewed in much the same light.

---

## The Death Penalty
(May 2, 2001)

If anyone in the United States deserves the death penalty, certainly it is Timothy McVeigh, the convicted murderer of some 168 people in the Oklahoma City Federal Building bombing on April 19, 1995. His will be the first execution carried out by federal authorities in decades. Hopefully it will be the last.

I say that not because I believe such executions will fail to deter further acts of terrorism by instilling the fear of God or even just a fear of death into potential terrorists, but because such executions will finally be seen as counterproductive. When we make a celebrity out of a murderer or a martyr out of a terrorist, we only promote more of the same.

McVeigh deliberately chose April 19th for the date of his crime as a protest against the Waco showdown in 1993—convinced that the U.S. government is an oppressive force out to suppress individual freedoms. In refusing to contest his own execution, or even requesting it be carried out, he hopes to prove his point. And he could be right at least if some of the long-standing attitudes prevalent in some of the fifty states become the policy for the whole nation.

Take, for example, Texas, which executed forty people last year [2000]. Compared to China, which admitted to executing 1,263 of its more than 1.27 billion citizens last year, your chance of being executed in Texas (with a population of about 20 million) is about one and a half times greater. Fortunately for those still awaiting execution on Texas's death row, the Texas State Legislature is looking at a moratorium to examine the evenhandedness of the practice. Yet one can only wonder.

In those states where Old Testament-style biblical fundamentalism seems to reign supreme, are we then to conclude that evenhandedness will also include the death penalty for idolaters (Deuteronomy 13:10), adulterers (Deuteronomy 22:22), abductors, or even those who strike or curse their father or mother (Exodus 21:15-17)? Hasn't the New Testament taught us anything?

So, too, the idea that the death of a murderer will somehow provide "closure" to the families of the victims is psychologically suspect. Even the chaplain to the Texas death row has expressed doubt, based on his long experience with those to be executed, that the victims' families, especially those who choose to watch McVeigh's execution on closed-circuit television, will find the peace they are looking for. The results, he says, could turn out to be quite the opposite.

One can only wonder then about a nation like ours that likes to call itself "Christian." Do we somehow think, ignoring what Jesus said about those who take up the sword dying by it (Matthew 26:52), that the cycle of violence can be broken by still more violence? Or do we really believe that God does not desire the death of the sinner but his reform (see Ezekiel 18:23 and 2 Peter 3:9)?

Or do we naively imagine that someone like McVeigh is going to repent in the face of a death that he imagines will make him a hero to every anarchist in the country? I suppose such miracles can still happen, and I'll pray that it does—but I wouldn't bet on it.

---

## New Year—New Era?
(December 7, 2001)

Remember the debate during the not-so-long-gone year of 1999 over whether or not the New Year's celebration of 2000 marked the beginning of a new (third) millennium or whether the proper date was really to be New Year's Day of 2001? Just to further muddy the waters, historians were all too ready to point out that if the starting point for all this year-counting really was the more probable year of the birth of Jesus of Nazareth, then the third millennium had already begun somewhere between 1994 to 1996!

Now, especially after September 11, 2001, all this debate seems quaintly academic and largely beside the point. Almost everyone seems to think we have just now truly entered a new era in the world's history, one in which all the old certainties of the past have come crashing down like the twin towers of the World Trade Center (or as some religious commentators have seen them, the twin towers of Babel) and that from now on the human race can never be the same.

Maybe so; perhaps we have really learned a lesson that will make this new millennium truly different. I really hope so. Still, from what I see happening around the world, and even in our own country, I'm not all that sure about such radical change. I still see a huge gap, even a widening gulf, between rich and poor, between the "haves" and "have nots" of this world, both within countries and between countries, with untrammeled free-trade, free-enterprise economics apparently making, at least for the underdogs, things even worse. Maybe this is only a temporary hiccup—something soon to pass. One might hope so, but perhaps more than mere hopes are necessary. When one is starving or homeless, even a case of hiccups may prove fatal.

I am no more hopeful about peace and justice for all. We hear politicians speak eloquently about the need for the nations of the world to pull together to fight our common enemy (terrorism) and then turn around and demand that they alone have the right to try such international criminals, as if the crimes were not against all humanity. Likewise, attempts to work together to eliminate the underlying causes that provoke many of these crises continually fall apart or are gutted of any effectiveness by one nation or another pleading its own "national interests," as if such selfish interests themselves were not the principal causes of the illness. Apparently we still do not trust one another enough to really make a common cause, even when ultimately our own individual futures are at stake.

In the face of this falling back into our old ways of doing things, we would do well to remember the warning of that not-quite-forgotten American philosopher George Santayana, who warned us that the price we pay for forgetting history is to be doomed to repeat it. Or to put it even more bluntly, as I think it was the British writer Samuel Johnson famously said, "Either we hang together" (in the figurative sense of cooperating) "or we shall hang separately."

---

## The U.S.A. "Under God"
(July 2, 2002)

The 9th District Federal Circuit Court decision barring the use of the words "under God" in the Pledge of Allegiance will no doubt be quickly overturned. Nevertheless, the political brouhaha that has erupted over this decision will continue to provoke further challenges over the role of religion in public life—as well it might.

I remember my own personal discomfort when the Lord's Prayer was recited along with the Pledge of Allegiance each morning at my public junior high in Connecticut in what I had always been told was the Protestant version ("for Thine is the power and the glory. . ."). In my ignorance I felt somehow disloyal to my Catholic roots, not realizing that this ending came from the Eastern Catholic/Orthodox liturgies (and was mistaken for part of the original Greek New Testament biblical text by the reformers). Even today, even after this Greek liturgical ending has been added to the post-Vatican II Latin or Roman rite Mass, those childhood memories of thinking of myself as the odd person out are still with me. So I can very well understand some people's discomfort at the public mention of God.

Nevertheless, should we excise every reference to the Creator or ultimate source of being that appears in our national heritage, including the Declaration of Independence, just because some people feel uncomfortable? If so, it would be hard to figure out where to stop.

However, it seems to me that by the terms "God" or "Creator" our founders were attempting to scrupulously avoid endorsing any particular religion. Whatever their original denominational affiliations, they were, at least in their public philosophy, what one might call "natural law deists." This view, roughly paralleling the philosophy of the Masonic Order, saw the Creator as the Grand Architect of the universe, the guarantor of individual freedom and equal rights before the Law. It is also a view that, however vaguely, reflects the biblical affirmation that not just humanity in general but even individual human beings are created in the image and likeness of God. All this is a quasi-religious belief that would be hard to justify from any scientific point of view.

One could argue, of course, that the majority of people in the United States no longer hold (if they ever did) such a philosophically neuter view of the deity. Still, this would be to miss the point. The idea was to skirt the issue of various religious and sectarian ideas and to find a common ground or foundation on which to erect the great American experiment. To begin systematically undercutting that foundation could be, if history is any sure indicator, a good way of causing the whole structure to fall down.

## On Church and State
(December 15, 2002)

While we are constantly warned against the danger of mixing religion with politics, the current state of the Church, as well as the quasi-religious hysteria of the American political scene, suggests that there is not a whole lot of difference between the two.

The Catholic Church is, for one, in really deep trouble over its cover-ups of clerical sexual misconduct and crimes—not just in the United States, but also in Europe, the UK, and elsewhere around the globe. Bishops, and even a few cardinals, have been forced to resign, if not for their own personal misbehavior then for their cover-ups and reassignment of priests who have seriously transgressed. It now appears that in its attempts to keep up appearances there is a paper trail of deception that leads back even to Rome. With the laity in a near state of open rebellion as each new scandal is uncovered, the Church faces an upheaval unprecedented since the Reformation begun by Luther five centuries ago.

Meanwhile, the United States, once admired as the world's most democratic country, has begun to be regarded as the world's pariah, no longer a shining example for other nations but a bully that feels entitled to dictate to the rest of the world what it must do to earn our favor and be considered our friends. Not to be with us is to be against us—certainly a hypocritical stance to take while our government refuses to be with the rest of the world when it comes curbing pollution, controlling nuclear proliferation, or even bringing international criminals to justice. And as our new officially declared national defense policy openly declares, no one may have weapons of mass destruction except, of course, ourselves and our friends—as if any nation should be any longer allowed to possess them! If ever there was an example of a nation operating under a double standard, in the eyes of the rest of the world it would be the U.S.A.

Yet, oddly enough, the cause of the problems of both the Church and the United States is remarkably the same—the self-corrupting influence of power. If we are told by scripture that the love of money is the root of all evil, is it not because gold and silver are evil by nature but because of the corruption and arrogance that such wealth tends to generate. Members of Congress and administration members are not so much corrupted by money as such (little of it stays in their own pockets) as by the influence that this money buys—the power to stay in office, and the prestige and the perks that the position affords. So too, in the Church, while the hierarchal salaries may be quite modest, the power and influence more than make up for it. After all, is there any single position in the world anywhere near the prestige of being pope?

If this is true, then all this suggests that the cure for this colossal mess can only come at tremendous cost in the form of some sort of terrible humiliation, and even then, it remains somewhat doubtful that cure can be in the end, successful. Perhaps there should be less doubt when it comes to the Catholic Church, which in one form or another has been with us for nearly two thousand years. As more than one historian has observed, any institution that has survived so much internal corruption for so long almost has to have had divine protection.

However, when it comes to political institutions, these tend to be much more short-lived. Although, as the old saying goes, "Rome was not built in a day," that ancient republic, especially after it became a continent-spanning dictatorship, fell completely apart in a remarkably short period of time. And as the English historian Lord Acton (1834-1902) once observed, "Power corrupts, and absolute power corrupts absolutely." Acton, who was a Catholic, meant this as a warning as to what might happen due to the expansion of papal power. Certainly his observation applies equally to matters of state.

Surely there is a lesson in all this for both America and the Catholic Church. Both are in dire need of a reality check: America in learning to cooperate with the rest of the world, not just in peace-making but even more fundamentally in both sharing and conserving the earth's resources with the other 95 percent of humanity, and the Church in restoring its own credibility (especially regarding the role of sexuality), in an increasingly crowded world.

## AIDS and Genocide
(July 30, 2003)

For some six months in 1994, approximately 800,000 Africans of Tutsi origin were slaughtered by Hutus in Rwanda and Burundi while the rest of the world looked the other way. Having lost eighteen U.S. Army Rangers in an ill-advised and risky attempt to capture a "warlord" in what was otherwise a popular famine-defeating humanitarian operation in Somalia, the U.S. president and the State Department refused to get involved anyplace in Africa and, in fact, even refused to admit that anything like genocide was taking place.

Today, what amounts to an even bigger genocide is taking place in Africa, this one not by means of guns and machetes, but as a result of AIDS. According to statistics gathered by the World Health Organization, of the 34.3 million people in the world who have come down with HIV/AIDS, nearly two-thirds (24.5 million) live in Africa. Of the some 19 million who have died from this dread disease so far (85 percent of them Africans), more than 2 million Africans died of it in 1999 alone. Another 4 million Africans came down with the disease in that same year. Already there are over 12 million AIDS orphans in Africa, and by the end of this decade there will probably be about 40 million parentless children on that continent while nearly 4 million African children under age fifteen will have themselves died of this disease.

The question needs to be raised: what does the rest of the world intend to do? Or will it simply look the other way? So far, the response has been meager. About $165 million is being spent on HIV prevention and AIDS patient care in Africa per year while about $2.3 billion per year is needed. Kofi Annan, the UN Secretary General, has repeatedly asked the richer developed nations to pledge $7 to $10 billion over the next five years.

The response of the United States, the world's richest nation, even before the current economic downturn, was a pitiful pledge of $200 million. Later on, under pressure from much less self-absorbed nations, we upped our pledge to $500 million, and lately our leaders are crowing about U.S. plans to give $1.1 billion. However, even that will be spread out over the next several years and will represent the U.S. commitment to the total Global Health Fund (not just for Africa) and will be directed partly to eradicating malaria and TB, not just HIV/AIDS.

Americans rightly pride themselves on being a religious people. Average church attendance in the United States probably outstrips any other nation or continent in the world (except perhaps Africa itself, where Christianity has been growing by leaps and bounds). Yet one can only question what kind of Christianity or level of religious understanding it is that consigns the human population of a whole continent to disease and starvation while, among other things, it lavishly feeds its own household pets. (According to industry-supplied figures, in 2000, U.S. citizens spent $27 billion on their cats, dogs, and other pets, with nearly half of that, on food—some of it even advertised as being "gourmet" quality!) Didn't Jesus have something to say about the injustice of throwing away what is intended for God's children as "food for the dogs" (Matthew 15:26; Mark 7:27)? Surely this is the kind of neglect that "cries to heaven for vengeance." So what should we do?

True, there is no cure, at least yet, for AIDS. Yet, even at the cut rate prices that some of the pharmaceutical companies have reluctantly agreed to, only some 36,000 African AIDS victims (out of 24.5 million) are being given life-prolonging drugs. Certainly we, the richest people in the world, could give more than just a few crumbs of compassion by sending pain-relieving medicines and helping doctors and nurses in Africa (most of whom earn less than $100 a month for their efforts) stay on the job. In Matthew's Gospel, Jesus warns U.S. that we will be judged by God on the basis of what we did for the "least of his brothers." Whatever else we think of Africa and the sorry state of its population, we must not be guilty of this new genocide by our indifference or neglect.

---

## Public Morality and the Ten Commandments
(September 6, 2003)

The federal court-ordered removal of Alabama Chief Justice Roy Moore's two-and-a-half-ton Ten Commandments monument from the lobby of the Alabama Supreme Court has become, in the eyes of many, a symbol of the antireligious or secular bias of modern American life. This is unfortunate, because to read this incident in this manner reflects a disturbing forgetfulness of the principles that have made the United States the leading light of freedom, including religious freedom, in the world.

When the United States was established, only one of the original thirteen states, Pennsylvania, still guaranteed freedom of religion. Maryland, originally founded in 1632 as a refuge for English Catholics, lost its freedom of religion in 1654 due to an influx of the same kind of Protestants who had forced Roger Williams, the founder of Rhode Island, from Massachusetts in 1635 because of his advocacy of religious freedom—but only for the likes of himself. Haunted by this history of intolerance, our founding fathers knew that, in forming a single nation from people with so many different beliefs, any attempt to establish an official national religion or church would spell the death of the still-struggling United States. Accordingly, the first amendment that had to be passed before the new Constitution could become law guaranteed that "Congress shall make no law respecting an establishment of religion or prohibiting the free exercise thereof . . ." (Article I, the *Bill of Rights*).

Nevertheless, isn't Judge Moore's monument an act of "free exercise of religion," especially if the people of Alabama voted him into office as "the Ten Commandments Judge"? Perhaps, but Moore's monument has a particular version of the commandments that happens not to be the version, the translation, or the numbering used by most Christians around the world. In other words, Moore's actions, whether he intended them to be so or not, amount to the promotion of a particular brand of Christianity, and this in the face of a population that includes people of many other faiths.

Granted, Moore probably did not intend this to be the case. In fact, I'm sure that in his mind these commandments represent the bedrock of Western civilization. Yet this is only true in part. Two other great classical currents also had a major role to play: the philosophical heritage of classical Greece with its ideals of democracy; and the great Roman legacy of rule by law. In this broader context, the Jewish *Torah*, much like the law codes of even earlier civilizations, must take its place among the many similar ethical codes that reflect what our country's founders called "the laws of nature and of nature's God."

Seen or used any other way, for example, as civil laws to be imposed on all people regardless of their individual beliefs, the Ten Commandments would become not, as originally intended, a source of human freedom but instead a cause of dissension and strife. If anyone has any doubts about that, one need only look to the Middle East, where another attempt to impose what the majority there considers to be divine law—the rule of Islamic *Sharia*—is turning that part of the world into a bloodbath. September 11th was only a sample of the kind of havoc that that sort of simplistic thinking can cause in today's complicated world.

## Reflections on Hurricane Katrina
(September 15, 2005)

In the aftermath of the devastation and suffering caused by Hurricane Katrina, we have seen an avalanche of finger-pointing—especially concerning the unnecessary deaths due to governmental bungling (local, state, and federal) and the failure to provide the means of evacuating people from the city of New Orleans in time.

Just as predictably, we have also seen a spate of theological opinionating, particularly of the sort that would see God's wrath or justice at work, apparently punishing the city of New Orleans for its fabled decadence and its people for their easygoing and sinful ways. However, if moral judgments are to be leveled regarding the conditions of life there, one might wonder if a good part of the blame shouldn't be leveled against America in general or in particular against its economic system. An acquaintance of mine who had been on assignment in India told me after visiting New Orleans long before the hurricane that the city reminded him of Calcutta with its yawning gap between the relatively rich and privileged and the throng of poor. That gap was exposed for all the world to see when the vast majority of whites managed to flee the city in their cars while a half million (mostly black) residents too poor to own a car were left to run (or swim) for their lives—leaving it mostly to the Coast Guard to try to rescue those who were left behind.

The perpetual problem of poverty ("The poor you shall always have with you," as Jesus predicted) aside, the question remains: what must now be done? Should New Orleans be rebuilt, and if so, to what extent? For many, especially those born there, this is an unthinkable question. Yet the world is filled with the sites of ancient cities that for one reason or another were abandoned as no longer inhabitable. Surely, slowly sinking well below sea level is one of those reasons!

Still, the optimist will object. Why not just keep building the levees higher? This is exactly what the U.S. Army Corps of Engineers has been asking to do for the past forty years. Yet, as scientists have been pointing out for years, the dangerous situation that has been building up in New Orleans for decades has been largely the result of the continued efforts of that same arm of government to artificially confine the Mississippi River within its channels and prevent the flooding that built up the wetlands that once helped protect the original city from storm surges from the sea. So while higher levees could undoubtedly prolong the city's survival for a time, in the long run, in view of the tendency of river delta land to sink coupled with the increased storm activity and sea levels occurring with global warming, the short-term solution looks more and more like a long-term formula for even greater disasters to come.

If the old adage that "God helps those who help themselves" has any truth to it, then common sense would seem to suggest that while the oldest parts of old New Orleans—which are actually still a bit above sea level—might be preserved, the other parts of the city should be rebuilt farther inland on higher ground. And while this new New Orleans might not turn out to be exactly a "New Jerusalem," it could reflect—again if we use common sense—a greater concern for the welfare of the urban poor.

---

# The Relatively Poor and Absolute Poverty
(December 21, 2005)

Although Jesus said "the poor you shall always have with you," this does not give us a license to ignore them. Quite the contrary, if we can believe the account of the Last Judgment in Matthew's Gospel (25:31-46), our neglect of the poor will surely lead to our damnation. How do we explain this seeming contradiction? How can the Catholic Church preach, as it has, "a preferential option for the poor" if the desired outcome would be to eliminate poverty, hence it seems the poor themselves in the process? The answer to that is, I think, pretty obvious. There are two kinds of poverty; one is absolute, the other only relative.

There will always be people who are, in *relative* terms, poor—that is, whose income and whose standard of living will be less than average. Even the socialist dream of "to each according to his need, and from each according to his means" assumes that some people are less naturally favored while others are more so. For them, the idea was to level the playing field, so to speak, so that everyone could live a life with at least of modicum of freedom and dignity. The fact that this has turned out to be an impossible dream does not negate its biblical origins. Christianity, like any religion, deals with ideals, and if these ideals have been replaced in the United States with "trickle-down" theories of economics, that does not negate the fact that all this remains in the realm of what might be called "relative prosperity and poverty."

Nevertheless, whether in secular or Christian terms, there can never be an excuse for *absolute* poverty—the absence of sufficient food, shelter, and food for survival. Yet millions in so-called "Christian" countries and billions of others around the world continue to barely live and not long survive under what can be barely called "civilized" conditions. How can this be?

I think that at this point we see the real clash between religion and science. It is not whether the creation accounts in Genesis—which were probably never meant to be taken as anything but metaphors—need to be taken literally. Nor is it a question as to whether the human species is descended from apes. It is, rather, a question of whether or not humanity can ascend beyond them. Those who would justify the continued existence of absolute poverty as being "in the natural course of things" would seem to show themselves to be little evolved beyond the apes, while those who have striven to eliminate even relative poverty (even when their dreams have proved wildly impractical) probably need to be counted among those who have most advanced humanity beyond the jungle and its ways.

---

## Religion and Society
(May 11, 2006)

Recently a paper published by Creighton University's *Journal of Religion and Society* has attracted some media attention. Written by Gregory S. Paul, it is titled "Cross-National Correlations of Quantifiable Societal Health with Popular Religiosity and Secularism in Prosperous Democracies." Although subtitled as being only "A First Look," the author seems to indicate that where the practice of religion is more prevalent, so too is anti-societal behavior.

The findings, drawn from a systematic evaluation of numerous studies made by sociologists around the United States and the Western world, are rather upsetting to those of us who like to think that religion is the foundation of a sound and law-abiding civilization. For example, while the United States remains the most openly religious of these modern societies, the homicide rate here tops practically all of the other countries studied, while the incidence of sexually transmitted disease, teen pregnancy, and abortion are anywhere from two to twelve times higher, depending on which state is involved—with the Bible Belt states leading the pack.

What are we to make of these statistics?

First of all, I think we should always have a healthy skepticism of statistics. While I'm in no position to contest the figures cited, one wonders if the conclusions drawn from them are accurate when the new democracies in Eastern Europe or the prospering economies of Southeast Asia, some of which are ardently religious, are left out of the picture.

Second, it should be pointed out that statistical *correlations* should not be confused with *causes*. When it comes to the latter, it may be that societal and economic inequality, which the author points out is greater in the United States than any of the other countries studied, drives some people to crime but others to religion.

Third, I would question whether the author's tendency to identify religiosity with rejection of evolutionary science—in other words, with biblical fundamentalism—is not inherently misleading. True, fundamentalists may also attend church more regularly, but why disqualify, as the author does, the fact that there are "especially low homicide rates in the more Catholic European states" as being statistically suspect or insignificant? Could it be that the author instead has confused certain beliefs, like creationism—which most Catholics reject—with Christianity?

Finally, I would like to make a suggestion that perhaps the correlations, if they mean anything at all, confirm what psychologists of religion and many theologians have long recognized: that there are different styles of religion that to some extent mirror different stages or levels of faith. If so, then the disturbing facts unveiled in this study may not be an indication that religion fosters unhealthy or dysfunctional societies but that religion as understood or practiced in the United States has some way to go before it reaches the level of a truly mature and socially responsible faith or faith-commitment.

---

## Abortion and Embryonic Stem Cell Research
(August 26, 2006)

Recently, a company calling itself Advanced Cell Technology, Inc. announced that they have developed a technique of removing individual stem cells from embryos without destroying the embryo. It was this company's hope that this new advance might bring about a truce in the hot debate over stem cell research and might even cause a reverse of President Bush's policy of blocking the U.S. of government money for research on lines of stem cells that are not already in existence. After all, if the embryo is not harmed in the perfected process, who could object to this new breakthrough in medical technology?

However it seems that there have been some very quick reactions to this news, particularly in the Catholic Church. Bishop Elio Sgreccia, head of the Vatican's Pontifical Academy for Life, pointed out that it is not only wrong to experiment with embryos, or even to create them in Petri dishes, but that the separated cell thus produced is, in effect, a clone, that is "a second embryo." Bioethicist Richard Doerfinger, speaking for the U.S. Conference of Catholic Bishops, accused the scientists involved of killing at least sixteen embryos in the course of their research.

From such sharp responses, it is easy to see why one expert, Dr. John Harris, professor of Bioethics at the University of Manchester, predicts that the conflict will never be resolved through scientific advance, because the issue is ultimately ideological. According to Harris, "the use of embryonic cells will only become non-controversial when it is accepted that the early embryo is of little or no moral significance."

Perhaps Harris is correct, but it is not because the early embryo is necessarily considered to be a full-fledged "person" or that it has a "soul" at this point. According to Rev. Tadeusz Pacholcyzk, Ph.D., a Catholic neuroscientist and ethicist, those are "very interesting intellectual questions, but they're not ultimately relevant." What is critical in the moral analysis, according to Pacholcyzk, is that we are dealing with an "embryonic human" at this point, "a being with the potential to become an adult" and "a bearer of human rights." According to this point of view (which echoes the approach taken by Pope John Paul II in his encyclical *Evangelium vitae*), it is wrong to manipulate the human reproductive process in any way, even for well-intentioned humanitarian purposes. Such utilitarian thinking has taken U.S. further down the same slippery slope that began with contraception (sex without reproduction) and has already resulted in widespread use of in vitro fertilization (reproduction without sex). From this point of view, asks Pacholcyzk, what would really be so wrong with reproductive cloning as well?

The problem with this critique, however, is that while it may seem to have a certain logical consistency on its side, it appears to be contradicted by what seems to most people to be common sense. For example, when the Church condones, even sometimes promotes, natural family planning (often called the "rhythm method") as a means of avoiding conception, many Catholics find it difficult to see where such a technique of birth control differs much from taking a pill, especially when the motives for doing either appear to be essentially the same. Likewise, when the Church allows "indirect abortion," that is, the removal of a "ectopic" or out of place fetus when it would endanger the mother's life, it is hard for most people to see how the sacrifice of an even less-developed embryo—which may have less than a 20 percent chance of developing to the fetal stage to begin with—cannot be justified when it contributes to the saving of a human life.

It may very well turn out that a breakthrough in the use of adult stem cells will turn out to be more efficient than using those taken from embryos. If that happens, one might hope that the furor over this issue would disappear. However, until that happens, it will be difficult to persuade most people, including most Catholics, that blocking all experimentation with embryonic stem cells is really consistent with the goal promoting human life.

---

## Capital Punishment
(January 16, 2007)

The recent decapitation of Saddam Hussein's half-brother, apparently an accident as he was being hanged along with another of Saddam's hated henchmen, underscores the barbarity of the use of the death penalty—however heinous the crime.

In fact, the use of the legal term "capital punishment" itself is a throwback to the days when the application of the death penalty literally meant to be relieved of one's head (*caput* in Latin). This was usually done by means of a sword or an axe.

While the ancient Athenians seem to have substituted the obligation of drinking poison, at least for eminent citizens like Socrates, the Romans considered decapitation something a privilege for its erring citizens. Lesser types, like slaves and noncitizens, were generally crucified, burned, or thrown to the lions for the people's amusement or education. This is why St. Paul, as a Roman citizen, was decapitated by the sword, where St. Peter, a noncitizen, was, at least according to an ancient Church tradition, crucified upside down.

One would think that after all those ancient horrors Christianity would have been against capital punishment from the very start. In fact, for the first few centuries of Christian history, the cross was virtually absent from Christian symbolism or art. However, after Christian emperors abolished crucifixion, decapitation remained the preferred method of execution in Europe, with burning at the stake reserved for witches and heretics. The English introduced hangings in the tenth century, but during the murderous reign of Henry VIII decapitations became common, and increased under "Bloody Mary" (Mary I)—who also reintroduced burnings—and "Good Queen Bess" (Elizabeth I), who added drawing and quartering to hanging for further terror and amusement.

Eventually the English apparently had enough of decapitations and opted for simple hangings instead. The American colonies mostly followed suit. In 1791 the French Revolution saw the introduction of the guillotine, a high tech (for its time) device that eliminated the problem of axe-men who couldn't aim straight. Meanwhile, Austria and Tuscany eliminated the death penalty altogether, and in 1846, Michigan led the way in the United States, abolishing it for all but the crime of treason. Wisconsin and Rhode Island followed Michigan's lead, but removed the death penalty for all crimes. However, the other, less progressive states eventually added firing squads, electric chairs, gas chambers, or lethal injection—this latter reminding one of the hemlock that Socrates was forced to drink. Two states still allow hanging.

One can't help but wonder when America as a whole will catch up with most of the world and abolish the death penalty altogether. Today, with the exception of a dwindling number of states in the U.S., it is mostly Muslim countries, with the exception of Turkey, and some leftovers from the communist world, that still execute many criminals instead of just locking them up for life.

Meanwhile, the Catholic Church has joined most of the rest of the Christian churches in opposing the use of the death penalty. The reason should be obvious by now. As one Iraqi, presumably a Muslim, commented after this latest gory fiasco, executions only promote more violence. The shame is that even after two thousand years, many Americans who like to think of themselves as Christians still don't get it.

---

## Universal Health Care: A Basic Human Right?
(August 25, 2007)

As the campaign for the 2008 presidential election heats up, one of the major issues is the health care situation in America. While technologically speaking the practice of medicine in the United States is among the most advanced in the world, yet, if one judges by our infancy death rate and over-all life expectancy figures, we fall far behind many of the world's more advanced industrialized nations. In fact, we seem to be the only country in this group that lacks a national health care system.

This rather startling fact appears odd, especially when the UN Declaration of Human Rights—which the U.S. lobbied very hard to achieve against the Soviet Union and some other objectors—lists (in Article 25) access to adequate health care as among these basic human rights. And even if the UN has little standing in many Americans' eyes today, is not this same right to adequate health care implicit in our own *Declaration of Independence* with its claim that "*all* men are created *equal*, that they are *all* endowed by our Creator with certain inalienable rights, among which are *Life*, Liberty, and the Pursuit of Happiness"? Note especially that "all"—which I have emphasized along with "equal" and "Life" in the above quote—does not exclude noncitizens, minorities, or others who cannot afford to pay for their health care.

Thus the major problem is how to make sure that all people, without exception, have an equal opportunity to enjoy this basic human right. Most of the world's most advanced nations (all of the G8 countries—with the exception of the United States and Russia), plus some that are still not very advanced have some form of a national health care system or what those who resist the idea here in the United States like to call "socialized medicine."

However, it seems that under this catch-all scare phrase there really is quite a variety of national systems. In some, as was the case in the former Soviet Union, all hospitals and clinics are run by the government and the whole staff, from physicians on down, are paid salaries directly by the government. The Soviet system, while maybe a bit crude by present U.S. health care standards, nevertheless managed to care more or less equally for everyone—unless of course you had been sentenced to die a slow death in a labor camp. Today it seems that, with the old system gone, Russians are now dying sooner rather than later, even without being exiled to Siberia.

In Canada, where I lived when I was in graduate school in the late 1960s and early 1970s, health care was "socialized" only to the extent of being a "single payer" system. Hospitals and clinics were run by various independent corporations, municipalities, religious orders, and the like, with most physicians in business for themselves. The hitch was that they could only charge so much per patient per procedure, with the upside being that the patient only needed to show his or her health care identification, which functioned like a credit card, with the balance paid for by tax money. According to estimates made at the time, huge savings were being made by Canadians in clerical overhead or accounting costs, compared to the freewheeling and often tangled U.S. system.

However, since then, on a recent trip back to Canada to visit friends, I learned that their system has become largely broken in many areas, with some blaming their particular province (each Canadian province administers its share of the national funding separately), or the particular party in power (one of my friends blamed the Conservative Party, presently in power in Ontario, for deliberately gutting the system in order to make it fail). Another blamed the rural physicians for having married wives from the big city who undermine their husbands' dedication to serving people who live in the "boonies."

This last explanation, as far-fetched as it may sound, nevertheless raises a good question. If receiving decent medical care is a fundamental human right—as well as, I think any Christian would agree, a religious obligation—then it does raise the issue of the medical establishment's motivations. While no one expects that every physician will sign up for a hitch with humanitarian organizations like Doctors Without Borders, it still raises the issue of whether or not a doctor, nurse, or other health care professional is in it just for the money or out of a sense of dedication, even a love of God and/or humanity. If it is only for the former, then the health care system, however efficient, has lost its soul. But if it is the latter, then however much broken, it should be fixable.

# Part 5
# Jesus and Christianity

This section, which contains the largest number of essays in this whole collection, is particularly concerned with historical Jesus and his relationship to Christianity, and its subsequent effects upon the world. Of central importance and mentioned several times in the course these essays is the recognition—even by the Vatican's own biblical scholars—of three levels or stages of tradition that can be found in the gospels and the implications this recognition might have for our understanding of the rest of the New Testament as well as subsequent theological developments. It is in light of these distinctions that these essays particularly focus on the relationship, as well as the tensions involved in the distinction between what many scholars see, on the one hand, as "The Jesus of History" and, on the other hand, "The Christ of Faith."

However, the first essay of this series, written specifically for the Advent-Christmas season, reflects an aspect of traditional teaching (the "divinization" of humanity) that is little appreciated in the Western Christianity, and which is approached from two more perspectives in subsequent Christmastime essays (2003 and 2007) on the Incarnation. This approach, when coupled with an evolutionary understanding of human nature, remains a key ingredient of my own attempts to rethink the relationship between the humanity and divinity of Christ.

One other essay ("Thoughts on the Interpretation of Scripture") ran much longer than the others and was originally split in two. It is published here as a single whole.

---

## A Gift from the East
(December 1, 2000)

If the most distinctive doctrine of Christianity is the "Incarnation"—the belief that God has taken on a human nature in Jesus of Nazareth—then the central task of Christian theology has been to explain not only *how* but *why* this is so. A number of answers have been suggested, but historically two explanations in particular have dominated.

One of these, most characteristic of Western Christianity (both Catholic and Protestant) has been based mostly on St. Augustine's interpretation of a passage in the Epistle to the Romans (beginning at 5:12).

From what St. Paul seems to have intended to be simply a contrast between the universal redemption won by Christ to the universal disaster visited upon the human race by the sin of Adam, there was developed an elaborate theology of "Original Sin" that had everyone headed straight to hell unless "justified" by Christ's "saving grace."

The other answer, most characteristic of Eastern (particularly Orthodox) Christianity, is based on a passage in the Second Epistle of Peter (1:4) and was developed by a whole host of the eastern church "Fathers" (theologians). It emphasizes the "divinization" of humanity—the transformation of our human nature so as to share in the divine nature itself. This *theopoeisis* or *theosis* (to use the Greek terms) was first of all accomplished through the act of God's own divine "Word" (God the Son) assuming our human nature.

In contrast to this Eastern theme, our Western Christian overemphasis on the story of Adam and Eve and the original sin seems to have saddled us with a pathological view of human nature and, in turn, led to a theology of "atonement" where, in its most distorted form, God was seen as an angry Father whose outrage could only be pacified by the bloody death of his Son. All this may lend itself to a kind of revivalist approach that leads to quick conversions but, in the long run, too often tends to alienate both those both those inside and outside the Christian fold. Especially today, for those of a more scientific outlook, how do we explain death (something that affects all living creatures) entering the world only because of the sin of Adam and Eve? Or how do we appeal to those of a more humanistic frame of mind with the insistence that human nature, due to the original sin, is entirely and irretrievably corrupt?

Not that Eastern Christians have ignored the inherited weaknesses of our human nature, but for them the "corruption" is primarily death itself. They see death as not so much the result of sin but the other way around, with sin, for the most part, being seen as the by-product of our natural fear of death. The selfishness revealed by sinful conduct (whether greediness, lustfulness, gluttony, or whatever) is seen as, for the most part, motivated by our *fear*, whether conscious our unconscious, of letting go of ourselves, and placing our destiny beyond death into the hands of God. Eliminate this fear by the prospect of sharing God's own immortality and you have already gone a long way in destroying the power of sin.

Perhaps this explains why for Eastern Christians it is not the feast of the Nativity (the birth of Christ or "Christmas"), that is the big holiday for this time of the year but, rather, the feast of the Epiphany (January 6 on our Western calendar—the "Twelfth Day of Christmas"), which celebrates Christ's "appearance" or revelation to the whole world of the promise of eternal life.

So maybe even while we continue to sing in our carols (if we haven't worn them all out by starting way too early, weeks before Christmas) about how God has "rescued us from Satan's power when we had gone astray" we need, perhaps even more, to continue the celebration by rejoicing in the ancient belief (as did even St. Augustine—Westerner though he was) once held by East and West alike that "God became Man that Man might become God!"

## Has Christianity Made Any Difference?
(December 7, 2001)

When the new millennium rolled in a year or so ago, there was some muted protest from non-Christians over all the hoopla. After all, was this not simply a kind of self-congratulatory bash on the part of those (the so-called "Christian" nations of the Western world) who despite their material and political success, were only making things worse for the rest of humanity? If we had any doubt about the seriousness of this dark undercurrent of resentment, September 11, 2001, should have erased this delusion forever.

Still, for all Christianity's failings, I think we have a right to speak out, even brag a bit. After all, look at what was, and to some degree still is, considered to be acceptable, even part of the "natural" order of things in a good part of the world still largely untouched by Christian values. For starters, there was the almost taken-for-granted "right" to kill unwanted children—whether before birth or not long after. And at the other end of the spectrum, there was, in not a few societies, the casual acceptance or even expectation of suicide when life seemed no longer productive or a person became a burden to the rest who were healthy. Although it took Christians most of two millennia to get around to it, the abolition of slavery and the granting of full human rights and dignity to women—including the rights to an education and equal pay for equal work—are no small accomplishment. Along with these advancements, while it may involve a struggle that at times seems beyond merely human capacity, there has been Christianity's championing of the ideal of life-long monogamy.

Of course, it may be argued that a lot of these developments were already "in the works" before Christianity came along, particularly within Judaism. And that would be at least partly true, as some early Christian writers stressed the argument that Christianity was, after all, the fulfillment of what already was humanity's highest aspirations. If, on the other hand, Islam also emerged partly from this same background, it nevertheless seems to have developed along much different lines, even if the Taliban movement is, admittedly, an extreme example. Nor have these "Christian" ideals ever been fully implemented, while some have become increasingly questioned and even eroded in what some now call "postmodern" or even "post-Christian" society.

Still, I think that we can be proud despite all our inconsistencies and sometimes outright failures. Time will tell. While we long ago gave up the illusion that God should be pacified by slaughtering animals, some still seem to think that society should exact vengeance by executing criminals. And although Jesus himself gave an example of resisting violence by refusing to use violence in return, we still seem to honor that ideal by claiming it is beyond us. Nevertheless, if such ideals can gain admiration, even in the non-Christian world, just imagine how much better a world this could be if Christians ever succeeded in living up to them!

---

## Atonement
(March 26, 2002)

One of the oldest human psychological traits is our need to make amends or reparations for whatever appears to disturb the order of nature or a relationship between persons. The ancient Hebrews, like so many other agricultural people around the world, offered sacrifices to God from their harvests as well as holocausts (burnt offerings) in reparation for sin.

This is problematic because it assumes that God is somehow like us. True, as the scriptures say, we are made in the "image and likeness of God." Yet as the prophets more than once pointed out, we err grievously if we think that God has any necessity for such offerings or that somehow we can earn God's favor in any way other than a "broken and contrite heart." As a result, Christianity's emphasis on the Redemption, seen as effected by the death of Jesus on the Cross as a "sacrifice" for our sins, presents problems as well. The temptation for Paul and the writers of the gospels to use such a theme to offset "the scandal" of the cross is understandable. That it was already there, "ready-made" in the Hebrew scriptures, so to speak, for their use, is obvious enough. Yet the question or the problem is do we really understand its deeper implications for us today? Do we, for example, use this concept as a way of escaping our responsibilities?

Luther and the other sixteenth-century church reformers seem to have sensed the problem when they attacked the Catholic notion of the Eucharistic rite as being a "sacrifice"—as if the offering of many "masses" day after day could atone for sin. Nevertheless, in their insistence on the "once for all" character of Jesus' offering of himself on the cross, they, in a way, only compounded the problem, driving us further back into the image of Jesus as a sacrificial victim (the "Lamb of God") who is made to suffer as a substitute for us who are otherwise (as the famous New England preacher Jonathan Edwards put it) "Sinners in the Hands of an Angry God."

Yet we must ask, is it helpful at all today to picture God in such terms? When people have done wrong, usually they are conscious of this and try to make amends. Still, if they are not so conscientious, does it really do any good to threaten them with hellfire and brimstone if the price of doing so is to have to picture God as some kind of mad tyrant or even a jilted lover? Can't a better image or likeness of God be found? I believe so, and it can be found in a very special word, which is "atonement" which literally means, in terms of the Germanic origin of this word, "to make as (or at) one." Biblical languages really had no real equivalent. The Hebrew verb *kipur* (as in "Yom Kippur"), often translated as "atone," really means "to propitiate," while the Greek word *exilaskomai* seems to convey the meaning of driving something away (a "scapegoat?")—which puts us back in the same old mindset, that of appeasing an angry God.

Accordingly, it seems doubtful that what humans have divided (by sin) can be magically be reunited by one man's death, even if he is also God's own Son. We can be made *whole* again or one with God only through *holiness*. So what Christians should do on Good Friday is not so much commemorate Jesus as a victim for humanity but live in communion with Jesus who lived and gave his whole life, even in his seeming abandonment, totally for and in union with God.

---

## James, the Brother of Jesus
(November 11, 2002)

The recent announcement (see the Nov.-Dec. 2002 *Biblical Archeological Review*) that a first-century stone ossuary or "bone box" had turned up in Jerusalem bearing the chiseled inscription translated as "James, son of Joseph, brother of Jesus" has brought back to life the old argument as to whether or not Jesus was actually born of a virgin.

The earliest written testimonies, the Gospel of Mark and the writings of St. Paul, seem to have no knowledge of such a miraculous origin of Jesus. Only the later infancy narratives found in Matthew and Luke make such a claim. And while the last of the gospels, that attributed to John, may be seen at most as possibly hinting at such a phenomenon, it takes quite a different and much more philosophical approach in explaining Christ's divine origins.

Even later Christian traditions seem split over the subject. Western (Roman) Catholicism has always proclaimed Mary as "ever-virgin" (even claiming that she remained a virgin during and after the birth of Jesus) and claims that James and the other so-called "brothers" of Jesus were at most cousins or even more distant kin. Eastern Orthodox Christians, on the other hand, while also holding that Mary was always a virgin, are of the opinion that this James (often called "James the Less" in contrast to the other apostle James, the brother of John) was indeed the son of Joseph, but by a previous marriage, hence a half-brother to Jesus. Protestantism seems even more divided, with fundamentalists insisting on the "virgin birth" of Christ, while the more liberal scholars tend to take Mark's reports about the mother and the brothers and sisters of Jesus at what seems to be their face value (see Mark 3:31-35 and 6:3).

All this seems to point to a new battle over the kind of symbolic language that by and large makes up the Christian creed. If "seated at the right hand of the Father" (to express Christ's eternal heavenly reward) is not to be taken literally, must "born of the virgin Mary" be taken literally as well?

To answer this question we must ponder the meaning of divinity as well as virginity in the ancient world. For the ancients, it was altogether natural that if a god were to become human it would be through the agency of a virgin, so that the divine paternity would be all the more obvious, while at the same time virginity was regarded as making one closer to God. So similar stories abounded in pagan mythology or even became attributed to the mother of Gautama, the historical Buddha. From this perspective another question can be asked: does God stoop to perform miracles to conform to ancient opinions, or is it that God (being God) can do anything he pleases, even if it grates against our current prejudices?

All this raises still another question as well, one about the usefulness of symbolic language in an age that has become addicted to what it believes to be "scientific accuracy"—even while it continues to search for meanings that science can never provide. Can such symbols as "virgin birth" and "resurrection" (or even "miracles" in general) continue to bear the weight or convey the meaning they once had?

One can only wonder if the paradox of trying to describe transcendent truth in terms of such material entities has not become more of a hindrance to faith than a help. And if this be the case, then what new kind of symbols are to take their place?

(Note: After laboratory tests were later carried out, archeologists believe that the inscription on the above-mentioned ossuary had been added more recently. However, this doesn't mean that the issues discussed in the rest of this essay are going to go away.)

## The Incarnation
(December 20, 2003)

In a world filled with various religions Christianity is perhaps unique in its claim that God has, in a very personal way, reached out to us, not just by revealing himself or giving us information or issuing commands, but rather by actually becoming a human being. Yet, is this assertion really believable any more, at least as it has been usually taught in the creeds and catechisms of traditional Christianity? Recent polls, even among many of those who still claim to be Christians, would seem to indicate otherwise. Most seem to think Jesus was a good and holy man, but "God incarnate"—how explain that claim today?

Actually, there has been two approaches to this claim all along, even beginning within the New Testament itself, either of which, taken alone can end up as an exaggeration, with both extremes long ago officially rejected as "heresies."

One of these, derived mostly from the Gospel of John, speaks of the *Logos* or divine "Word" (understood as the eternal Son of God) coming "down from heaven" and taking on human *carnis* or "flesh"—hence the term "incarnation." Yet this view, still emphasized by traditional or conservative churches, when taken too literally, all too easily ends up in the errors where Jesus is either seen as God appearing among us in a human shape (docetism), or else as a kind of half-divine, half-human hybrid (monophysitism). In neither case is Jesus seen truly as a human person, with a human mind and will.

The other view, which is derived from the other three gospels (but particularly from Mark, who leaves out the Christmas story altogether) sees Jesus as adopted by God through the descent of God's Holy Spirit, not unlike the granting of the Spirit to other humans, but to a degree that made Jesus worthy to be called, in a very special way, "The Son of God." In this case, Jesus is seen to be merely human, even if a lot holier than most. It is this view (early on known as "adoptionism" or "Nestorianism"—after its reputed founder) that dominates so-called "liberal"—and many would say "watered-down"—Christianity today.

The question remains: can these two approaches, both of which can find their roots in the New Testament, be reconciled in such a way that the resulting polarization of Christianity that has for a long time resulted from them—even after the Council of Chalcedon in 451 attempted to heal the breach—be avoided?

Perhaps the key lies in reconsidering what makes us humans in the first place. As I see it, we only become completely human, that is, fully what God intends us to be, through the power of God's Holy Spirit in our lives. We are made up of body, mind (or "soul") and spirit, but that last, the human *spirit*, is more of a longing, a capacity (like an empty cup) waiting to be filled with God's life or Spirit, and until that happens, we are still in the process of becoming fully human beings.

Once we admit this, might it then not be possible to see the uniqueness of Jesus to consist in his humanity having been fully "completed" by the Holy Spirit, and this having been so—unlike in our own case, which generally takes a lifetime—from the first moment of his existence? In this way he, in his human nature, is constituted as the person who fully embodies the divine Word or Wisdom (personified in the later Old Testament writings), but now revealed as the new or "Second Adam" (as St. Paul describes him) the perfect prototype of the "image and likeness of God" that we humans are all called to be.

Does this mean that Jesus would have been fully conscious of this unique privilege? I do not think so. In fact, the gospels (even that of John to some extent) give us the impression of a Jesus who like us, struggles to carry out the will of God—whom he calls his "Father"—and to do this, he must, just like us, go through the all too human process of suffering and death before his true identity is fully revealed.

Yet even if only this be true—that Jesus was totally like us in his human nature and person, except that God accomplished in him something entirely new—then Christmas could be seen the birthday, not just of Jesus Christ, but the beginning of a new and final stage in the evolution of humanity. Thus on Christmas we celebrate the birthday of Him whom God made divinely human so that we can become humanly divine.

## Thoughts on the Interpretation of Scripture
(November 4, 2004)

When one looks at the divisions that split Christianity today, whether it be evangelical "fundamentalism" versus the "main-line" churches, or traditional or "orthodox" versus "progressive" Catholicism, or even the historical divide between Catholicism and Protestantism in general, I think the real cause of the division is not so much whether persons are theologically, or even temperamentally a "liberal" or "conservative" in their thinking—although this psychological factor obviously has a part to play in it. Instead, I believe that the major theoretical or ideological source of the division lies in the question of *historical consciousness*, that is, whether the historical perspective is really present or not, or even if present, in what particular form it takes, particularly when dealing with the sacred scriptures.

This question became particularly evident at the time of the Reformation. While reaction to institutional corruption as well as political and national rivalries played the most visible role in the reform movement, the theoretical basis for the Reformation lay in the intellectual revolution that began in the Renaissance and continued into the period that congratulated itself as "the Enlightenment." During this period, several major changes took place in the intellectual world. One was the movement to go back to the sources of European civilization, whether of the classical texts of Greco-Roman antiquity or the original texts of the Holy Scriptures. The other, the counterpart to this, was to translate these original texts into the current vernaculars to be widely disseminated through the miracle of the then newly invented printing press. From this combination was born the belief that Christianity could be reformed or purified by returning to its original, strictly biblical, roots, unencumbered by the encrustation of centuries upon centuries of tradition.

Of course, the project of the reformers did not turn out to be that simple. Luther, who preached a doctrine of *"sola gratia, sola fide, sola scriptura,"* nevertheless, to his dismay, found himself struggling with the issue of the canon—which books really belonged to the Bible?—as well as with the more radical reformers, whom he believed went too far by failing to interpret those books according to the received tradition. The Catholic "counter-reformers," on the other hand, found themselves forced to resort to a two-source theory of revelation, one that spoke of both scripture and tradition. In subsequent centuries, these two directions of approaching scripture have appeared to widen the gap, not only within Protestantism but also within Catholicism.

The crucial issue is whether or not to read and interpret scripture in terms of its historical context (that is, according to the scientific-critical approach) or "canonically" (that is, with the conviction that the Holy Spirit guided the Church both in the initial selection of books as well as in their interpretation—including the development of ideas or practices that are not clearly or explicitly contained within the texts themselves). I'm convinced that the other divisions in Christianity, as well within the various churches themselves mostly come down to this. And if this is the case, is there a way of overcoming these divisions? I believe that there is. It consists in *looking to scripture to see how it interprets itself.*

To use a quick example, take the Catholic Church's (or the various other churches') interpretation (or reinterpretation) of Jesus' remarks concerning divorce and remarriage. That Jesus was against the practice as being contrary to the divine intention is pretty obvious, even to the majority of scripture scholars today. Yet Mark's addition (regarding women who divorce their husbands—something that was back then impossible in Jewish society), Matthew's exception clause (allowing for it in the case of *porneia*—whatever that word really means), as well as Paul's decisions regarding converts married to pagans—all these are obviously scriptural interpretations or even reinterpretations of what Jesus seems to have originally said, which is that, generally speaking, Jesus was dead against it. The rest, whether it be Mark's extension of the prohibition, or Matthew's and Paul's loopholes allowing for divorce and remarriage in certain circumstances, are scriptural *reinterpretations* made as a concession to (or in Mark's case, as a buttress against) human weakness.

Or take another example, one that is perhaps a bit more threatening to institutional claims, the assertion that Jesus intended to found a "church" (specifically the Catholic Church). Did he really? Or was it that his *qahal* or gathering of disciples within Palestinian Judaism, especially after it found acceptance among gentile converts associated with the Jewish diaspora, only became a new religion after Palestinian Judaism definitively rejected it? It seems to me that if one reads the claim (based mostly on Matthew 16:12) the first way (which is to say "canonically"), then one is admitting the concept of an on-going revelation, which is indeed what one sees in the later epistles where the "church" has already become something far beyond the group of followers Jesus seems to have had in mind.

However, with this admission, the problem becomes one of deciding or proclaiming when this ongoing revelation ceased. This, in turn, creates a dilemma, for if one answers (as the traditional doctrine says) "with the death of the apostles," then how justify later decisions that go beyond, or even contradict, what the apostles laid down (for example, clerical celibacy, the exclusion of women from church office, or other ecclesiastical practices that may have changed in the course of history).

On the other hand, if one says that the decisive power extends beyond the death of the last apostle ("Whoever listens to you listens to me" Luke 10:16) then what are the limits? Why can't the Church demand clerical celibacy on the one hand or decide to ordain women—in other words, change the tradition? Thus it would seem at this point that church authorities cannot avoid being driven back to the gospels to try to discern the mind of Christ. Yet if one is to do that honestly and realistically, then must not one take the historical-critical perspective as well? In other words, what this all boils down to is asking the "WWJD" question, that is, even allowing for changed circumstances, "What would Jesus do?" And in that case, it would not be the canonical, but the historical reading of scripture, that should be the most decisive.

---

## Dogma
(October 2, 2005)

Only a few letters separate the Greek noun *dogma* from the Greek verb *dokeo*, but there seems to be a world of difference between the two. The former, which came to us from the world of politics and government, means a "decision" or "decree." The latter, which came from the realm of philosophy, means to think, to hold an opinion, to believe, or even to just "suppose." The tragedy is when, in the realm of religion, such opinions or beliefs are turned into dogmas or litmus tests of faith.

I say this because when one reads the gospels, for the most part one looks in vain for any such thing. Jesus seems to have been much more concerned about how people treat one another than whether or not they held strictly orthodox views concerning the nature of God. And even if he did himself believe in the resurrection of the dead (not all Jews in his time did), still, the point was to emphasize the reward that awaited those who live a godly life. And it was this promise (of eternal life) and the example of his followers' love for all humanity and for one another that gradually converted the pagan world.

Yet even as that conversion progressed we can find this other ugly dogmatic side of religion beginning to emerge. There are even hints of it in some of the other writings in the New Testament—which shouldn't surprise us, because by the fourth century, even before the official list of books in the Bible was fixed, we find various factions within Christianity not only at odds but even occasionally killing one another over the question of the correctness of their beliefs. Among them were such esoteric questions as to whether or not the Son (Jesus Christ) was of the "same nature" as the Father or only "similar" to him—a difference of only one tiny letter in Greek (*homoousios* versus *homoiousios*)! And then it took the intervention of a Roman emperor to enforce the former—a clear case where religious beliefs had entered into the world of politics and dissenters did so at the risk of their lives. Yet, considering the fate of Jesus, whose religious teachings threatened the political order, should we be surprised?

I have long held that religion is so important to people because it is what gives ultimate meaning or purpose to their lives. Still, let's face it: if a particular religion seems to justify the persecution or destruction of others, then no matter how theologically correct its beliefs may seem to be, it will turn out to be a curse on the human race. On the other hand, no matter how strange some beliefs may seem (for example, the Jains in India who believe every living thing, including tiny gnats and bugs, contain divinity and consequently go to great lengths to avoid killing them) they may reflect, in their own bizarre way, the kind of love that Jesus had in mind. So too, the kind of world-transforming pacifism that the Hindu Mahatma Gandhi preached and practiced was inspired both by the gospel of Jesus and the writings of the Russian religious dissenter Leo Tolstoy, but growing up where Gandhi did, he was no doubt also inspired by the example of the Jains.

There are those, of course, who see such a blending of ideas as a kind of dangerous kind of religious "syncretism" that could lead to moral "relativism." Well, perhaps: but in the face of dogmatism, then, I say, perhaps the world needs more of this kind of tolerance of and even the occasional blending of beliefs!

## Cooked Books?
(December 18, 2005)

Recently, Bart D. Ehrman, a highly respected scholar of the New Testament and early Christian literature at the University of North Carolina, was interviewed on NPR about his latest book, just released in November, which is provocatively titled *Misquoting Jesus: the Story about Who Changed the Bible and Why.* In the radio interview, Ehrman used the well-known discrepancies between the stories of the conception and birth of Jesus as found in the gospels of Matthew and Luke as prime examples of how early Christians "cooked" the original evidence, as slim as it was.

This new book sounds like a more popular version of the themes aired in one of his earlier books, *The Orthodox Corruption of Scripture: the Effect of Early Christological Controversies on the Text of the New Testament* (Oxford University Press, 1995). Yet there can be little doubt that this latest book by Ehrman, who describes himself as having grown up as an "Evangelical Christian" but now as "a happy agnostic," could have a disturbing effect on a lot of Christians—much more than *The DaVinci Code*, a mystery novel that only pretended to be based on historical facts. Ehrman is a serious scholar with some ten books to his credit and his conclusions, although sometimes arguable, are based on widely recognized evidence.

Should devout believers be disturbed by such historical detective work? Perhaps we should be. Certainly the new pope, who appears to have great reservations about the effects of modern biblical scholarship, seems concerned. Even the late Pope John Paul II—no doubt prompted by the former Cardinal Ratzinger—openly complained about Catholic theologians who fail to adhere to what he called "the canonical interpretation of Scripture." By this he meant that they were paying too much attention to the scripture scholars and neglecting scripture as it has been traditionally interpreted by the church.

Still, need the choice be between biblical fundamentalism and/or Catholic traditionalism (which increasingly seem to be bed partners) as against serious biblical "criticism" or scholarship? Need one either end up either a "true believer" or else an "agnostic" (at least when it comes to

Christianity), or, even worse, an "atheist"? I really don't think so. If the scriptures have been tampered with, all the more that we need to cut through the veneer of cherished misconceptions and pious beliefs that have obscured what one progressive theologian, Johann Baptist Metz, has called the "dangerous memory" of Jesus and the impact these "memories" should have on the world.

Why "dangerous?" I think it is because if we discovered who Jesus really was, and even more, if we actually became serious about living the way he said we should live, there would be a real revolution—not just moral/ethical, but even political-economic (because ethics, put into practice can affect everything else). How else to explain the continual recurrence of war, the systematic violations of human rights, the unjust hoarding of the world's goods that results in widespread poverty and famines, even among those who claim to be "Christians"? While not every cause of human misery can be eliminated, so much more could be done. In fact, to the extent that Christianity or the distortions of Christianity have contributed to the mess we now have in this world, it is imperative that we go back to its beginnings to reexamine and rethink what Jesus really was about. Otherwise I fear that what that great apologist G. K. Chesterton said about not blaming Christianity because "it has never been tried" will be more a curse than an excuse.

## Schweitzer's Radical Christianity
(January 24, 2006)

It has become increasingly clear, as scholars have critically studied the origins of Christianity during the past century or so, that the religion *of* Jesus, who instead of trying to found a new religion was attempting to reform an old one, very quickly turned into a new religion mostly *about* Jesus. As the famous Protestant biblical scholar, missionary doctor, and musician Albert Schweitzer (1875-1965) saw it, all the indications point to the conclusion that Jesus, like his predecessor John the Baptist, was proclaiming the imminent end of the world and much like John, met an untimely end. This was because the preaching of Jesus, like that of John, threatened the status quo and especially those who were in religious and political power. Unlike the case of John, whose disciples, faced with the fact that final judgment day had not yet arrived, were left with a ritual of repentance and a memory, the disciples of Jesus were soon convinced that their Master still lives and that the Kingdom of God has already arrived, at least in principle, in the new movement and its followers who soon became known as "Christians." So the result was that where Jesus preached not about himself but mostly about the Kingdom of God coming to earth, his disciples instead ended up preaching mostly about Jesus or the Christ himself.

Was Schweitzer right? If he was, or was even close to being right, then a great deal of what Christianity is about has to be rethought. For if he and others like him were correct, then the Jesus uncovered by historical scholarship (the "Jesus of History") might have had little resemblance to the Jesus worshipped by Christians (the "Christ of Faith"). If so, Christians will be forced to either put up or shut up, that is, to either start acting like Jesus (which includes turning the other cheek, loving one's enemies, sharing all one's worldly goods with those in need, and the rest) or else forget about calling themselves "Christians."

All the indications are that Christianity, whether in its traditional or more conservative forms, be it Roman Catholicism and Eastern Orthodoxy on one end of the spectrum or American-style Evangelicalism and various "fundamentalist" groups on the other, is resisting any such reassessment. In fact, one suspects—judging from the gospel verses they decide that Jesus couldn't have said—that even most of the members of liberal groups, like the so-called "Jesus Seminar," find themselves in a similar bind.

Perhaps this is understandable. No one, no matter how open to new ideas, or in this case recovering old ideals, is comfortable making the changes these ideas might demand. In other words, when it comes to one's own back yard, everyone, no matter how liberal, tends to be a conservative.

So if there is a major crisis in Christianity today, especially in the affluent West (whether it be Western Europe or North America), it is not because of "liberal" biblical or historical scholarship. It is rather because such a rediscovery of who Jesus really was would demand a radical change in our lifestyle and standard of living if we would claim to be his followers. For some like Schweitzer, who went back to school and earned an M.D. in addition to his Ph.D. and eventually was awarded the Nobel Peace Prize for his humanitarian work, it could even mean such a radical change as giving up a university position to go off and serve the poorest of the poor in a clinic in Africa!

---

## Did Jesus Have Faith?
(January 29, 2006)

This question probably strikes many Christians as strange. However, if Jesus was, as is often said, "like us in everything but sin," then it would be, it seems to me, even more strange if he didn't have faith.

Yet the fact is that almost from the very beginning of Christianity, my question has been considered generally out of bounds. In fact, when one fairly unknown theologian toward the end of the fourth century happened to write something on the subject, St. Augustine, the single most influential thinker in Christendom, denounced that theologian as a "heretic." It seems that the great Augustine could admit that Jesus could be hungry or thirsty, or even tempted just like us, but drew the line at the idea that, just like the rest of us, Jesus might have needed to have faith. To Augustine's way of thinking (like that of many Christians) if Jesus was truly divine, he must have known the answer to everything. And if that is the case, how could Jesus be said to have had faith?

Of course it is possible to simply say that Jesus had, humanly speaking, "faith" in the fundamental gospel sense of that word, which is a loving trust in God. I think that is obvious to anyone who consistently reads the gospels and mediates upon them. As the story (in Matthew 8:21-28) about St. Peter trying it out tells us, one can't walk on water unless one really trusts that God will not let him sink!

Yet did Jesus have faith in the sense of holding certain religious beliefs? Again I think it is clear that he did. For example, he seems to have believed that the end of the world (or was he just predicting the destruction of Jerusalem?) would come very soon. Yet when Jesus was asked for an exact timetable as to when whatever he was talking about would take place, we are told that he answered that even he didn't know the exact day or the hour (Matthew 24:36; Mark 13:32).

Perhaps even more significant regarding this whole question, Jesus apparently defended his belief in angels and even more importantly the resurrection of the dead—things that not every Jew of his time believed in. In fact, he seems to have bet the whole meaning of his life on that resurrection taking place. How much more faith can one have than that?

So if all this is the case, and Jesus had faith in every meaning of that term, how could he also be the very "Son" or "Word" of God?

Maybe this answer is too simple, but it seems to me that if Jesus really was God's special "Word" given to the human race, then that word or message is that if we too wish to be God's "sons" or "daughters," then we too must live by faith. In fact, I think that even Augustine was saying much the same when he wrote that "the only Son of God became a man that the many sons of men might become sons of God."

Just substitute "Word of God" for "Son of God" (for that is what John, whose gospel Augustine was writing about, prefers to call him) and update the "sons of men" to "humans," and I think you'll see what I mean. It simply comes down to saying that if we really become people of faith, trusting, even risking, the meaning of our life on God and God's plans for this world, then we too will be found worthy to share God's kingdom with Christ.

---

## The Gospel of Judas
(April 10, 2006)

The much-heralded discovery of a third- or fourth-century copy of an Egyptian translation of the so-called "Gospel of Judas," has the Christian world in a tizzy of speculation. Actually discovered by an Egyptian archeologist back around 1975, it was sold to an antiquities dealer in Cairo and terribly mistreated (kept in a shoe box!) for some twenty years until finally sold to some reputable scholars who, funded by the National Geographic Society and another foundation, have painstakingly reconstructed the crumbling manuscript.

So what should be our reaction to this new discovery?

First, we should understand that the existence of this document is nothing new. St. Irenaeus, bishop of what is now Lyons, France, back around the year 180, knew about this supposed "gospel," apparently in its Greek original, and considered it worthless. So the media hype that it is "authentic" is highly misleading—unless by "authentic" one simply means that it is a genuine third-or fourth-century copy of what today we would consider to be a forgery.

Second, examination of its contents shows it to be, like the other so-called Lost Gospels (those of Thomas, Philip, Mary, and a document called "The Gospel of Truth"—all found in Egypt back in 1945), typically "Gnostic" in content. Early Christian Gnosticism was a movement that was especially popular in early Christian Egypt and that generally divided things between a "good" world of pure spirit and an evil material world. Typically, in this "Gospel of Judas," Jesus tells Judas that he wants him to do what he has to in order to get rid of the "man"—that is the mortal body—that veils or obscures his real (spiritual) identity. In other words, like so many of the earliest deviations from the accepted gospels, the writer of this secret document believed that Jesus was a divine being only more or less pretending to be a human.

Finally, we have to remember that according to the four canonical or accepted gospels (of Matthew, Mark, Luke, and John) Jesus did in fact send Judas on his errand, which is to say that Jesus knew he had to die to accomplish what God intended and allowed the least trustworthy of the twelve he had chosen to betray him to his inevitable fate. Still, to claim, as does this "gospel," that all this was plotted out in detail in a long conversation between Jesus and Judas, and that Judas quickly wrote it all down in what now appears as a twenty-some page long manuscript before hanging himself, seems to be stretching things more than a bit.

If nothing else, this latest discovery confirms basically three things. First, that there was a wide diversity in the first few centuries as to just how Christianity was to be understood, with esoteric fringe groups especially trying to present alternative interpretations opposed to what was the earliest tradition. Second, it illustrates, yet again, that what we tend to think of as the foundation documents of Christianity, that is, the four Gospels and the other documents found in the New Testament, were selected from a host of competitors because they reflected or accurately reported what the majority of Christians knew or already believed to be true. And finally (third), if nothing else, it proves that even after some two thousand years, the memory of Jesus continues to both fascinate and disturb people—enough that there seems no end of the attempts to reinterpret both his life and message, and even his death, to suit our own prejudices.

---

## Essential Christianity
(August 18, 2006)

More than a half a century ago, the Oxford professor and writer C. S. Lewis wrote a small book with the title *Mere Christianity*. Recovering from a prolonged adolescent bout with atheism, Lewis sought to explain his regained belief in Jesus and his return to Christianity in language that almost any member of any church, or anyone open to belief, might be able to understand.

The problem with Lewis's generic version of traditional Christianity, however—at least as I see it—is that it was, even back then, largely out of touch with the really serious biblical scholarship that had been going on for at least a century before his time. The result is that while Lewis's fine book may be fairly convincing to those who long to turn back to an imagined era of an undivided Christianity, much of it remains problematic for those who are aware of the real historical background of how the gospels came to be or how the traditional creeds were formed.

For example, today serious biblical scholarship recognizes at least three distinct layers or stages of tradition that can be found within the four gospels. The first layer consisted of collected recollections—including many miracle stories—about what Jesus said and did. The second layer, sometimes called the apostolic *"kerygma,"* is a summary announcement of the meaning of life and death and resurrection of Jesus as they apply to us. The third layer, the one that accounts for the existence of four separate gospels, consists of differing theological and other thematic interpretations designed to address the concerns of different audiences—for example, in Matthew's gospel, the need of converts from Judaism to understand how Jesus fulfilled the promises found in the Old Testament. Unfortunately, most of the fourth gospel, that which is attributed to the Apostle John, seems to be made up of this third level of theologizing, presented (despite the sharp contrast in language with the other three gospels) as if Jesus said all these words himself. So too, it almost goes without saying, the rest of the New Testament, especially the epistles or letters to the various churches, belong to these last two layers of the tradition. Paul, for example (except for his recounting of the Last Supper narrative), has next to nothing to say about the words or deeds of Jesus but instead seems almost entirely absorbed in disciplinary and leadership issues and in theological arguments, such as the relative importance of faith as distinguished from "works."

With all due respect to Lewis, I do not think that the future of Christianity lies in trying to reach a doctrinal consensus that, despite surface differences, Lewis believed somehow exists. Instead, I think that only a radical reassessment of who Jesus really was, and what he actually taught and did, can serve as a sound basis for a renewed and vital Christianity that will be essential for the well-being, even for the survival, of the world. What we need to do, then, is engage in serious study and debate, disentangling and sorting out the different layers of tradition and various and sometimes conflicting themes found within the scriptures to rediscover the historic Jesus who inspired the Christian faith.

Yet first, for this effort to bear fruit, we must most of all pray, perhaps more than ever before. If nearly two thousand years of Christian history proves anything, it is that doctrine or dogma divides. It is only prayer and sacraments—if we don't get into arguments about how many there really are—that unite.

## Inventing Christ
(September 26, 2006)

In 1768 the French skeptic Voltaire wrote a poem in which appeared his famous line which when translated reads; "If God does not exist, it would be necessary to invent Him." Since then, other skeptics have taken their turns at interpreting this statement, but it seems clear from the whole poem that Voltaire, a deist who distrusted all organized religion, was arguing for religious tolerance. He did so on the basis of what can be known for sure about God from what is evident in nature—as well as for the need for an anchor for the moral universe.

It seems to me, however, that one might take Voltaire's argument one step further. We might claim that unless Christ exists, we would be forced to invent him as well.

My argument? Well, it has become more and more evident, especially since Voltaire's time, that the past existence or beginnings of the universe depends on the existence of some First Cause or God—otherwise, what was it that "banged" or caused the big bang? Yet it is also becoming more evident, as science progresses, that the universe has only a limited and ultimately doomed existence. Eventually the universe, and everything in it, including humanity—if we can manage to keep from blowing up our home planet in the meantime—is going to be snuffed out in what scientists call a "heat death," meaning the exhaustion of all energy, and with that, the cessation of all life.

Of course, back when people used to believe we really have immortal "souls" or are that we are heavenly spirits just spending a few years trapped in material bodies, even this problem wasn't of any major significance. However, science has pretty much dispelled those quaint notions as well. So what is left for us? Not much, unless we are satisfied with the image of a God who put the whole process of evolution into motion just to keep himself amused until he gets bored with this show and turns to something else.

Instead, this is where Christ—or at least someone like him—comes into the picture. We need someone who can demonstrate, by achieving it himself, that death, whether it be of the universe or simply of ourselves, can be truly overcome. Otherwise, for us humans at least, everything is lost.

Of course, the job description is exacting. It takes a very special person. A mere wise man or prophet, be he Socrates, the Buddha, Moses, or Mohammed, is not enough. They can only point to the truth as they see it or as it might be revealed to them. For that matter, not even Jesus of Nazareth—that is, Jesus as seen by the historians—can make the grade. It is only when Jesus is seen as the Christ of faith, the Son of God, who "dying destroyed our death, and rising restored our life," that he can truly accomplish the job.

---

## End Time
(December 3, 2006)

For the past century or so, a debate has raged among New Testament scholars as to whether or not the passages in the gospels that seem to predict the end of the world were really spoken by Jesus or were simply placed in the gospels by the writers to reflect early Christian beliefs on the subject. Some claim that Jesus never said these words or that at the most he was predicting the destruction of Jerusalem—an event that actually did happen twice, first in the year 70 when the Roman army sacked the city after a long siege, and yet again in 135, when they finished the job, literally "not leaving one stone upon another."

On the other hand, there are those who believe that these passages really do repeat much of what Jesus actually said and that Jesus foresaw these traumatic events, such as the destruction of Jerusalem, as simply one of the signs that God's new kingdom was at the point of arriving. Certainly this seems to be the way that the first Christians understood the matter.

If this is true, and Jesus really did expect history to come to a sudden end this way, then, quite obviously, we have a major problem. In fact, so did the early Christians, especially after a generation or two, when they began to realize that the world really wasn't about to end as soon as they expected. This problem is especially evident in the last books added to the New Testament, the Second Epistle of Peter and the Book of Revelation.

So what are we to make of all this today? Mainstream Christianity has for a long time straddled the question by claiming that God's new kingdom or order of things has in fact *already* arrived—at least in principle—with the resurrection of Christ. Still, on the other hand, it is *not yet* fully accomplished until Christ arrives again at the very end of time "surrounded by angels, and seated on the clouds of heaven." The difficulty with this view is that it only prolongs the problem faced by the early Christians, not only periodically stirring people up by means of wild-eyed claims that the world is about to end but even tempting some people to promote its ending by staging a final showdown battle, which the Book of Revelation (16:16) calls "Armageddon."

Perhaps there is another solution. It is to recognize that, humanly speaking, Jesus himself was not certain about the divine timetable (see Mark 13:32 or Matthew 24:36), but that nevertheless, we faithfully follow him in his conviction that God intends there to be a better future and that it is God's will that it be soon. Not only this, but we must also realize that God has forbidden us to bring the world's history to a catastrophic end, either by slowly destroying the earth's capacity to sustain human life or suddenly by continuing to play "Russian roulette" with our arsenals of nuclear weapons. Instead, we must realize that God has entrusted us with the task that Jesus himself has given us, which is not so much about selfishly "saving our souls." Not that this latter isn't important. Nevertheless, it is something that will take care of itself, yet only on condition that we accomplish what Jesus taught us to pray and work for—that God's will be done here on earth "as it is in heaven."

## The Knowledge of Jesus
(December 9, 2006)

A week or so ago, I sent out one of these short essays—one dealing with the problems associated with conflicting Christian beliefs about the end of the world. In it I suggested that one way to deal with the confusion regarding the "End Time" was to entertain the possibility that while Jesus accurately predicted the destruction of Jerusalem in the year 70, not only his followers but even he himself may have been mistaken in his predictions as to when the end of the world would arrive.

This suggestion—first made by the biblical scholar and later Noble Prize-winning missionary doctor Albert Schweitzer back around 1900—raised a few eyebrows, to say the least. Yet the reactions, both then and now, also reveal how deeply one of the earliest heresies to afflict Christianity still affects the belief of many Christians today. That heresy was called "docetism" (from the Greek word *dokeo* meaning "to think"—but in this case mistakenly, thus to "appear" or "seem") because it held that Jesus was God in a form that only seemed or appeared to be human, as if Jesus was nothing less than almighty God walking around on earth in a suit of human clothes. Later on, after the Council of Nicea (325 AD) had further emphasized Christ's divinity, this same old heretical tendency took a new more sophisticated form technically known as "monophysitism" (from the Greek *mono* for "single" and *physis* for "nature"). It held that Jesus was a kind of amalgam of divine and human natures, thus implying, among other things, that everything God knows, Jesus also would have known, and that he could not have really "suffered" in any psychological sense of the word, but only that at most his body could feel physical pain.

As a result of this situation, the Council of Chalcedon had to be held in the year 451. It is mostly famous for its "one person, two natures" description of Christ, which made it into our catechisms but, unfortunately, not into any of our usually recited creeds. Even more disturbing, the insistence at Chalcedon that these two natures remain permanently conjoined, but "unconfused" or unmixed in the person of Jesus Christ is almost never quoted—probably because it makes the mystery of who Jesus really was during his life here on earth even more mysterious than it already is.

Whether or not this explanation of the Church's official doctrine makes it any easier to entertain the idea that Jesus might possibly have been mistaken—of course, only "humanly speaking"—about the divine timetable for the end of the world is, of course, merely a matter of opinion. It could be, as St. Ephraim the Syrian once suggested, that Jesus was being deliberately ambiguous, just to keep us "on our toes." Or it could be that most early Christians, not being all that familiar with Jewish apocalyptic literature of that time, somehow got it wrong.

Yet it seems to me that to deny the possibility that Jesus himself, in terms of his human knowledge, could have been uncertain or in the least bit mistaken, amounts to what might be seen as still another revival of this old docetic tendency. And what is perhaps more disturbing, at least to my mind, is that when this tendency affects our thinking this way it ends up, to a large extent, confusing particular beliefs or the interpretation of these beliefs with the life of faith. Even worse, it destroys the challenge of following in the footsteps of Jesus, who the Epistle to the Hebrews (12:2) reminds us—despite the often misleading translations of the phrase—is "the leader and perfecter of faith."

# The Tomb of Jesus and the Body of Christ
(March 4, 2007)

The recent presentation on the Discovery Channel of "The Lost Tomb of Jesus" seems to be just the latest exhibit in a series of sensational claims that will supposedly rock the foundations of Christian doctrine and beliefs. Maybe so, but to do so the evidence, presented by Hollywood movie producer James Cameron and Israeli-born Canadian writer-director Shimcha Jacobovici, will have to be a lot more convincing than that presented so far.

First, this discovery is not new from the archeological standpoint. In 1980 ten ossuaries (bone boxes) were found in an underground chamber at a construction site in East Jerusalem. They were routinely emptied of their contents (which were reburied) and stored in a warehouse of the Israeli Antiquities Authority. In 1996 an archeologist got around to writing an article about the inscriptions found on six of the ossuaries, which consisted of the names Yeshuah (Jesus), Miriam (Mary), Judah, Joseph, Matthew, and another variant of the name Mary—"Mirianene e Mara" or Miriamne. These were all fairly common names in the first century. There are three or four different Marys mentioned in the New Testament, at least three different Judahs, two Josephs, and several persons named Matthew or Matthias. And as for the name Jesus (or *Yeshuah* in his own language), neither was that unique. It was simply the then-current Aramaic pronunciation of the Hebrew name *Yehoshua* or, as we now pronounce it, "Joshua." All that might be inferred from this collection, according to the Israeli government archeologists, is that the excavators had stumbled upon a typical cemetery vault of that period.

Historically speaking, even if this was the crypt belonging to the family of Jesus, why would his most famous "brother," James—reputedly the leader of the Christian community in Jerusalem—be missing from the family tomb or left there with his bones unmarked? (Back in 2002, Jacobovici promoted the claim that another ossuary once held the bones of "James, the son of Joseph and the brother of Jesus," but chemical analysis indicated that the inscription had been recently faked.) And even if this were indeed the final resting place of Jesus, why did the Roman occupiers go to such great lengths to destroy the location where the first Christians believed Jesus had been buried (the present site of the Church of the Holy Sepulcher) yet leave this cemetery alone?

Let's suppose that, contrary to all the above, somehow these ancient relics could be proved to be the remains of Jesus of Nazareth and his associates. Then what? Would the foundation of Christian faith be thereby destroyed? Perhaps it would be for those whose beliefs are founded on a naïve or literal reading of the gospels. Although these documents appear to report physical reappearances of Jesus after his death, even there these are described as a temporary state, prior to his being taken up "into the heavens."

Yet, what does this mean—that Jesus is now floating around somewhere up in space? One might hope that by now, believers might have grown out of such childish concepts. Indeed, for St. Paul, who wrote even before the gospels were written, the risen Christ is no longer a material body but a "life-giving spirit" whose "body" is now his Church made up of its members joined to him through Baptism and his living presence in Holy Communion.

Viewed from this spiritual-sacramental perspective, I think, the discovery of the body or bones of Jesus would make no real difference to the essence of faith. While such relics would undoubtedly be the object of great devotion, still, in the end, they would be of no more lasting significance than an abandoned house or a cast-off suit of clothes.

In fact, because of the media hype involved, perhaps we might even end up thanking these promoters, regardless of what their motives may be. If nothing else, the stir they have caused might just end up challenging Christians to think about their faith more deeply and maturely.

# Buddhism and Christianity
(April 5, 2006)

There is an old French proverb that says "The more things change, the more they are the same." It struck me that this proverb is especially applicable when it comes to comparing Buddhism and Christianity, which, although to begin with could not seem more unlike, nevertheless, as time passes, the more the history of the two religions resemble each other in surprising ways.

Certainly the ideas of God held by the two religions could not seem to be more different. In fact, strictly speaking, Buddhism is "atheistic," at least in the sense that it claims no knowledge of a personal Creator of any sort. For Buddhists, everything that happens is a result of "dependent origination"—more or less random combinations of causes and effects in a universe that apparently has always existed and always will exist. Thus, we are but momentary existences within an eternally recycling universe.

In fact, according to the teachings of Siddartha Gautama (the original Buddha or "enlightened one"), the belief in a permanent "self" or "soul" is only the result of an illusion, a spell that must be broken before we can achieve nirvana—perfect peace or enlightenment.

In practice, however, things have turned out very different. Among most Buddhists, the ancient Asian belief in successive reincarnations of the self remains unaffected by these teachings. In fact, the Buddha himself, far from being simply a wise man and a teacher, has been, especially in many of the popular Mahayana or "Great Vehicle" sects of Buddhism, gradually turned into the incarnation of ultimate wisdom, is prayed to as a savior, and is even given the kind of worship due to God.

In addition, the histories of the two religions show strange parallels. While both movements began with individuals who were engaged in reforming or purifying their own ancestral faiths (Hinduism and Judaism, respectively) both movements were eventually favored by political rulers (King Ashoka in India and Emperor Constantine in the West), each of whom attempted to spread them throughout their empires and beyond. Yet, paradoxically, both religions have all but disappeared from the lands in which they began.

Finally, both religions have undergone radical reform movements. In Buddhism this happened very early on when the Theraveda Buddhists—meaning those who follow "the teaching of the elders"—attempted to bring Buddhism back to what Gautama actually taught. They succeeded only in Ceylon (Sri Lanka) and in a few small countries in southeastern Asia. Because of that, the Theravedins are rather derisively called "Hinayana" (the followers of "the lesser vehicle") by the Mahayana Buddhists everywhere else.

In the West, the Reformation—which tried to bring Christianity back to the simplicity of reliance on "scripture alone"—has led to what seems to be an unending argument about what the scriptures really teach. As a result, perhaps today more than ever, there are biblical scholars, both Catholic and Protestant (and even a few who are Jewish), who, like the ancient Theravedin monks who insisted that only the authentic teachings of Gautama be taken as the norm, are busily engaged (many think futilely) in trying to determine what Jesus actually said and did.

One can only wonder, from all this, what it is in the human mind that causes this ceaseless struggle between the tendency to expand the claims of religious doctrines and the opposite tendency to purify and simplify the teaching back to what it was to begin with. I suspect that what we are seeing in all this is really the struggle in our own minds between the way we'd like things to be and the way they really are. Yet I also suspect that in this contest, it is the popularizers (the Mahayanists), the ones who preach what most people want to hear rather than what they really need to hear, who are going to win. Nevertheless, in either case, it seems to me that the Theravedins, the purists who are most intent on returning to the sources, are always doomed to be regarded as the "Hinayana"—followers of the lesser and, because more difficult, the least popular way.

Or could it be, on the other hand, that God, in his providence, has actually accomplished in Jesus that for which most Buddhists and the followers of other religions only dreamed? Either way, it may very well be, as Thomas Merton believed, that the future of religion in this world will depend on Christianity and Buddhism understanding and learning from each other.

---

## The Incarnation Revisited
December 25, 2007

If one believes in a loving God, or simply in a God who cares, then the Incarnation, the belief that God took on human form or came to us as a man, makes perfect, logical sense. Or at least it does in theory. Indeed, an incarnation of this sort might be seen as a reconciliation between what Pascal called "the God of the philosophers" and "the God of the prophets."

The first (God in the eyes of the philosophers and, we might add, of many of the mystics), is seen as "the prime mover" (Aristotle), the "first cause" of our existence (Aquinas), indeed, "Being in itself" (Augustine), the "ground" of being (Eckhart) who is immanent or within, but not identical to, creation. This is the kind of God whom the modern philosopher A. N. Whitehead also saw, a God who not only initiates the whole creative process, but is fully present within creation, and who also "persuades" or draws it toward its final consummation.

The second, God as pictured by the prophets, at first seems quite the opposite. Remote, totally "other," or transcendent in principle, he is nevertheless passionately, sometimes even violently engaged with his creatures, especially humankind, personally rewarding both individual persons or whole communities for their obedience, yet periodically withdrawing his presence and punishing them for their transgressions.

It would seem then, just as the philosopher Hegel pointed out, that in the incarnation of God in Jesus Christ we have the synthesis that both combines yet transcends the opposition between the thesis of God as conceived in the minds of the philosophers and what seems to be its antithesis in the God of the Old Testament prophets. Indeed, what we might see presented in the New Testament is a Jesus who is not just the "Image of the invisible God" but the very presence of the God whom the whole universe cannot contain, yet is nevertheless concretely, individually, personally, and fully realized in this one human being.

However, all this is fine in theory. It is on the practical level that the Incarnation seems to be a contradiction in terms or an outright impossibility. On the one hand, how could God, even a God who is present in all of creation, become so confined in space or time? Or, on the other hand, how can a human being—even if he is Jesus Christ—possibly possess divinity (as it says in Colossians 2:9) "in all its fullness"? Either way, what sounds fine in theory seems almost ridiculous, even blasphemous in practice—that is, unless we totally rethink what it means to be fully human.

Here is where I think the answer lies. Each of us is still on the path to becoming fully human. Indeed, Aristotle described us as "rational animals"—yet how much of the time do we even succeed in acting rationally? In much the same way, we are called to be sons and daughters of God, or even, as the Second Epistle of Peter (1:4) puts it, "to share in the divine nature." In other words, we are here on earth to become something more than what we actually are in terms of our physical and even our psychological or mental existence. Human nature is, in its present state, incomplete or open-ended. We are called to be more than we are; each one of us, in fact, is called to become divine, or like God, immortal.

This is why, in one form or another, we find the early Church Fathers insisting, even repeating over and over again, almost like a mantra, that "God became man that man might become God."

Of course, today we might want to rephrase it in more gender-inclusive terms (as well as give credit to the "Church Mothers"). Yet none of this should be allowed to distract us from understanding the real meaning of the Incarnation. Jesus was sent to us not in the form of God pretending to be a human, but as "the Second Adam" (as St. Paul calls him), the man who embodied fully in himself the divinity that each of us is called to share, even if, as of yet, only partially.

# Part 6
# The Church and the Churches

Although closely connected with the preceding section, the essays contained in this part concentrate on the institutional aspects of Christianity, particularly on the doctrinal issues and other problems which beset its various divisions today. In this context, the term "Church" (capitalized) generally refers to entity described in the Nicean Creed as "one, holy, catholic, and apostolic" while "church" or "churches" (whether in the plural or singular) can refer to the local congregation, regional or national bodies, or the various denominations within Christianity. Whether the former fully exists (or even "subsists"—see the next-to-last essay on "Pope Benedict and the True Church") or ever did in terms of what the Nicean creed actually had in mind, might be open to question. So while not going so far as the theologian Paul Tillich, who thought that all such institutions or organizations are "inherently demonic," we might say that the difficulties they face from within, due to their own inherent weaknesses, merit serious attention.

However, the approach taken here, much as in the previous section, keeps coming back more to the scriptural basis of Christianity with much the same critical factors (historical consciousness, layers or stages of tradition, etc.) at play.

---

## Women in the Church
(Jan 12, 2001)

Recently, the defection of former president Jimmy Carter and his wife from the Southern Baptist Convention, as well as the practical breakdown of any further progress toward reunion between the Roman Catholic and Anglican (in the U.S.A., Episcopal) churches, underscore the division that is occurring between churches, and even within various churches, over the acceptance of women into the ordained ministry.

Biblical fundamentalists and diehard traditionalists, of course, can always point to passages in the Bible (like those found in 1 Corinthians, chapters 11 & 14) that forbid women to speak in church or even to attend with their head uncovered. On the other hand, the New Testament speaks of "deaconesses" and ancient documents have been uncovered that prove that this term refers not just to charitable service to the Christian community but to an ordained role in early Christian worship. Some historical researchers claim to have found evidence even of female Christian presbyters or "priests." Meanwhile, the Episcopal Church in the United States has even gone further and ordained a few female bishops! (Can you imagine what this could mean for Catholicism? After all, the pope is not what he is because he is ordained as "pope," but because he is ordained or appointed as Bishop of Rome.)

The problem, then, seems not to be simply what the Bible says (which in itself seems inconclusive) nor simply a matter of tradition, some of which is based on rather weird ideas—like Aristotle's opinion that women were misbegotten (that is, defective) males. Since that kind of argument is clearly bizarre, others have retreated to the claim that since Jesus picked only males as his "apostles," only males can be ordained to officially function in church. Others, finding that argument weak, since being an apostle (that is "emissary" or missionary) is not the same function as presiding at worship, argue that only a male can adequately do the latter job, since in some church theologies the presider should represent Christ. Yet, in that case, must not all presiders wear beards? Still others argue that the presider must first of all represent the congregation, which in that case would argue that at least half the time the presiders should be female!

All this suggests that what we have at work here is simply a reluctance by males to admit that they've largely run out of excuses for keeping women "in their place." In a religion that proclaims that in God's eyes there is no real distinction between "Jew and Gentile," between "freeman and slave," or between "male and female," and as the consciousness of women regarding their basic human dignity increases around the world, it is hard to see how those Christian churches that continue to bar women from the ordained ministry can expect that they are going to retain the loyalty of half of the human race.

---

# The Rapture Craze
(July 7, 2001)

The astounding success of Tim LaHaye's "Left Behind" series of religious novels, which feature people being snatched up or "raptured" into heaven—much to the consternation and bewilderment of those left behind—has produced another type of consternation and bewilderment, especially among those whose Christian beliefs are a bit more traditional or "mainstream."

Actually, what we are seeing here, in a novel form, is quite an old story in Christian history. In his classic work *Enthusiasm*, Ronald Knox traced the ups and downs of repeated outbursts of millennial expectations along with Pentecostal-type revivalism, starting with the Montanists in the middle of the third century and on down through medieval times, even to the "Great Awakening" in America, especially in the 1840s when people climbed up on house tops and barn roofs to be better poised for takeoff into heaven.

Often such beliefs have been mixed with predictions of an Armageddon or final battle between the forces of good and evil—much as has been more recently seen in the "Watchtower" type of publications or the tragedy that took place in Waco not many years ago.

Most of this kind of belief and speculation has taken its inspiration from the final book of the New Testament, generally known as "The Book of Revelation." This book, which has often, but probably wrongly, been attributed to the Apostle John, speaks of itself as a "prophecy." However, it actually belongs to a special class of writings generally described as "apocalyptic"—from a Greek word referring to what is "hidden" or what is yet to be revealed. It is not "prophecy" in the classical sense of the word like the writings of the prophets Isaiah and Jeremiah. Instead these apocalyptic writings are a type of underground literature that was written in a kind of code consisting of symbolic representations of what were back then current events, mostly to console people who had no longer any control over what was happening to them. Good examples of this kind of writing are parts of the Old Testament Book of Daniel (which is not listed among the prophetic books in the Hebrew Bible but among the "Other Writings") and many of the other books that are rejected by more traditional Jewish scholars but were found in abundance among the Dead Sea Scrolls.

Nor did this kind of highly imaginative literature find easy acceptance into the New Testament. Many of the early Christian bishops and scholars argued against considering the Book of Revelation as part of the Bible, and even today, the Greek Orthodox Church relegates it, at best, to being a kind of appendix.

While it contains some truly stunning images and inspiring lines, this book also contains a hodgepodge of vindictive and damning passages that hardly exude the spirit of Christian love and which, as Carl Jung and other psychologists have pointed out, seem to have a special appeal to those who feel marginalized, helpless, or "ripped off" by society at large. Nevertheless, the Book of Revelation, and even LaHaye's novels, like the various millennial cults that have preceded them, perhaps do serve a useful purpose. They remind us that although the gospels tell us that the Kingdom of God is already "within" us or "among" us, it is still not yet complete.

However, what these writings so often fail to tell us—and it is in this that they most differ from the classical prophets and the gospels—is that in the meantime it is our responsibility to help make this a better, more just, and more loving world. Can we really expect that God will treat us mercifully if we sit back waiting for God to destroy the world or to "rapture" us out of disaster's way after we have failed to do our part?

## Clerical Celibacy?
(March 1, 2002)

If nothing else does, the current pedophilia scandals rocking the Catholic world, especially here in the United States, must eventually force the Roman Catholic Church to seriously question its current policy of almost exclusively ordaining unmarried men. Certainly, some married men are pedophiles (in fact, recent statistical studies show that most pedophiles are married men). However, the alarming accounts of so many supposedly celibate priests having committed such crimes against children and adolescents points to an extremely serious situation. So the question must be raised: does celibacy tend to lead to pedophilia? If we understand what religious celibacy is and begin to better understand pedophilia, both the cause of the situation and its solution becomes clearer.

The word, pedophilia, is derived from the Greek words *philos* meaning "love" and *paidos*, meaning "child." Currently our society understands it as inappropriate behavior of a sexual nature toward a child or adolescent. Various psychological theories attempt to explain such behavior. Many professionals think that directing sexuality toward children results from an inability to engage in a personal, mature, adult relationship.

Celibacy (from the Latin term *caelebs* meaning "unmarried"), especially religious celibacy as a dedicated state of life, is much more than simply the physical state of remaining single or abstaining from sex. It must also involve a psychological willingness to give one's life totally to the service of God and humanity. Still, even that is not enough; celibacy also requires the spiritual strength (a God-given "grace" or "charism") of being able to live according to that dedication. Sometimes this is termed a "calling" or "vocation" to celibacy.

Early on in Christian history, this vocation began to be especially cherished. It was expressed first of all in the consecration of virgins and soon after in the emergence of the first monks (from the Greek word *monachos*, describing "one who lives alone"). When persecutions ceased and bloody martyrdom was no longer a threat, Christians saw celibacy as a way to witness to their faith. All this was seen as part of trying to live as much as possible like Jesus and what seemed to be his recommendations (see Matthew 19:12) and those of the Apostle Paul (1 Corinthians 7:32-34). The effort by the Western Christian church to require priests to be celibate began as far back as the third or fourth century. Most Eastern Christian churches required this sacrifice only of their bishops.

There has often been a problem with following the ideal of celibacy for the sake of the gospel, because it also attracted people with unhealthy motives. Some were fleeing, for various reasons, any involvement with the opposite sex or at least avoiding the obligations of married life. Others may have been attracted to it by reasons they may not have been able to admit even to themselves. And it seems that this problem is compounded when celibacy is required for ordination, for not everyone who feels called to the priesthood may necessarily have the gift or charism for the celibate life. Then, in addition, we live in a sex-saturated society that regards sexuality as a commodity, a form of entertainment and self-gratification—something that brings added pressures on even those who are trying to live according to the spirit of the Gospel. In the face of this triple whammy, is it any wonder that there are, perhaps even more than ever before, frequent deviations from the ideal of celibacy?

If so, then it seems that the solution, as far as there can be one, must address all three of these problems. First of all, it will be necessary for the Catholic Church to separate the call to priesthood from any requirement to live the celibate life. A much clearer distinction needs to be made between the monastic or celibate religious life and the call to be ordained a priest.

Second, those responding to what they believe is a call to priesthood, and even more, those responding to what they believe to be a vocation to celibate life, must be subjected to much more intense psychological scrutiny and spiritual preparation for their calling. This increased screening and preparation will benefit both the candidates for priesthood or dedicated religious life and those whom they will serve.

Finally, and perhaps most important of all, Christian churches need to work together to try to better understand human sexuality in the light of Christ's teachings. Hopefully, this better understanding will help all people to appreciate their sexuality as a great gift from God. While perfect adherence to such high ideals can probably never be completely accomplished, still much of the current immaturity, deviations, and perversions of this treasure can be prevented.

## Systemic Failure
(December 21, 2002)

Recently, in the face of the clerical sex scandals within the Roman Catholic Church, the question is increasingly being asked whether there is not something seriously wrong within the system.

Until now, the official line of response, as well as that of more conservative critics, is that what we have here is the accumulation of decades of individual moral failings, and at most a more or less pervasive policy of sweeping these failures under the ecclesiastical rug. In other words, if there is anything that might be described here as "systemic," it is a policy of denial of just how serious the problem really is.

This is why it is so very hard to get any real information from official church sources. At best, what we have is some educated "guesstimates," some of which range from suggestions that true pedophiliacs (those who sexually abuse children) and ephebophiliacs (those who abuse youths) are about only half as common among Catholic priests as among the male population in general, to estimates that somewhere between 20-50 percent of priests are homosexuals but only a minority of these (at most 20 percent) prey on adolescent boys. Richard Sipe (a widely quoted authority on the subject) also claims that over 50 percent of the Catholic clergy, whether "straight" or "gay," is sexually active—that is, failing to live up to their obligations to live a celibate life—and that most of these, when honestly confronted, state frankly that they do not intend to live up to their vows.

If these figures are anywhere near accurate—or even accurate by half—then clearly this is no longer just a situation where individual failures to live according to an ideal have become alarmingly common but, rather, that we have a situation where there is a widespread breakdown of the whole celibate ideal within the Roman Catholic clerical system. This conclusion is doubly inescapable when it has become obvious that even when faced with these figures, the authorities decide to bar those they deem most liable to failure (homosexuals) even while insisting on the discipline (celibacy) which seems to attract them.

As for the rest, these authorities also seem oblivious to the fact that overworked, isolated, and lonely heterosexual priests will be more liable to fail as well. Apparently they believe that they can also detect those who are most likely to fail years, even decades, before such failures are most likely to happen—certainly a good trick if one can pull it off (or else a true act of faith).

While no one ever said that everything about religious beliefs and practices have to make perfect sense—indeed, part of the pitch has been in it making no sense unless God exists—still, one would think that at least some concession to common sense would help. Apparently the bishops are too preoccupied with their own self-preservation (the Vatican seems determined to depose any bishop who might start ordaining married men without special permission) to figure that out.

## Christian Unity
(March 2, 2005)

If one really believes in a Christ who prayed "that all may be one," and that there might be "one flock and one shepherd," then one must conclude that one of the biggest failures of Christianity, and that one of the biggest sins of Christians, is the complacency, indeed even pride in their divisions—divisions that find Orthodox divided from Catholics, Catholics from Protestants, and Protestants themselves segregated from each other into divisions and subdivisions almost too numerous to list. In addition, within each separate church or denomination we find so-called liberals divided from conservatives or radicals at odds—oddly enough when one considers the "root" meaning of the latter term—with traditionalists. Why or how can this be?

One answer is human nature. Much of the time we humans like to gain or hold on to our own sense of self-worth as individuals by trying to be different than others. Witness, for example, adolescents who try so often to be as different from their parents as possible, even at the price of slavishly imitating someone else.

Another answer might be the diffusive nature of "nature" itself. As life develops it spreads out across the face of the earth, and as it spreads it tends to develop differences. Eventually these differences evolve into separate species. It is the same with human language. Regional accents develop into separate dialects, and given enough time, dialects become separate languages, and sooner or later, people not only can't understand each other but don't even think much alike—even to the extent they end up killing each other over their differences. All of this is natural, and to a large extent can't be helped. Yet somehow, all this has to be overcome, especially for the sake of world peace.

However, I think there is also a theological distortion that has complicated things. We Christians have gotten the relationship of beliefs to conduct, and of faith as distinguished from love, all backward. There are "these three" St. Paul tells us: "faith, hope, and love, but the greatest of these is love."

Faith, as well as the beliefs that are involved, is but a provisional or passing thing, seeing only partially or obscurely. Beliefs are like looking through a piece of cloudy glass or by means of a mirror that is defective or even distorted. Love, on the other hand, is not just a means of achieving a goal (like faith or hope) but an end or goal in itself—indeed the goal of all religion, which is God, and as St. John tells us, "God is love." Thus the central goal and the chief commandment of religion is not correctness of belief but, rather, "to love the Lord our God with all our heart, strength and mind" and to love our neighbors (as we love ourselves) as the embodiment of God's love around us. If beliefs held in common help us to do this, then such beliefs are useful. Still, if our beliefs divide us from each other, then they are more a hindrance than a help, more a curse than a blessing. Yet that is exactly what seems to be the case today. What then are we to do?

Early on in Christian history, the great St. Augustine pondered this problem and came up with a formula we might well remember and take to heart; "in essentials, unity, in non-essentials diversity, but in all things charity." In other words, in terms of the Christian faith, there are a few essentials, most of them enumerated in the Apostles' or baptismal Creed. Perhaps all the rest should be considered non-essentials, helpful in adapting the faith to various cultural groups or to certain times but hardly absolutes.

Essential unity need not involve uniformity. Indeed, uniformity may not be what God has in mind at all—after all, just look at nature, which despite its variety, forms, as it were, one vast interconnected organism. Why can't Christianity also be like that?

## Pope John Paul II
(March 2, 2005)

Perhaps it is far too early to try to give an accurate historical assessment, but those who have already begun to call the recent pope "Pope John Paul the Great"—even though only two other popes have ever been given that title—may not be too far off in their judgment. Like Pope St. Leo the Great, who turned back the barbarians from the gates of Rome to save the still-struggling beginnings of Christianity in Europe, Pope John Paul II is largely credited, through his support of the Solidarity movement in his native Poland, with the eventual downfall of Soviet communism. And like Pope St. Gregory the Great, who was perhaps the greatest pastoral theologian of all the long line of popes, John Paul, not just because of his extensive travels throughout the world, but perhaps even more because of his extensive writings (which, unlike some other recent popes, he has largely written by himself), will surely be remembered as philosopher and theologian who reached out to address the most vital concerns of all of humanity.

Nevertheless, I think that when it comes to assessing the effectiveness of his extraordinary term as pope, John Paul would first of all want us to judge him in terms of those popes whose names (like his immediate predecessor) he took: Pope Paul VI and Pope John XXIII before him. Like John XXIII, whose revolutionary council he participated in, John Paul has worked hard to open the "windows of the Church" to dialogue with the whole world and all humanity. And like Paul VI, to whom fell the task of completing the council that John XXIII had begun, John Paul had to wrestle mightily with the currents of modernity and the expectations that council unleashed, none of which has been an easy task. Indeed, to a large extent, it still remains an unfinished job.

Some will take him to task, no doubt, for the contradictions that have resulted from this effort. Socially progressive (in the tradition of most modern popes) John Paul nevertheless remained (again like most modern popes) doctrinally conservative. Glorying in the power and influence of the Church, he nevertheless openly and sorrowfully confessed and apologized for its failings in the past. Openly advocating and calling for a more collegial structure in the Church (in keeping with the Vatican II documents he helped shape), he often seems to have let the Vatican bureaucracy get away with just the opposite. Championing the dignity and freedom of all human beings, he nevertheless has insisted upon adhering to customary ways of looking at things (such as the role of women) that often rankled those who see things quite differently.

At this point comes the question to everyone's mind; how shall we ever replace him? I think that in more than one sense, John Paul is irreplaceable, but not just because he was a unique, highly talented individual. I think it is also because the papacy itself has become too big a thing for any one man to fill—which fact is, I think, the cause of the contradictions within his tenure. It combines (as the now-discarded papal tiara or crown once symbolized) three quite distinct jobs: first, Bishop of Rome; second, Patriarch of the Western Church; and third, the center or symbol of unity for all Christendom. When these three jobs get confused, which they have over time, real problems result, particularly those that occur when union or "communion" gets confused with uniformity. As a result, the person who will fill his shoes, I predict, will only be successful to the extent that he is able to distinguish between these three quite different functions, and act accordingly. Who this man might be, I have no idea. Nor would I want the responsibility of having to choose him, but we must pray mightily for those who do have that responsibility.

---

# Catholicism or Papalism?
(March 4, 2005)

The great stir surrounding the death of Pope John Paul II, or, even more, the great amount of commentary from pundits and experts of all sorts, makes one wonder: what is the soul of Catholicism? What is it that really makes Christianity "catholic" at its core? Or on the other hand, what makes Catholics different from others who call themselves "Christian"?

For many, the answer seems obvious: it is the belief that Jesus Christ made St. Peter head of his church in his place, and that the pope, as the successor of St. Peter, is, as they say, "the Vicar of Christ."

It may surprise one to find out that this has not always been the case. True, we find that early on the Church of Rome, the place where Peter is said to have been martyred in 64 AD, was generally considered to stand in a special place of eminence in respect to the rest of the churches in the Christian world and that, accordingly, its bishop held a certain special prerogatives and responsibilities. Yet the idea that the bishop of Rome should be considered the "universal pastor" whose decisions could override the consensus of the rest of the Church was relatively new, defined only in 1870 and even then not accepted without protest. Similarly, the idea that bishops must be appointed by the pope is a recent innovation.

How did all this come about? In some aspects, it was due to political factors, both the result of the growing power of churchmen in the West after Constantine moved the imperial capitol east to Byzantium in 320 AD, followed by Charlemagne's efforts to create a new "Holy Roman Empire" with the help of Pope Stephen in 800 AD, and to suppress what was left of the other ancient rites in Western Christendom in favor of the Roman model of Christianity. This move, in turn, set the stage for the thousand year old split between the highly centralized Roman Church and the more diversified and autonomous regional churches that make up Eastern Orthodoxy. It also largely produced the conditions which, along with the rise of the various European nation-states, led to the rise of multitude of separate Protestant Reformation churches.

In the face of all this divisiveness, what then does it mean to be "Catholic"? While it is clear as far back as the second-century (in St. Irenaeus' treatise on *The Proof of the Apostolic Teaching*) that Rome was even then considered a preeminent witness to what was considered to be orthodox doctrine, it still remains to be proved—especially to the Eastern Orthodox—that the Church of Rome has remained faithful to that task. Today, Roman Catholics seem to automatically assume that loyalty to the pope guarantees catholicity. Yet even as late as the fourth century (but still six centuries before the split that severed East from West) St. Cyril of Jerusalem could characterize the Church as "catholic" because "it has spread throughout the *entire* world . . . teaches fully and unfailingly *all* the doctrines which ought to be taught . . . to *all* classes of people . . . cures *every* type of sin . . . and possesses within itself *every* kind of virtue . . ." (*Catechetical Instruction* 18:23, emphasis mine).

No mention of the pope—why? I would venture that the reason for this omission is that Cyril wished to emphasize the aims or goals of the church as being truly *katholikos*, that is to say literally "pertaining to the whole," "universal," or "all-embracing." Having a pope is not an aim or goal; it is only, at best, a means employed in the attempt to maintain unity. Yet, if history is any criterion, it has often been a failed means. Not that ecumenical councils have always resulted in complete unity, but at least their batting record has been somewhat better. In contrast, almost every major move by a bishop of Rome, especially those carried out or initiated *ex cathedra*, that is, in virtue of his authority apart from a general council, has inevitably lead to yet further divisions within the Church or Christianity in general.

Nevertheless, one must wonder if any of these means, whether councilor decrees or "infallible" papal declarations, have really served Christian or Catholic unity. Have not most of them gone far beyond the teachings of Jesus himself? If so, why has this happened?

I believe the reason is obvious. Given any teaching or idea (or ideal) there is bound to be elaboration over time. This is entirely natural, perhaps even necessary to meet the needs of any given period in history. Yet is it necessary that these elaborations become dogma? In fact, should not the aim be to keep going back to the original inspiration, even as vague as that may sometimes be? After all, to "define," in the original sense of that word, means "to set limits to" rather than to further elaborate.

Given all this, and especially considering the sorry history of Christian infighting, I would suggest that the greatest thing any council or pope could do to bring about truly catholic unity would be to call all Christians back to the simplicity of the gospels. To the extent that the papal office itself is misconstrued as being the heart or soul of Catholicism rather than its servant, we are in danger of distorting the meaning of what it is to be truly Catholic.

---

## Divisions
### (March 5, 2005)

At the root of the doctrinal divisions that dog Christianity there lies one fundamental division that causes all the rest. The late Pope John Paul II put his finger on it when he complained about the neglect of the "canonical reading" of the sacred scriptures. What did he mean by that?

When the term "canon" (derived from the Semitic word for a "reed"—often used as a measuring stick or ruler, hence "law") is used regarding the scriptures, it usually refers to the question as to what books belong (or don't belong) in the Bible. For example, the various Gnostic writings we hear so much about today were books that were rejected by the early Church as doctrinally misleading or unsound—thus "uncanonical." However, this is not primarily what the pope was referring to. Rather he was speaking about how the Bible is to be interpreted or understood. "Canonical" in this sense means more or less "traditional," this in contrast to what is often called the "critical" understanding resulting from modern biblical scholarship. It is often what splits fundamentalist Protestants from "main line" Protestants and conservative Catholics from "liberal" ones. And it is here, and not over the argument as to whether certain books should be considered "apocrypha" or not, that the real division lies.

This division that probably exists to some extent within the Eastern Orthodox community as well, though perhaps is a much more muted form, because the cause of this division lies in the rise of the *historical consciousness* that was the product of the Renaissance in western Europe and the so-called scientific enlightenment that followed, movements that scarcely affected eastern Europe and the Middle East. It was this awareness of change relative to the passage of time that made the Protestant Reformation intellectually attractive, with its call to return to "scripture alone" (versus "tradition") as the sole authority for belief. However, it was also the cause of the rival sectarianism that followed when people no longer had a tradition to guide how the Bible should be interpreted.

Yet there is a deeper problem still, one that the Reformers seem to have largely overlooked. It is the existence of different layers or stages of tradition that make up the texts of the scriptures themselves—for example, the general recognition among scholars today that the gospels contain three such layers or stages; at their base the memory of the words and deeds of Jesus, then the proclamation of the meaning for us of his life, death, and resurrection, and finally the particular cultural and theological slant employed by each of the evangelists to convey his message (the reason there are four gospels and not just one). The discernment and sorting out of these layers is a tricky business, and one that has immense implications for our understanding of Christianity. For example, was Jesus a charismatic but martyred prophet of a soon-to-happen "end time" (the picture we are most apt to draw from the synoptic gospels, especially that of Mark) or was he instead the eternal "Word" of God "made flesh" conscious at all times of his divine identity (the impression given by the style of his speaking as attributed to him by John)?

Faced with such a challenge, we basically have only one or the other of two roads to take. Either one can believe that the Holy Spirit has all along been guiding Christianity in a way that should leave us content or undisturbed in our traditional beliefs, no matter how much they may seem to be shrouded in "mystery" or even contradictory at times. This is the way of "canonical" reading or interpretation and belief. It is also the way of "orthodoxy" and traditional Catholic belief.

Or else one may believe that the Holy Spirit may be challenging Christians to use the gift of critical biblical scholarship as the primary tool of discovery of who Jesus really was and to try to understand what he means for us today. This was the route attempted by the original Reformers, but it was abandoned by their followers when their tools proved inadequate to the task at hand. Today, it seems, thanks to more than a century of intense effort, I believe that what the Reformers aspired to do has become increasingly possible. We only need the confidence that the Holy Spirit will give us the courage to persevere in the task.

## Catholic Disbelief
(January 5, 2006)

A recent Gallup Poll taken from a sample of Catholics around the United States revealed that nearly half of them do not take very seriously the Church's claims to speak authoritatively on matters dealing with sex and marriage. When asked what beliefs and practices among a selection of twelve suggested they thought were most identifiably "Catholic," belief in the Resurrection of Christ and concern for the poor vied for top place, with belief in the Church's teaching about Mary as "the Mother of God" (in other words, Christ's divinity) and adherence to the sacramental system (Baptism, Holy Communion, and the rest) rivaling for second. At the very bottom of the list was adherence to a celibate male priesthood. Next to that, near the bottom, agreement with the Church's condemnation of abortion and disapproval of the death penalty was only slightly ahead of its rules on contraception, divorce and remarriage.

This suggests several things. Most obvious is that the Church's credibility on matters of sexuality is shot and its authority on matters of life and death nearly so. And judging from the direction that legislation has been taking in Europe, even in the so-called Catholic countries, one gets the impression that a similar poll there would yield much the same results, even if with some significant differences—for example, in Europe the death penalty is just about universally outlawed, yet "Catholic" Spain recently approved same-sex marriages.

Another impression is that when compared to many other parts of the world, Catholics in the United States, like those in other in comparatively rich industrialized countries, may take their faith (where they still claim it) "with large dose of salt," so to speak, when it comes to what they consider matters of personal, especially sexual, morality. And the poll indicated that the younger and the more educated the respondents were the more these differences surfaced.

Of course, some may point to the top of the list to emphasize the bright side of things as a confirmation that the really essential elements of Christian belief are still intact. True, but it is always easier to say you believe in something rather than live up to the tougher implications of those beliefs and the moral requirements of Christian living. With this in mind, the Church has generally been quite forgiving.

Nevertheless, I see real trouble down the line. It has been reported that the new pope has long held the view that the Catholic Church must continue to insist on doctrinal conformity even if the price of doing so will be to shrink in numbers. It has also been reported for some years that those in charge of the Vatican have more or less written off Europe, and more recently North America, and are placing their bets on the burgeoning growth of Catholicism in Africa, certain parts of Asia, and most of Latin America. Yet, what will happen when these parts of the world gradually become more industrialized and affluent?

My own guess is that unless the official Church, especially the Vatican, becomes more attentive to what its younger and more educated members (especially those in the United States and in Europe) are saying, that its future, even in the rest of the world, is going to become, sooner or later, more and more limited. As Jesus said, "Many are called but few are chosen." Nevertheless, if those who are supposed to be doing the calling don't understand the thinking, or even the language, of those to be called or if they can't come up with more persuasive reasoning to change their thinking, then the future of worldwide belief in the Church as a moral authority doesn't look very promising.

---

## The Original Mistake?
(February 24, 2006)

It seems to me that the original mistake of Christianity, especially in the Western church, was to have concocted a doctrine of "Original Sin" out of ancient biblical legends and made it into its primary rationale for the story of Redemption. This mistake, which is like a cancer in the gut, eats away at the credibility of Christianity and has led to all kinds of misunderstandings, ranging from the reason Jesus died (projecting human psychological needs on God) to belief in the eternal damnation of all those who are not baptized Christians. It has led not only to frantic—even if often heroic—missionary efforts but also much too often to conquests, wars, persecutions, and inquisitions. It has also encouraged a kind of infantile blame game where, when all else fails, instead of accepting full responsibility for our actions, we end up claiming that "the devil made us do it!"

How did this situation ever come about? Many trace it to St. Augustine, who, not knowing Greek very well, mistranslated a famous but rather tricky passage in the Epistle to the Romans (5:12-21) where the Apostle Paul drew rather loosely on the second chapter of Genesis. Paul's obvious purpose was to extol Jesus as a second beginning for the human race—contrasting the new life brought by Christ to the death that, according to the ancient legend, was introduced by Adam. Still, as a third-level theological motif (compared to the first level teachings of Jesus in the gospels and the earliest—second level—summaries of the "good news") this comparison of Christ to Adam should have been balanced, as it was in the Eastern Christian churches, by other theological elaborations, such as Christ as the "Light of the World," the "Word" and the "Image" of God, or, as found most often in the New Testament, God's "Suffering Servant" or "Son."

Today our understanding of human origins and the phenomenon of death is entirely different than Paul's. If there is chaos and disorder in the universe, and a corresponding human tendency to sin, it is not because our earliest human ancestors broke some divine law (although we can be sure they probably broke many of them) but simply because we are, after all, creatures who carry so much of the genetic "baggage" that we inherited from our ancestors who were less than human. Understood from this point of view, "Redemption" is not so much a matter of "forgiveness"—though no doubt we need that as well—but even more divine empowerment to follow the example of Jesus and complete the process of becoming that "image and likeness of God" that God has intended us all to eventually become.

Oddly enough, it was the writings of these same two which, when read too hastily, may have led us astray that might also provide us with the quickest remedy or correction as to what our redemption is all about. For Paul has also told us, in the same letter where he compares Christ to Adam, that it is not just ourselves who crave immortality but the whole universe that seeks its fulfillment in God (Romans 8:18-25). And it was Augustine who, despite his gloomy pessimism that saw all humanity as damaged goods, also wrote "Our hearts were made for you O Lord, and they will not rest until they rest in you."

The moral of the story is that we must read on. No one thing that is written, even by an apostle or a saint, can say all that might be said.

# Pope Benedict and the True Church
(July 17, 2007)

Recently, Pope Benedict XVI signed on to a new document issued by the Congregation for the Doctrine of the Faith (CDF), the Vatican office that he headed for a long time before he became pope but now is headed by an American Cardinal, William Levada. This new document is apparently intended to try to downplay the Vatican II statement that the church intended by Christ "subsists in the Catholic Church, which is governed by the successor of Peter and by the Bishops in communion with him although many elements of sanctification and of truth are found outside of its visible structure" (*Constitution on the Church*, 8). It also seems designed to avoid possible misinterpretations of another document from that same Council which stated, that the Church recognizes "some, even very many of the most significant elements and endowments, which together go to build up and give life to the Church itself, can exist outside of the visible boundaries of the Church itself . . ." (*Decree on Ecumenism*, 3).

It seems that this current attempt to roll back Vatican II started in 2000, when the present pope, while still head of the CDF, had issued a document titled *Dominus Jesus* ("The Lord Jesus"). In explaining how these other elements are found outside of the Catholic Church, he nevertheless went out of his way to remind theologians that the other churches (here is meant the Eastern "Orthodox" churches—apparently because they are not in communion with Rome) are "defective" or even, in the case of many Protestant communities, not fully "churches" in the proper sense of the word (because, at least in the Vatican's eyes, they lack a valid line of succession in Holy Orders). Needless to say, this 2000 document, which was given an official seal of approval by Pope John Paul II, upset not only the very traditional Eastern Orthodox churches, but also many ecumenically minded Protestant theologians and more liberal Catholics.

According to an interview that Ratzinger gave, while still head of the CDF, he defended his interpretation of the council by claiming that the concept expressed by the term *subsist* is much more restrictive than simply existing: it means to exist "in itself." Thus the Cardinal went on to explain that the Council meant to say that the being or existence of the church intended by Christ is something broader than the Roman Catholic Church, but that within the Roman Catholic Church, this broader church (as he put it) "acquires, in an incomparable way, the character of a true and proper subject." In other words (at least it seems to me unless there has been a mix-up in the translation), the church intended by Jesus is something much bigger than the Roman Catholic Church—which, in turn, seems to imply that the Roman Catholic Church itself needs to become a whole lot more inclusive!

Yet if this is so, why repeat this same idea, this time using his new authority as pope to stress what he sees to be an essential difference between the Roman Catholic Church and all others? One would think that the Roman Church, which more than all others claims the quality of catholicity or universality, would be more concerned with promoting Christian ecumenism, which has already fallen on hard times over such dicey issues as women's ordination, is stymied by resurgent nationalism in Eastern Europe, is being overrun by Islam in the Middle East, and is being replaced by enthusiasts in Latin America who have little or no regard for traditional Christianity. Instead, what we seem to be getting from Rome is a renewed obsession with drawing more boundaries to keep the Roman Catholic Church separate from other Christian churches and more rules to keep the clergy separate from the laity, despite the fact that before long the laity may be all that is left. Instead of turning outward in its mission to the world, which is what Vatican II and ecumenism were all about, what we see is a turning inward in retreat from the world's real challenges.

I think that we all, whether Catholic, Orthodox, or Protestant, have to admit that as long as there is division between us, we all, including Jesus himself, end up the losers. Unless the Evangelist got it wrong (see John 17:21), Jesus prayed that all his followers be one, just as he and the Father are one—realizing that his message would be effective only to the extent that his disciples remained united. The sin and scandal of Christian disunity, while it often poses as "fidelity" to the word of God, is all too often just the opposite. Of course, human nature being what it is, there will always be a tendency toward division and schism. To the extent that we retreat from our responsibility to overcome this tendency, we fail to be Catholic or even truly Christian.

---

## The Church and Change
(November 21, 2007)

"In a higher world it is otherwise, but here below to live is to change, and to be perfect is to have changed often." (John Henry Newman)

It seems odd that traditionalist Catholics, who otherwise tend to think of the famous English convert to Catholicism, John Henry (later Cardinal) Newman (1801-1890) as one of their great heroes, so often forget his insightful saying. In fact, it seems to be one of their most central dogmas that Catholicism cannot change, and that if that be so, then the changes introduced by the Second Vatican Council mark the departure of the Roman Church, and with it, every pope after Pius XII, from true Catholicism.

Yet it seems that Newman, who painstakingly drew out the implications of his statement in his long *Essay* [actually a large book] *on the Development of Christian Doctrine*, thought quite the opposite. Following the lead of the old comparison to the growth of the human body that was used by the fifth-century monk and scholar, St. Vincent of Lerins, Newman showed how doctrines must gradually develop in order to meet the needs and challenges of an ever-changing world.

However, the problem seems to be that this change is rarely smooth and that it often proceeds by fits and starts in what otherwise remain long periods of stagnation. That the Second Vatican Council was such a breakthrough, after several centuries of doctrinal deep-freeze following the Protestant Reformation, and especially after the intellectual repression brought about by the "Modernist" crisis in the early 1900s, almost goes without saying. If anyone doubts this, one need only look at the Church's turnabout in its official stance toward Judaism, which amounts to a repudiation of convert-making to recognition of Jews as our elder brothers and sisters in the faith. Or consider its greatly altered understanding (some might say to the point of outright rejection) of the old doctrine that held that "outside of the Church there is no salvation."

Yet there are those, most notably the present pope, who are trying to minimize the differences. Why is this? Some think it is a misguided effort to win back those who refuse to admit any change at all. If so, judging from the ultraconservative reaction to his reintroduction of the Latin Mass, his efforts seem to be destined to being written off as tokenism.

Others think that this is simply the reaction of an old man to what now seems like the naive excesses of youth—indeed, the future Cardinal Ratzinger, now Pope Benedict XVI, was seen back in the 1960s as one of the guiding lights of this new Catholic reformation. That excesses did occur, there can be no doubt. When people are treated as children for long periods of time one should not be surprised that when finally given some freedom they will act like a bunch of adolescents.

Nevertheless, my own opinion, not discounting the elements of truth in the above, is that Newman was right, and that in a world that is constantly changing, the expression, or even our understanding, of eternal truths also has to change with it. However, the unfortunate side effect of this phenomenon, as Newman also noted, is that those who are ahead of the rest in recognizing this need for change, or even promoting it, are going to be inevitably denounced as troublemakers, even "heretics."

# Part 7
# Islam and the Middle East

From January until May of 1981, I lived as a visiting scholar at the Ecumenical Institute for Advanced Theological Studies at a location known as "Tantur" south of Jerusalem, within a stone's throw of the border between Israel and the Palestinian (but Israeli controlled) West Bank. It was during a period of relative calm (the Israeli invasion of Lebanon had not quite begun and the first *intifada* was five years off) and I was able to travel by bus with some Israeli tourists to Egypt, thanks to the Camp David Accords. Nevertheless, I returned home filled with foreboding of the violence that would soon erupt, but found that, even after the assassination of President Sadat of Egypt by Muslim fanatics a few months later, that very few people in the U.S. cared to listen to what I had to say. Nor did they have any appreciation of the dangers of what was perceived by the Muslim world as unconditional American backing of the Israeli presented to world stability or peace. No doubt September 11, 2001 (see the second essay in Part 3) finally got the attention of America, but it remains questionable as to whether Americans still have begun to understand what it is that drives the conflict or what it may take to finally bring peace in the Middle East.

---

## Islam
(October 13, 2001)

It is said that the term *Islam*, which literally means "submission," is derived from *salaam*, the Arabic word for "peace." Thus, a *Muslim*, literally meaning one who has "submitted," should be, almost by definition, a man or woman of peace. If so, then the murderous dedication of Middle Eastern Islamic militants to their cause seems to be almost beyond our comprehension. How can people engage in such calculated murder-suicide? How can they—as some of their terrorists have put it—"love death more than Americans love life"? How is it that a religion that is said to be dedicated to bringing peace and order to society can be made into an ideology of war and self-destruction?

In order to understand this gross deformity of a major religion we have to try again to understand the difference between faith as a personal commitment and particular beliefs as expressions or interpretations of that faith. Because we continually tend to confuse the two, allowing doubt about our beliefs to undermine our faith commitment, we are left completely dumbfounded and even confused in the face of self-sacrifice by people who are so completely dedicated to their cause. The bungling of the FBI and the Federal Alcohol, Tobacco, and Firearms agents at the Branch Davidian showdown in Waco, Texas, was typical of this incomprehension. It was similar to the way that Americans were shocked by the dedication of Japanese kamikaze pilots during World War II.

For the average American (as well as probably the average European), faith tends to be little more than a eternal life insurance policy, something with which we hedge our bets just in case the ancient beliefs about heaven and hell turn out to be true. It is hardly something most people—especially people who are well-off as we are—are prepared to die for.

How do we explain this kind of total dedication to a cause? If religion is, as psychiatrist Viktor Frankl wrote, the "search for ultimate meaning" and "faith is trust in ultimate meaning," then the problem or question is in what exactly that trust or faith consists. Is it a trust that there really is an ultimate meaning for life, one that is something beyond what we are able to conceive in our own puny brains or write down in our own books? Or is it a belief that we alone possess the one true answer—one that might even be imposed on others rather than discovered in the process of living our lives?

I think there is a big difference between the two. It is the difference between a reasonable faith and what too easily turns into religious fanaticism. And I think that it is what makes all the difference over what the Qur'an or Muslim holy book calls jihad or "struggle"—whether it is to be understood, on the one hand, as the struggle to put our own lives in order, or the struggle to defend our society, or, on the other hand, turns into a murderous "crusade" under another name.

---

# The Holy Land
(April 4, 2002)

Polls indicate that a large proportion of the American public believes that religion is increasingly the cause of much conflict throughout the world. Yet more sophisticated analysts are apt to point out that many other motives, ranging from the struggle for economic rights and political power to outright racism, all posing under the guise of religion, are the real cause of these conflicts. If only people would really and sincerely live according to their religious beliefs, then, these experts say, there could finally be peace. Unfortunately, the situation in the Holy Land gives lie to that liberal delusion. While economic problems and racial stereotypes undoubtedly play a role in the present Israeli-Palestinian conflict, at the very center of all this violence stands religion.

To begin with, there is the biblical belief that God has given this land to the Jews as their very own. According to the first five books of the Bible, God promised this land to the Israelites, commanding them to expel its former inhabitants, either by driving them from their lands or by slaughtering them when they could not be driven out. And then, according to the earliest historical books of the Bible (Joshua and Judges), God repeatedly punished the Jews whenever they failed to carry out this command, or when they compromised, either by retaining the former inhabitants as slaves or by drawing up peace treaties with them instead.

Likewise, the New Testament is not without its own share of blame for the current situation. While the exile or major deportations of Jews from the Holy Land were carried out by the pagan Babylonian and Roman empires, later on, under the Christian rulers, the few remaining Jews were either forced to convert, driven into exile, or, in the fury of the Crusades, slaughtered in retaliation for what was regarded to be Jewish collaboration with the Muslims. All this was justified by what Christians claimed was the accursed state of Jews and their collective guilt for having crucified Christ.

Nor does the story stop there. Even the beginnings of Jewish resettlement of the Holy Land began primarily as a result of religion. First, religious intolerance caused the Jews to be driven from Spain beginning in 1492 and the Muslim Turks began to give Jews refuge in their former homeland. Second, it has been largely Christian guilt over our failure to halt the Nazis' murder of some six million Jews that allowed, even encouraged, the massive immigration of Jews to the Holy Land and the formation of the modern state of Israel, despite the fact that this new "final solution" could only lead to the further tragedy we are seeing now.

If this bloody history proves anything, it is that, for better or for worse, religion is still a very powerful, perhaps even the most potent, force in the world. Right now we are seeing this fact demonstrated at its very worst. Yet if this is true, might it be that only religion can solve the problems it has created? If so, then we need to radically rethink and reform religion to make it into a still more powerful instrument for peace.

---

## Christians in the Middle East
(October 22, 2002)

Despite the disaster of the Crusades, Christians living in the Middle East have generally managed to live or at least coexist in peace with their Muslim neighbors. Perhaps this is because they had no other viable choice. Yet Islam itself generally taught that other "People of the Book" (that is, Jews and Christians) were to be treated with respect—as long as they were willing to go along with the political dominance of Islam. In fact, many Christians faithfully served Muslim rulers throughout the ages. A major part of the official bureaucracy of the Turkish Ottoman empire was staffed by Greek Christians. So too, much of the civil service of the Egyptian government is still made up of native Egyptian (Coptic) Christians who probably constitute at least 10 percent of the Egyptian population and who have historically belonged to the wealthier and better-educated class. Christians still form a visible minority in Syria, so much so that the state of Lebanon was carved out of Syria to be a haven for them. Iraq once had nearly a million Christians, one of them, Terak Aziz, even serving as Saddam Hussein's foreign minister.

Middle Eastern Christians have also been persecuted, sometimes unmercifully, when the West tried to interfere with the political or religious—often they are one and the same—order in the Middle East. The Crusades and the Muslim reaction to them were only the beginning. The deportation, mass starvation, and outright slaughter of up to 1.5 million Armenian Christians by Turkish Muslims in 1915 and shortly thereafter is even now still denied by the Turkish government, even though it declares Turkey to be a secular state. Meanwhile, any public display of Christianity is strictly forbidden in Saudi Arabia, a country whose ruling class has made Wahabism—the fanatical fundamentalist brand of Islam favored by al Qaeda and Osama bin Laden—the state religion. And in Pakistan, another haven of Islamic fundamentalism, Christian churches and charitable institutions are being increasingly targeted and Christians (both Pakistani and foreign) are being killed. Nor has this anti-Christian violence been confined to the Middle East. The same has been true in the Far East, particularly in Indonesia where Christians have been persecuted for years, and in Africa, especially in Algeria, where the Christian institutions and personnel left behind by the French are considered fair game by Muslim extremists.

I recount all this history, ancient and modern, as a warning. The United States seems perilously set on blundering into a situation that it barely understands. And the consequences will probably prove disastrous for all of us. Are Americans (who are only about 5 percent of the world's population) prepared to invade not just Afghanistan and Iraq but the whole Muslim world (about 20 percent of humanity) to impose our will? Are we prepared to stay there and protect the millions of Christians who will otherwise surely suffer as a result? If the fate of Palestinian Christians (most of whom have left their country as a result of U.S.-backed Israeli policies) or the plight of the Christian population of East Timor, who suffered for years while the United States backed and supplied arms to their Indonesian oppressors are any indication, we can conclude that we Americans are about to get our feet stuck in a tar pit, one from which it will be almost impossible to extract ourselves without leaving behind a large pool of Christian (as well as Muslim) blood.

## The Religious Roots of Conflict in the Middle East
(November 11, 2002)

Until recently, the idea that religion might cause many of the world's future conflicts was not taken all that seriously. After all, had not the sophistication of modern civilization rendered religion more or less obsolete? Religion might be consoling or beneficial in some, mostly sentimental, ways, but that it could be a real motivation for war or violence was very much doubted. Indeed, this opinion is still very much alive, especially when it is obvious that religious identity is often being used as an excuse or even as a scapegoat to avoid the more obvious causes of conflict, causes like social and economic injustice, the political suppression of minorities, or outright racism.

However, in the present circumstances, especially after the catastrophe of September 11, 2001 and continued attacks by Muslim terrorists since then, is it any longer possible to write off the real causes of such violence as simply a Middle-Eastern reaction to Western expansionism, or even the wounded pride of what had once been one of the world's greatest and most advanced civilizations?

Many have begun to ask what had long been a taboo question: Is there something inherently violent in the religion founded by Mohammed? Wasn't Islam (a word that literally means "submission") founded on the concept of the forced conversion of whole peoples or societies in the name of Allah/God?

However, before we attempt to answer questions like that, I think we need to focus on three elements that are to some extent shared by all three of the faiths (Judaism, Christianity, and Islam) that trace their origin back Abraham.

First, there is *monotheism* or belief in one god, not many gods. This is certainly Judaism's major contribution to the history of religion. Still, is it (or need it be) also the major cause, as it has all too often been, of intolerance of others' beliefs? Is it possible to have a monotheism that does not judge other beliefs to be automatically wrong and a cause for discrimination against them?

Second is what is sometimes called *supersessionism*, the belief that in the divine plan one religion is destined to replace another. Historically this has been Christianity's own understanding of itself in respect to Judaism, but one that in turn that seems to have been inherited by Islam and that has come back to haunt Christianity with vengeance.

Finally, there is scriptural *literalism* (sometimes called "fundamentalism"), the belief that the Bible, or in the case of Islam, the Qur'an, is the direct word-for-word message of God, and thus to be followed exactly, with as little reinterpretation or adjustment as possible on our part.

Each one of these traits needs to be examined carefully, and critically, especially to see if they really mean what people have tended to think they mean. Otherwise, if history is any indication, religions, especially those that trace their origin to Abraham, may well deserve to be sidelined as a major hazard to the future peace and well-being of the human race.

---

# Abu Ghraib and Moral Bankruptcy
(June 14, 2004)

The recent revelations at Abu Ghraib prison near Baghdad and similar stories now coming to the surface from elsewhere in Iraq and Afghanistan have exposed to the world what the National Council of Churches (USA) describes as "a moment of moral bankruptcy."

"Moral bankruptcy" may be an apt description. However, are we talking about only a *moment*? As the trail of responsibility for these outrages leads ever higher up into our government, it is becoming obvious that what happened at Abu Ghraib is just one particularly horrible example of the kind of thing that has been going on all along, especially since 9/11, when the U.S. government started imprisoning suspicious residents in ways that violate the UN Universal Declaration of Human Rights (once championed by the United States over the objections of the Soviets) and started detaining captives elsewhere in various ways designed to avoid full compliance with the Geneva Conventions.

However, it would probably be a mistake to pin all the blame on the Bush administration, even though its refusal to ratify the establishment of the International Criminal Court (which could try Americans for violations of the Geneva Conventions if we failed to try them ourselves) and its dismissive attitude toward the United Nations have certainly not helped matters. The fact is that almost from this country's beginning, Americans have always tended to speak in grandiose terms about human freedom, equal rights, due process, and the like and yet in practice often fall short in protecting these ideals, especially when it comes to applying them to people thought to be different from ourselves. In other words, even while we've been a nation of high ideals, we've also tended to be very much a nation of hypocrites.

How has this come about? Certainly it is human nature to fail in this way. Ideals somehow get translated into the self-delusion that we are morally superior simply because we value these ideals. However, I think that the often-repeated claim that America is fundamentally a "Christian nation" has added an additional note of arrogance to our self-delusion. As a result, we tend to see ourselves as divinely commissioned "missionaries" and to be both an example and a means of bringing our ideals to the rest of the world. Such a belief has generated a tremendous amount of self-righteousness in the American mind and, with it, a tendency to end up getting involved in things that are beyond our ability to solve. Iraq is just the latest case of this.

Yet there is still something else. The higher our ideals, of course, the more tenaciously we defend them. However, when it comes to Christian ideals, then we run into a real problem, because unless our faith in these ideals (such as the ideal of nonviolence) is really strong, in times of danger we are all too apt to forget these same ideals and betray them by using many of the same tactics as our enemies, thus falling into the immoral fallacy of believing that the end justifies the means. This has been particularly true from World War II onward, when, like the Nazis and the Japanese, we started bombing civilian targets. Then, during the cold war, we engineered right-wing military coups and political assassinations (as in Chile), taught friendly regimes more sophisticated "interrogation techniques" (as at the School of the Americas) and turned a blind eye while death squads (as in El Salvador, Guatemala, and Argentina) carried out their "dirty wars." So now should we be surprised to see American troops engaged in some of the same tactics we taught others?

One can only hope that the spectacle of what happened at Abu Ghraib will finally wake America up to the fact that once we compromise on our ideals or fall victim to the delusion that "God is on our side," too often we become no better, perhaps even worse when judged for our hypocrisy, than those who would destroy us.

## Iraq's Christians
(September 26, 2004)

One of the unintended but first victims of America's rush to war in Iraq has been its Christian communities. From the first-reported civilian casualty (a young Christian boy) in the U.S. Air Force bombings of Baghdad before the invasion to the recent bombing on a Sunday morning of five Christian churches by Muslim extremists, Iraqi Christians have been exposed to new dangers unknown during the long, even if brutal, reign of Saddam Hussein.

The Chaldean Catholic Church (to which most Iraqi Christians belong) is among the oldest Christian communities in the world, and its official language of worship of remains Chaldean Aramaic, a variant of the language spoken by Jesus. Even though they were always small in numbers, squeezed between the Byzantine Empire on one side and the Persian Empire on the other, Iraq's Christians still managed to send missionaries as far as western China about eight hundred years before European Christians did. Until recently, when so many of them fled elsewhere, Chaldean Catholics numbered over a million in Iraq, and, along with the Syrian Orthodox and Armenian and Greek Catholics (and even a few thousand Protestants), were protected by the secular Baathist regime from persecution by the Muslim majority. While there was some displacement of Christian families in the north (where Saddam was trying to resettle Arab families in the oil-rich Kurdish territories) the only severe restrictions on religion under the Baathists were against the Shia Muslims, who revolted against Saddam at the first President Bush's urging, hoping to unseat Saddam without the cost of American lives, but at a deadly cost to the badly outgunned rebels.

Now, increasingly fearing the worst as Muslim extremists have begun to target Christians, thousands of Iraqi Christian families have fled to Syria, where a similar Baathist regime, despite its dictatorial ways, ensures Christians the freedom to practice their religion. Thousands more Iraqi Christians who are lucky enough to have relatives in the United States are besieging them to intervene with our government to grant them special emergency immigrant status. They fear, quite rightly since the United States has agreed to Iraq now being officially declared an "Islamic Nation," that American-style democracy (if it ever comes to Iraq) will almost certainly result in *Sharia* (Islamic Law) becoming the law of the land, with Christians ending up as a more or less persecuted minority (less than 3 percent of the population) in an Iranian style "Islamic Republic."

Did the U.S. government have any idea of how this was likely to play out? With all the Middle East experts available to give advice, it certainly should have. The Vatican clearly tried to warn the United States, even sending a special envoy to Washington before the war to try to reason with the Bush administration. However, subsequent revelations have made it abundantly clear that our government long had a very different agenda in mind, one that if pursued as planned will almost guarantee (even if this result was not intended) that the last remaining Christians will be forced to leave Iraq—much as is already happening to the Christian community in the Holy Land.

Does this mean Iraqi Christians wish that Saddam were still in power? Probably not. Still, it does make one wonder if the American-administered cure, at least as far as Iraq's Christians are concerned, has not turned out to be far worse than the illness.

---

## Muslim Outrage
(February 7, 2006)

The insensitivity of the Danish newspaper that first published the cartoons of Mohammed and the stupidity of those European papers that republished them after the predictable outrage, are only equaled by the thoughtlessness of those in the Muslim world who are reacting in a manner that confirms the reasons for the ridicule in the first place.

Not that violence is something to be laughed at. Nor is the ridicule of others' beliefs a minor thing, even if it is based on what seems to most of the world to be an excessively strict interpretation of the second of the Ten Commandments (or the second part of the first Commandment—depending on which system of numbering one uses) as forbidding the making of images of any living being and not just attempts to picture

God. Nevertheless, the point of most of the cartoons, which seemed to be aimed at what the rest of the world perceives to be an inherent Islamic tendency toward violence, is only reinforced when the Muslim reactions are predictably violent.

Not that we should expect such ridicule to be accepted passively. When one gallery in the United States just a few years ago displayed a crucifix suspended in a bottle of urine and called it "art" and another displayed a picture of Mary and the infant Jesus decorated with elephant dung, many Christians were outraged. Yet no fatwas were issued or buildings firebombed.

Such acts of retaliation have never been compatible with the Christian ideal. In fact, one of the earliest surviving depictions of the crucifixion was among graffiti found scratched on a wall in Rome showing a person kneeling before a figure on a cross. In it Jesus is pictured with the head of a donkey, and the caption reads "Alexamenos worships his god." Still, we hear of no riots breaking out over it. Instead, for several more centuries Christians suffered such ridicule and slander, and even crucifixion, burning, being thrown to lions, or other horrible tortures before the blood of all these martyrs who refused to strike back eventually resulted in the conversion of most of the inhabitants of the Roman Empire to the Christian faith.

No doubt there have been periods in Christian history when blood would have been spilled over such insults, especially when, after that mass conversion, the mistake was made, again and again, of uniting church and state. However, history has taught Europeans and Americans, as well as much of the rest of the world, that too close an alliance between religion and politics is unwise. Such violent reactions to insults only escalate into more violence and mayhem and eventually lead to a world that becomes unlivable for all. Perhaps Islam, as the youngest of the world's major religions, has simply not lived long enough or has been isolated from the rest of the world for too long to have learned that lesson.

Maybe this incident, unfortunate as it is, will move Muslims, as well as certain Christians and others, a bit closer to understanding and accepting—however much they or we may not like it—what it takes to live in peace with the rest of the world.

---

## The Sunni vs. Shiite Division
(February 28, 2006)

The violence currently convulsing Iraq, especially following the demolition of the famed golden-domed Shiite shrine in Samarra, is nothing new. It goes back some twelve centuries, to the very foundations of Islamic society. The Shiites (*shia* meaning "division" or "sect" in Arabic) insisted that the future leaders of Islam must all be descendants of Mohammed, while the Sunnis believed that their rulers must be those who most faithfully follow the *sunna* or "traditions" written in the Koran (Qur'an) and the Hadith or other traditions. This division erupted into bloodshed when the grandson of Mohammed, Hussein (no relation to the present Saddam), was defeated in battle in the year 680 and his brother Hasan was reportedly murdered not long after. Since then, the Shiites have believed that a *mahdi* (meaning "one who is guided") will return to restore God's order of things, with various divinely guided *imams* ("leaders") taking his place in the meantime. In contrast, the Sunnis have long maintained that the only true mahdi is *Isa* or Jesus—a belief that no doubt comes as a great surprise to most Christians!

Arguments as to who the genuine imams are have greatly divided the Shiites down through history, giving rise to many radical religious and political movements. In many ways, Shiism can be seen as a kind of messianic movement within Islam, just as Christianity began as a messianic movement within Judaism. The main difference in this comparison is that where Christians far outnumber Jews in the world, Sunnis far outnumber Shiites in the world of Islam, except in two places—Iran, which is about 90 percent Shiite, and Iraq, where Shiites are almost 60 percent of the population.

This basic division within Islam, as well as all the subdivisions within these two major groups, is barely noted in the usual "World Religions 101" textbooks. Nor have the basic textbooks paid much attention to the rise of "Wahabism"—what might be called a kind "Sunni fundamentalism"—that has turned out to be, in the form of al Qaeda, just as lethal as Shiism's famed *Hashshashim* ("Assassins"). The only thing that the textbooks seemed to get right was the overall Muslim belief that the religious and political order should be one and the same. Unfortunately, all this has come much too late as a sobering lesson to those who hope to promote democracy in Iraq or elsewhere in the Middle East.

The only upside to all of this violence may be that the Muslim world will now finally learn the lesson, just as the Christian world did, that fanaticism of any sort—be it Jewish, Christian, Muslim, Hindu, or Buddhist—is a disaster for human society, and that differences in opinion have to be peacefully accommodated by a much clearer wall of separation between government and religion.

## Can Islam Change?
### (April 1, 2004)

We have recently seen an attempt by Muslim hard-line clerics in Afghanistan to have a man condemned and executed because of his conversion to Christianity. And we have also seen the success of the Karzai government in extricating itself from having to carry out such a sentence. All this illustrates a fact that is often overlooked—that while people, like most everything else in nature, change, the traditions and institutions they create change only with great difficulty.

We see this in our own society where, because of major changes in the makeup of our population, the way various groups of people think, and the changed circumstances of modern life, serious conflict erupts as to how our Constitution should now be interpreted and applied to the realities of contemporary living. So a great deal of energy is expended, maybe even wasted, either by conservatives trying to force people back into literal compliance with the laws or by liberals trying to reinterpret the laws to mean something that was never intended.

Now if this is a problem with a tradition that took form only two hundred years ago, can we expect it will be any less a problem with a religion that took form thirteen hundred years ago? One would hardly think so.

Yet if we go back another thousand to two thousand years before that, to the millennium during which the Hebrew scriptures were written, we find that major changes did take place not just in the Hebrew people and way they lived their lives, but even in the way they understood their religion. In fact, at the end of that period approximately two thousand years ago, so radical was the change that what amounts to two almost entirely new religions emerged. One, which might be called the "conservative" reaction, is what we now think of as Judaism. The other, a much more liberal movement, was the beginning of what we now call Christianity. And, as we well know, there has been an ongoing struggle between those who keep trying to change things and those who want to keep things the same within both these descendants from the ancient Hebrew religion.

Now we see a similar struggle going on within the third descendent of this ancient Hebrew faith, which is, in fact, Islam. However, many today seem to think that Islam, unlike Judaism and Christianity, can never change or adjust itself to modern life. They point out that Judaism and Christianity both have "constitutions" (their Holy Scriptures) made up of many books compiled by different writers expressing various interpretations of God's ways and God's will. Instead, Muslims have largely rejected their own historical religious roots—claiming that both Jews and Christians got it wrong—and have substituted a single book, the Koran (Qur'an), which they believe was dictated directly by God and in fact involved no human "author."

Of course, if this were really true, then there seems there can be hardly any room for varied interpretations. In fact, it never works out quite that way, even within Islam. What happened recently in Afghanistan is in fact happening every day, perhaps in less dramatic ways, within the Muslim world over many other issues. So while change may be much more difficult for them because of the seeming inflexibility of their beliefs, the fact is that deep down human nature remains pretty much the same and that change is inevitable. In the meantime, instead of threatening them with sanctions, invasions, or worse—which only stiffens their resolve to never change—we in the West, even while we protect ourselves, need to be patient.

---

## Apocalypse Now?
(July 21, 2006)

Back when the modern state of Israel was first being conceived by secular Zionists like Theodore Herzl (1860-1904), there were ultra-orthodox Jews who had grave misgivings about the whole thing. To them this idea of a modern secular Jewish state was presumptuous, perhaps even tantamount to blasphemy, since only a future messiah sent directly from God could restore the Jewish homeland that had been destroyed by the Romans in 70 AD and yet again by the Romans in 135. Until then, the ultra-orthodox believed that Jews, scattered around the world, must continue to suffer as a result of their repeated infidelity to God. Even today there is a small group of Jews living in the shadow of the walls of old Jerusalem who, although they must live under Israeli law, refuse to recognize the modern state of Israel—at least until such a time when the Messiah finally comes.

There already were small Jewish settlements here and there in Palestine under the Turkish Ottoman empire. Yet it was the British, who with Arab help, had defeated the Turks during World War I, who had, unknown to the Arabs, promised the Zionists to work for the eventual establishment of the Jewish state. Understandably the Palestinians, who now felt they had been betrayed by the British, resisted, so much so that the British plans had to be put on hold until the influx of Jewish refugees after World War II put so much pressure on the British that they were forced to give in and the UN, in 1947, sanctioned the creation of the state of Israel. Foolishly, in 1967, the United Arab Republic (Egypt and Syria) thought it could destroy Israel and lost miserably, which gave the Israelis the opportunity to expand their borders—borders that the UN only provisionally recognized, leaving the West Bank and the Gaza Strip to the remaining Palestinians while the rest of them had fled, mostly to Jordan and Lebanon.

Today, several wars later, we see the remainder of these refugees and their descendants, who probably far outnumber the Israelis, regaining their determination to return to their homeland and to eliminate the modern state of Israel. They see this state, as one Egyptian Christian told me, as just the latest instance of Western "colonialism"—this time American, rather than European—in the Middle East. Our incursion into Iraq only confirms this view, and despite our claims of trying to spread democracy, the American reluctance to join the rest of the world in calling for an immediate cease-fire in Lebanon is seen as undermining one of the few democracies that actually exists in the Arab world.

Some see the present crisis as the beginning of a new world war, this time between the Muslim world and the modern secular West. I don't believe it is quite that bad, at least not yet, although the potential for nuclear confrontation is already there, with our old friends the Pakistanis already having proudly produced the first "Islamic bombs" and the Israelis refusing to confirm or deny what everyone knows—that they have enough of them to wipe any Muslim country off the map. But all of them—one fifth of the world's population? One dares not think so.

So where do we go from here? One cannot help but wonder whether those old ultra-orthodox Jews were right: there can be no restoration of Israel, or for that matter, any peace in this world, before the Messiah comes—or from the Christian viewpoint, comes again. In any case, it seems to me that slim chances of peace that once seemed possible under the first Camp David and the Oslo Accords are long gone. Wiping out Hamas in Gaza or Hezbullah in Lebanon will at most only give temporary respite. As the Middle Easterners like to say, "Terrorism is the war of the weak; war is the terrorism of the powerful."

As long as the United States and Israel wage war on terrorists rather than addressing the injustices foisted upon the weak, we can only expect terrorism in return. Until that realization finally sinks in, it may well be that the fate of Israel and of Jerusalem predicted in Matthew's Gospel—the so-called "Little Apocalypse" in which we are told that "there will not be one stone left upon another"—will be repeated yet again.

## Regensburg: Did the Pope Misspeak?
(September 18, 2006)

The furor that has erupted over Pope Benedict's September 12 homecoming talk at the University of Regensburg, where he once taught theology, should remind us—as well as the pope—of a number of things.

For one, the pope should be reminded that such talks to academics, even if not meant as a formal lecture, are not easily understood by average persons or even, perhaps, by reporters who are forced to write in sound bites. Anything that is said is apt to be taken out of context and come out distorted, even to the point of seeming to say the opposite of what was meant. The context of the pope's talk was not Islam and Christianity, much less jihads, as the press might have it, but rather can be found in its title, which is "Faith, Reason, and the University: Memories and Reflections."

Second, the inflammatory quote about Islam and the horrors it had caused was from one of the last Byzantine rulers discussing the problem of religion and violence with a Persian scholar before what remained of the empire was destroyed by the Ottoman Turks in 1453. However, it was only cited by the pope in contrast to another quote, this time from the Koran itself. Sura 2: 256 reads "There is no compulsion in religion," which seems to imply that faith that is forced by any means other than intellectual persuasion and personal convictions is not faith at all.

Third, it is apparent that the real reason for using these contrasting quotes was that the pope was trying to ask another question: why is it that faith and reason have become so divorced in the modern world, even to the point where theology is no longer given a serious place among the "sciences" in many universities today? His answer to that question is complex but started with what he called "a turn toward voluntarism" that began in the late Middle Ages, and was reinforced by the Reformation and the liberal theology of the nineteenth century in Christian thought. This "voluntarism" is the belief that religion is a matter mostly of will, emotions, and sentiment and that reason or logic has no proper place in religious belief.

Fourth, we must ask ourselves what the antidote for this sorry state of affairs might be. In his talk, Benedict himself argues that Christianity, almost to begin with, was an amalgam of Hebrew religion with Greek rationality—a tendency that can even be found in the Greek ("Septuagint") version of the Old Testament. Then quoting the beginning of John's Gospel, he reminds us that the *Logos* or "Word" also means "reason" and to not act "with logos" is contrary to the nature of God. When Christians or Muslims begin to describe God in terms of sheer willpower, we're headed for trouble, big time.

Finally, we—and this includes the pope, who seems to have failed to mention it—as well as Muslims, must remind ourselves that it was due to the Islamic world, particularly the Persian scholars and philosophers of medieval times, most of whom were persecuted by their own fundamentalists, that the works of Aristotle that had been lost during the early Middle Ages were finally rediscovered in the West. It was Aristotle's insistence that the study of nature must be the foundation of philosophy—in other words, that before you delve into metaphysics, you'd better get your physics right—that paved the way for the scientific revolution in the West. Unfortunately, theologians in both the East and the West, both Muslim and Christian, soon forgot this lesson and failed to keep their physics up-to-date.

In reaction—remember the Galileo affair?—modern science began to deny metaphysics and religion altogether. It is this great divorce between science and religion, and between faith and reason, including the current debate over evolution, that explains a lot about the present mess we're in.

---

# The Annapolis Initiative
(December 1, 2007)

Israeli Prime Minister Ehud Olmert says he is an optimist. And Palestinian President Mahmoud Marzen ("Abu Abbas") isn't saying. With Olmert's scandal-ridden administration barely holding together a shaky political coalition government, and Marzen's corrupt Fatah party having completely lost control of Gaza to radical Iranian-backed Hamas, it is hard to believe that anything substantial can come out of what the Bush administration has called "The Initiative" that was staged in Annapolis, Maryland, this past week.

While the purpose of the meeting was to revive the 2003 "Road Map" that was supposed to lead to a two-state solution to the Palestinian-Israeli conflict, the use of the word "initiative" almost sounds like an admission that we have to start all over again to try to use America's influence to bring peace to this most critical area of the Middle East. Yet the fact is that America, bogged down by its ill-considered invasion of Iraq, and faced with having to go back with greater force to finish the job it began in Afghanistan (and maybe even invade northwestern Pakistan to accomplish it) has largely lost whatever political influence once had to control events in the a Middle East. In fact, the Israeli prime minister was almost defiant in his denial, when asked in an interview, how much influence America still had over Israel's policies and politics.

Be that as it may, none of this must distract us from the challenge that the Israeli-Palestinian conflict poses. It, even more than oil, is at the heart of the resentment the Muslim world has toward America and Western Europe. While they are all too happy to sell us their oil (as long as it isn't being taken from them at gunpoint) the existence of the state of Israel in their midst is, to their mind, little different from the Latin Kingdom of Jerusalem set up by the Europeans during the time of the Crusades. The only difference is that while the Crusaders generally came to terms with what was by then the mostly Muslim inhabitants of the Holy Land, the modern Israelis have, for the most part, by one way or another, succeeded, over the past sixty years, in driving the Palestinians off of about three-quarters of what they believe to be their own ancestral lands. What that means is that any peace process or reconciliation has to overcome an accumulation of three generations worth of bitterness and resentment—something that anyone who knows the Middle East and its culture also knows is well-nigh impossible without what is truly a "conversion" in the literal religious sense of that word, a complete change or mind and heart.

This is where the real challenge lies. Judaism, Christianity and Islam are *historical* religions, in that they are not built primarily on philosophical views or vague spiritualities, but on what they each firmly believe are historical events or revelations given by God to humans in the past. Our claims as to what actually happened may differ somewhat, but as Mohammed himself attested, we are alike in that we all claim to worship the same God and are, as he put it "people of the book." The problem is that to the degree that we focus on that past as it was subsequently lived, our differences are accentuated, and largely become intractable and fixed on this increasingly crowded planet.

All this suggests that the key to peace is not so much justice as *mercy*, the ability to treat people with love and compassion, no matter what their ancestry may be or what may have been the sins of the past. In other words, while we may not be able to forget the past—nor should we lest we end up repeating it—we must learn to forgive, and to the degree possible (which can never be completely adequate) make amends for the harms that were done.

Yet of all virtues or qualities, true mercy may be the most difficult to come by—especially if it is not to be granted in an attitude of superiority by those who dispense it, as if they are not also in need of it as well. This is where the new initiative begun at Annapolis must lead all of us. Perhaps this may seem like we are asking for a miracle. Still, after decades of neglect, dishonesty, disappointed hopes, and outright failures, it will take the miracle of real conversion. Either that or another failure will surely lead to catastrophe.

# Part 8
# Spirituality

The general topic taken up in this group of essays has to do not so much with any specific religion but with spirituality—understood as the cultivation or promotion of the spiritual dimension of the individual person—whether within, or even apart from, a particular religious tradition from which it may, or may not, have originated. The approach here is not so much theological as it is psychological; that is, it has to do with the kind of mentality we bring to our efforts and the psychological dynamics that are involved in spiritual development. As such, this section also deals with distortions of the religious sense, as well as some of the basic rules of spiritual growth and maturity.

---

## Spirituality and Therapeutic Religion
(July 27. 2000)

Sociologists like Robert Bellah in his 1985 book *Habits of the Heart: Individualism and Commitment in American Life* have characterized our civilization as "therapeutic"—that is, as being dedicated to and largely obsessed with the goal of personal fulfillment and self-contentment. One of the places this is most evident is in our choice of a religion or a particular church. Americans increasingly seem to be no more committed to a particular faith or belief system than they are to living their whole life in one community or even with one husband or wife. Instead, religious affiliation or its replacement by some variety of home-grown "spirituality," more often than not, is chosen (and frequently changed) merely on the basis of what makes us "feel good inside."

Not that there is anything essentially wrong with therapy or healing as such. The Lord knows there is enough trauma and suffering in life. Healing and consolation are certainly worthy enough benefits of a religious faith. Nevertheless, can "feeling good" about one's self be the principal goal of belief?

Not if we follow the reasoning of Aristotle, the great philosopher of *eudaimonic* ethics (literally, "good-spirited" rules of behavior), who taught that while pleasure is a sign that we are heading in the right direction—that is, not acting contrary to our nature—common sense and experience show us that pleasure alone cannot serve as goal by itself. Too much pleasure, especially for its own sake, is like too much food or drink. Eat or drink too much and you'll get sick to your stomach or even eventually destroy your health.

So, too, if we follow the logic of religion when it comes to our spiritual health. Just as worship in its truest sense involves forgetting ourselves or at least acknowledging ourselves as dependent on a "Higher Power" in the universe, so too, the healing and comfort of religion can only come as a by-product or fringe benefit of having committed ourselves to something beyond ourselves. Anything less than this commitment to the Other who is totally "beyond" us ends up in what amounts to idolatry—the worship of a god who is fashioned primarily in the image of our own needs.

This is not to say that a faith must make us feel miserable in order to be considered genuine. Rather, it is a question of emphasis. As Gautama, the Buddha or "Enlightened One," put it, we can only achieve the peace of nirvana through *anatta*—that is, through first denying one's self. So too, Jesus warned (in six different places in the gospels) that is only when we are willing to "lose our life" that we will "save" it; in other words, by forgetting ourselves we find our true self. In this, he was echoing the Old Testament prophets who gave "comfort to the afflicted," but also saw it as part of their job to "afflict the comfortable."

As the world's most comfortable society, we Americans need a spirituality that demands much more than just making us feel good about ourselves. And this is why, for those who seek spiritual growth and enlightenment, one of the most important rules has been that we must "Always seek first of all the God of consolations, rather than the consolations of God."

---

## Commitment
(August 2, 2000)

Thirty or forty years of commitment to a marriage, a vocation, or any cause seems like an awful—that is, a truly "awe-inspiring"—period of time. Indeed, once the fifty-year mark is reached, we can say for all practical purposes it is a whole lifetime. And that is just the problem. For unless one is blessed with the unusually rare situation where every moment of those years is a joy, such commitment does not come easy. How then is such commitment possible?

In the forty-some years that I have thought about my own commitment to my calling, one thought keeps coming back. And it is that in terms of eternity, a whole lifetime is but a drop in the bucket. Conversely, for those who are unable to conceive of an eternity, committing oneself to something or someone for a whole lifetime is tantamount to "putting all one's eggs in one basket." No wonder they hesitate. It is not so much the lifetime as such that is the problem, but whatever does or doesn't come after.

Eternity, strictly speaking, is not just a long time; it is, literally speaking, completely out of time. So there is some truth to the oft-repeated advice, "you only live once—so . . ." Yet if we believe that this "once" extends all the way into eternity, then no mere lifetime, no matter how long, comes even close to what lies beyond. And it is the conviction that how we live now, how committed we are, and how faithful we are to that commitment, that makes all the difference. Or as the philosopher Nietzsche put it; given a sufficient *why*, we can endure any *what*.

Yet all this is hardly easy. It seems there is a real paradox at work here. In fact, when one thinks about it, it is rather easy to make a commitment to something that is perceived as unchanging. Take God for instance (who is, as scripture says, "the same, yesterday, today, and tomorrow"). God will never let us down, providing we are doing our best. Still, even that is not always easy. Both times and people change, and unless we are able and willing to adjust to these changing conditions and relationships, nothing, and certainly no promise, not even one made before God, is likely to last. In fact, we can almost guarantee that the longer we live the more things will change. The only question, then, is whether we are strong enough to adjust to change. If not, the firm "forever" of "until death do us part" will have been largely replaced by the easy ambivalence of "whenever." In this way, in our time, it seems, commitment has been largely replaced by convenience.

The answer or antidote, of course, is "faith." Without faith, there can be no real faithfulness. Yet faith, which is at root "a loving trust," is itself a "stretch"—a reaching out beyond our beliefs and imagined certainties toward what is, at least in this life, unattainable. Faith is, at the same time, a risk, a gamble in which we wager the whole meaning of our lives on what is not yet completely certain. For if it were a sure thing, then what need would there be for commitment?

# Hypocrisy
(September 3, 2000)

When we call someone a *hypocrite*, what exactly do we mean? We mean, generally speaking, that this person, whether they be preacher or politician, public authority or private person, is insincere, putting on a show, pretending to be something other than what they really are. And of course, to the extent that we all try to show off the best side of ourselves—do we not all dress up a bit to impress others or do we not often swallow our feelings rather than come right out and say what we are really thinking?—are we not all a bit hypocritical? Thus it seems that there is a little bit of the hypocrite in all of us. So the problem with hypocrisy of this common sort is not so much that it exists. Civil society would be impossible without a certain amount of it. Instead, the real challenge is in understanding how this tendency functions and the limits of its usefulness.

Hypocrisy is born in idealism. It is the result of failing to live up to what we aspire to be. The Pharisees of Jesus' time were not so much evil men as good men whose idealism was misplaced or had gotten out of line. They had, as Jesus said, replaced God's commandments with human conventions, substituting their own elaborate rules of conduct for the more fundamental obligations of human life. And in doing so, they had become *hyper* or overcritical of others while becoming increasingly *hypo* or undercritical of themselves. They had become experts in finding specks of sawdust in other people's eyes while they had a whole plank of lumber lodged in their own.

What then should we do about this? Give up our ideals? Perhaps we do need to examine them to find out whether or not they are realistic and make appropriate adjustments when necessary. Yet to give them up entirely would, I think, bring human evolution to a grinding halt. Repeated failures to keep peace in this world hardly mean that we should settle for perpetual war. Nor should the inevitable imbalance between the haves and have-nots in this world mean that we should give up on the struggle to make this a more just world. What we need to do, I think, is to sit down and examine carefully where our idealism (or sometimes lack of it) has gone wrong.

However, we must begin with ourselves. True or authentic religion has always begun with a confession of sin. Without the admission of our own failures there can be no genuine progress toward a higher ideal. The person who says that he or she is not conscious of any sin or failure in his or her own life is either inhuman—perhaps superhuman?—or else just plain naive. In any case, meeting with others, admitting our failures, and trying to do something about it (in other words going to church) is, in most cases, the first step on the path toward making this a better world. No doubt, there are a lot of hypocrites to be found in churches and other religious establishments. Yet at least (if they are heeding the message of religion) they know they are hypocrites. Unlike those who avoid church because as they say it is filled with hypocrites, churchgoers at least have a handle (the criticism of other churchgoers) on what it takes to overcome the hypocrisy built into daily life in the world.

A preacher I once heard over the radio put the case quite succinctly: we go to church not to pretend that we are better than anyone else but simply to practice, at least for a short time, what we should be doing for the whole rest of the week!

---

## The Devil You Say?
(September 4, 2001)

For better or for worse, Christianity took root in a world obsessed by the devil—the belief that most, if not all, human ills, whether physical, psychological, or moral, were caused by evil spirits of one sort or another. Even philosophers like Plato and Aristotle believed that the human soul was driven by various *daimonoi* or "demons," whether for good or for bad. Likewise, religious thought of the time was dominated by a metaphysical, even theological, dualism that saw the universe in terms of an epic battle between two cosmic forces, the good or "divine" and the bad or "diabolical." Late Old Testament-era literature, like much of that found in the Dead Sea Scrolls, is filled with such imagery, as is the New Testament Book of Revelation. The mythical serpent of Genesis became identified with the fallen angel "Lucifer," and just as divine messages became personified as "messengers" (angels) so too temptations became personified as the tempter—in Hebrew *Satan*. What for us is largely explainable in psychiatric and psychosomatic terms was, for the authors of the gospels and many others of that era, evidence of diabolic possession. Apart from this kind of understanding, how else could even Jesus have made himself understood?

Unfortunately, the exaggerations of such a mind-set soon dominated Christian spirituality, for according to this dualistic thinking, the body and its appetites (especially sexuality) were seen as almost inherently evil. One of the early Christian sects, the Messalians, even went so far as to teach that each human soul was inhabited by a personal demon—after all, if one believes in a specially assigned "guardian angel," why not a specially assigned tempter as well? The early monks and hermits went off into the deserts of Palestine, Syria, and Egypt not just to find God, but, first of all, to engage in personal combat with these evil spirits, while their publicists (like St. Athanasius in his famous "Life of St. Anthony") played up this aspect for all it was worth.

Today, of course, we at least think we know better. We know, for example, that in terms of psychological growth, dualistic thinking characterizes not only our earlier growth stages, but especially that stage when a person is first emerging from collective or inherited groupthink to take a position or stand of one's own. At this point in life—including the life of institutions or cultures—everything has to be clearly defined in terms of black or white, yes or no, true or false. Especially if one is still in a struggle with one's own personal demons, there can be little tolerance for shades of gray. In addition, there is the psychological phenomenon of "projection"—attributing to others our own inner attitudes or accusing others of possessing our own faults.

The disturbing thing about all this is not the inspiration it gives comedians (Flip Wilson's "The devil made me do it!") but the opportunity for self-evasion of responsibility it affords. As the "Desert Fathers" (and Mothers) soon discovered (much like "Pogo" in the comic script), the real enemy is us. Solitude, quicker than anything else, makes this evident. Too often society or constant company becomes the escape of those who can't face themselves. And in turn, the society or institution is made to serve as a refuge to avoid facing up to the real evils in the world. And we must make no mistake; evil is very much a reality. Perhaps the psychiatrist Carl Jung was on to something when he suggested that Christianity had erred in describing divinity as totally good and neglecting the "shadow side of God" (although I personally think a fuller understanding of the evolutionary process yields a more satisfactory explanation for the evil in the world).

However, as for "Satan" and the other "devils"—if there really are such beings—I think it is best just to ignore them. For if Christian tradition is correct in attributing the devils' fall from their angelic status to their pride, then the logic of human experience would seem to dictate that we ignore them altogether. After all, for those who are filled with pride, there is no worse fate than being treated as if they didn't exist!

## Religious Extremism
(October 15, 2001)

Recently, as reported in a short news segment on National Public Radio, several scholars of religion put their heads together and came up with six characteristics of religious extremism. In light of the world's present problems, where so often religion plays an important role, it might be well worth our effort to seriously consider their list.

First: almost all such movements are addicted to scriptural *fundamentalism* or, more exactly, to a literal interpretation of their holy books. This is true not just of some Christians (and even some Jews) with the Bible, but perhaps even more so of Muslims when it comes to the Koran.

Second: *apocalypticism*. Many religious extremists pay special attention to prophecies and predictions of catastrophes leading to the "end times." With Christians, this tendency shows itself in a fixation on the Book of Revelation (the last book in the New Testament), almost to the exclusion of all other books.

Third: a *siege mentality*. Extremists often see themselves as an embattled or persecuted minority. This condition is certainly evident in the thinking of many in the third world, who see their civilization as being swallowed up and destroyed by Western culture, with its strong emphasis on individual freedoms and material success.

Fourth: a *single identity*. Extremists seem to lose a sense of the multiple aspects of life and the varied roles they must play in regard to them. Instead they seem obsessed by a single thought or idea. They tend to have what we might call a "one-track mind."

Fifth: the influence of a strong-willed or *charismatic leader*. Without such a leader, the tendency toward extremism generally remains only an individual quirk.

Sixth: the temptation of *wealth or power*, or at least the fear of losing whatever economic advantages one might already have.

While these scholars admitted that something like these same six tendencies can also be found in non-religious forms of extremism (think, for example, the way dedicated communists hung onto every word that Marx or Lenin ever wrote), the big difference is that in religious extremism, all these factors are combined into the conviction that "God wills it"—which was the battle cry of the both of Muslim warriors in their jihads and their Christian counterparts in the Crusades.

Which of these six characteristics is most important? I suspect that it depends on what religious movement one is talking about. The third item (a siege mentality) would seem to me to be a much larger factor in the Muslim world's conflict with the rest of us than is the second (apocalypticism), although Muslims also believe that there will be a "Last Judgment" at the end of the world. However, as far as I know, Hindu extremists in India have no such visions of a final showdown, but instead see themselves as economically threatened by Christians, a factor that has played a similar role in Protestant vs. Catholic tensions and violence in Northern Ireland.

Still, despite regional variations, I suspect these experts are very much correct—enough that I think we should make an effort to examine each of these factors more closely. Often, behind what we take to be religious extremism there is a great deal more than what first meets the eye.

---

## Prayer
### (November 21, 2001)

Prayer, in the strict sense of asking God for favors, would seem to be a nonsensical activity. After all, if God is the all-wise, all-knowing, all-powerful entity we claim God to be, the idea that we can change God's mind seems contradictory, if not outright childish. Nonetheless, throughout history, humans, even those who are not otherwise religious, have almost universally engaged in such prayer, at least in moments of crisis. As the old wartime saying had it, "there are no atheists in foxholes." So how do we explain prayer, or defend the practice?

Theologians, in particular, have long wrestled with the issue. Thomas Aquinas, who assumed that God always wants what is best for us, taught that what prayer really does is to dispose us to accept God's will. In other words, instead of changing God's mind, we end up changing our own. So if we are so crass as to ask God to give us a Cadillac, real prayer will probably change us enough to be perfectly happy with anything that runs reliably on four wheels—or to see the benefit of walking instead.

However, take something much more serious, like life or health. Does prayer do any good? Recent medical research says most definitely, "Yes." Mind and body are intimately connected. A prayerful mind soon becomes a peaceful one, while an anxious mind only makes matters worse. Stress produces not only hypertension but also a host of other physical problems, and makes the body more vulnerable to invasion by pathogens of all sorts.

Of course, these examples are a "natural" explanation of the power of prayer. They hardly involve miracles. So we still have to face the question, can prayer reverse the course of nature, can it literally "move mountains"? One answer is, of course, that if God is God, and God so wills it, the mountain will be moved. (Supposedly St. Nicholas of Myra, the fourth-century bishop who became our "Santa Claus," actually did pull off that kind of miracle—but, of course, that is only a legend.) The other answer is that such mountain-moving is only a metaphor for tough cases, like changing human minds, starting with our own. Still, if the so-called laws of nature are, at least according to quantum theory, more like statistical averages (what goes up usually, well over 99 percent of the time, comes down) rather than absolute rules, who knows what influence mind might have over matter as well?

All in all, however, I think St. Augustine had the best approach. He saw prayer as primarily an expression of our *desire* for God. Likening the human heart to a sack or container, Augustine saw prayer as a kind of exercise by which we slowly stretch the walls of this container, increasing its capacity to receive God's power or grace. This divine influence first of all changes our minds so that we ourselves can become instruments of God's will. If this is true, then these theologians are only echoing Jesus, who told us that "those who ask shall receive" . . . not just "good things" but, even more, according to St. Luke's rendition of this saying, they shall receive "the Holy Spirit." And if that is the case, then it is not just ourselves who pray but, as Paul tells us in his letter to the Romans, God's Spirit that prays within us. At that point, who can place limits on what can happen?

---

## Solitude
(March 11, 2002)

The great Indian thinker and patriot Mohandas Gandhi once wrote that "He who would be friends with God must remain alone . . . or else make the whole world his friend." Gandhi, of course, was reflecting on the age-old experience of his own Hindu tradition, but he was not unaware that this same paradox is found in the Bible and in other religious traditions. Solitude is one of the surest paths to God. Nevertheless, so too is service of one's fellow human beings—perhaps the more the better.

Need this paradox express an either/or choice? Those first Christians who left the world to live in the desert or the wilderness (*heremos* in Greek, hence our word "hermit") did so to be entirely alone with God. Yet soon others joined them in great numbers, so many in fact that some of the first monasteries were more like large villages, as also were the later abbeys in Europe, with their extensive land holdings, industries, hospitals, and schools, compared to the kind of isolated or walled-in enclosures we think of today

Yet no doubt a tension remains within this paradox. The heart of monastic vocation is still to be found in solitude. The term monk (*monachos* in Greek) means someone who, even though he may live in a community, still, since he is unmarried, essentially lives alone. And even though, early on in Christian history, there also began to be small communities of hermits, the model remained that of the anchorite—the true solitary, the one who literally lived *anachoros* or "apart."

Why is this? Could it be that despite all the pitches on "community" and "fellowship" and "communion," religion is essentially, as the philosopher A. N. Whitehead put it, "what one does with one's solitude." What each one of us is, as an individual, is ultimately between us and God, and that no amount of "do-gooding," however wonderful, can make up for it if that direct connection between ourselves and our Creator is lacking. Even the "communion of saints," whether here or in heaven, depends, first of all, on our personal union with God.

This is not to say that in some way the fruits of this personal union with God can be hoarded for one's own exclusive use. Quite the contrary, they must be shared in one way or another. The reclusive John the Baptist became the public witness to Christ. The hermit Benedict became the "Father of Western Monasticism" and, through his many followers, as well as through the efforts of the many missionary monks from Ireland, the preserver of European civilization at a time when the barbarian invasions plunged that continent into the Dark Ages.

So when it comes down to Gandhi's paradox, maybe it's not an either/or proposition. Instead, it is only when one learns to live solely for God that one becomes truly capable of befriending all.

---

# Seeing
(March 14, 2003)

Remember the line in the old American revival hymn "Amazing Grace" that says "Once I was blind, but now I see"? This hymn was written by a New England sea captain who had once been a slave trader, but once he had began to realize what he was really doing, repented of the evil he had done. Certainly he had seen, firsthand with his own eyes, the misery of the human cargo he was carrying across the ocean from Africa, yet it was years before he really saw, that is, *understood* the moral depravity of his trade.

From this it is evident that to simply see with one's eyes is far from really grasping the truth. We know, for example, that physically speaking, sight comes from little energy particles, called "photons," registering on the retina of the eye, which in turn cause nerve impulses to be transmitted via the optical nerve channels to the brain. Yet the picture we actually see in our mind is a construct of the brain itself, and what we think we "see" is largely determined by what we are used to seeing or even by what we think we ought to see. This is why sometimes certain people just don't see what seems obvious to others and why, sometimes, some people see things that others don't. As many prosecutors and judges can testify, even eyewitness evidence can prove to be highly subjective. Two witnesses can see the same event and yet give completely contradictory accounts. And yet, once we sift through all the evidence, we can generally manage to arrive at the truth.

If so, why can't we do the same when we confront so many issues that are the occasion of such fierce debate, whether they be economic, political, scientific, religious, or even just personal or within the confines of the family? Isn't it because something else other than the objective truth is at stake?

For example, take the ongoing debate between evolutionists and creationists. Die-hard evolutionists claim that the circumstantial evidence for evolution is so overwhelming that only the most stubborn (or stupid) observer could fail to see that evolution is all but proven scientific fact. Yet many of their opponents no longer rely on a literal interpretation of the Bible but on more sophisticated arguments for "intelligent design." They point out that there are still large gaps in the supposed circumstantial evidence, and they claim that if the evolutionists were true to their own scientific methodology (which demands replication under laboratory conditions, in other words, eyewitness evidence), that they would acknowledge that evolution is at best a mere theory (a "likely story") that never can be proved.

Yet suppose for a moment we grant, for the time being, that both are at least partially right. Obviously, the existing circumstantial evidence would seem to indicate that evolution on a very large scale has occurred. Otherwise there is just too much in nature that is completely unexplainable, even (as I see it) in theological terms. On the other hand, some of the leaps or crossings of the evolutionary "thresholds" (like that from non-life to life) seem to remain statistically so improbable that it is hard not to see some kind of design or even "invisible hand" at work.

So then, why can't the two sides come to some sort of agreement? Might it not be that for some reason or other they, like the Yankee slave trader had for so many years, don't really want to see the whole picture or the full meaning of what is before their eyes?

## *Shabbat Shalom*
(May 13, 2003)

When Constantine the Great issued his famous edict in Milan in 313 AD, he did not initially make Christianity the official religion of the Roman Empire. Instead, his "Edict of Toleration" gave equal rights to all religions to exist. Yet what Constantine did next to tilt the empire toward Christianity was to officially make what Christians called "the Lord's Day" into a legal holiday by forbidding the carrying on of government business and commercial transactions.

In effect, Constantine gave imperial recognition to the Middle-Eastern idea of dividing the lunar month into four seven-day periods and with it, introducing the Jewish concept of *Shabbat Shalom*, the Sabbath peace or day of rest. Until then, the week as we now measure it was unknown to the Romans, who scorned the Jews as being "lazy" for refusing to work one day out of seven. Instead, the Romans let their slaves do all the work all through the month while they themselves enjoyed a perpetual holiday. Constantine's decision to legally establish the Christian version of the Jewish Sabbath, and with it the week as we now have it, became one of the foundation stones of European civilization—so much that even wars were often interrupted to observe a truce on Sundays!

Today, even as we demand longer weekends for relaxation and recreation, it seems we hardly give the origin of this age-old custom a second thought. A large number of people, especially in our country, still flock to church on Sunday (or even the evening before—another custom borrowed from the Jews whose Sabbath begins at sundown the day before). Still, how many of these same Christians then immediately flood the nearest major discount store? Jesus may have healed the sick on the Sabbath and told us that the Sabbath was made for our sake—and not the other way around—but would he who drove the money-changers out of the Lord's House approve of the Lord's Day being given over to "business as usual"?

Here I think we have to try to strike a balance. No one wants to go back to the puritanical "blue laws" that practically put life on hold on Sundays by confining all movement or activity to church-going alone. On the other hand, I doubt if even the most ardent secularists would want to go so far as the post-revolutionary French who from 1793-1805 tried to abolish the week (and with it the Lord's Day) altogether and replace it with three ten-day periods to make nice even thirty-day months followed by a five or six day New Year's binge. Not even atheistic Soviet communism went that far!

How much of our present lack of balance is driven by business? Some years ago, auto salespersons in Michigan refused to be forced by their employers to work weekends. This should tell us something. Even if one is not religious, there is something disturbing about a business that refuses to give its employees a break or, even if it is a necessary business (people have to eat, even on Sunday), fails to pay them extra for that sacrifice. Yet even here there is a danger, especially if one is attracted to Sunday or weekend work because it might pay more. Then the danger comes from the temptation of making money one's major goal in life to the exclusion of all other values. Maybe that is why in the Ten Commandments the observance of the Sabbath is right up there near the beginning—along with the prohibition of idolatry in all its other forms.

On the other hand, how much of America's present disregard for keeping the Sabbath (whether is be Sunday for Christians, Friday for Muslims, or Saturday for Jews) comes not from a the worship of the false god of money but, rather, from the general loss of our sense of "creatureliness," that is, our dependence on a greater reality in the first place? How else do we explain devoting a whole day or even a whole weekend to our own *re*-creation without any reference to the Creator?

---

## What Does It Mean To Be Christian?
(January 10, 2004)

The discovery of the Dead Sea Scrolls in 1946 revealed that there was, back in the time of Jesus, a greater amount of variety of religious beliefs among the Jewish people than we had previously suspected. What we understand to be Judaism today is merely the last survivor of what had been a whole cluster of various beliefs and practices that once existed among the Hebrew people.

In much the same way, the 1945 discovery of a cache of ancient manuscripts, hidden in a cave above the Nile River near the Egyptian town of Nag Hammadi, has confirmed what scholars had long known—that within the first couple of centuries following the time of Jesus there was even more of a variety of conflicting beliefs among those who were calling themselves "Christians." Some thought of Jesus as merely a particularly wise teacher, much like a Jewish Socrates. Others thought of him as a prophet and wonder-worker like Moses or Elijah. Others believed him to have been a kind of divinely sent "extraterrestrial" who only appeared to be, but really wasn't, human.

It seems no wonder then, that when the Roman general Constantine took control of the whole empire in 312, one of the first things on his agenda was to try to bring some unity among all these popular but conflicting interpretations of Jesus among those who called themselves "Christians." The result was the official doctrine hammered together at the great council of bishops held at Nicea in 325 under the watchful eyes of Constantine and the solders of his imperial guard. From then on, all those who did not consider Jesus to be, in the words of the creed issued by that council, "God from true God, Light from true Light, of the same substance [i.e. nature] as (God) the Father" were to be considered "anathema" (condemned as heretics), and that their writings were to excluded from that collection of early Christian writings that we now know as "The New Testament."

Today the situation is not much different. Traditional Christians seem to think that anyone who does not accept the literal meaning of the words of the official creeds must be denounced and shunned as heretics, while modern evangelical Christians, in particular, seem to think that all those who have not had a "born again" experience hardly deserve to be called Christians to begin with. Meanwhile, polls or surveys of Americans reveal that about two-thirds of those who think of themselves as Christian remain as confused as ever about these doctrinal issues, while the Unitarian-Universalists even went so far as to declare their church as not being "Christian," if that is what is necessary to be independent of such straight-jacket denominational thinking.

I can sympathize with that reaction. Years ago, I was in the habit of visiting an acquaintance who was not a member of my church, nor even a churchgoer, but, at a relatively young age, was dying of cancer. On one of these visits, I decided it was time I asked him about his relationship to

God and what he thought this might mean in regard to his eternal destiny. His answer was very simple. "I believe in God" he said, "and that God sent Jesus to us to show us how to live, and I have tried to live accordingly." Then he added that he was content that God would know what to do with him and that the only thing he was really worried about was what would happen to his wife and children.

In all my years in ministry and in teaching Christian doctrine, I must say that I've never heard quite so simple and profound a profession of faith. Certainly I would have liked to have seen him within my church, and to have shared our sacraments with him, but knowing personally how good a man he was, I would defy anyone who would consider him not to be truly a "Christian."

## All Souls
(October 31, 2005)

It almost goes without saying that most humans throughout the ages have held some sort of belief in life after death. Even some of the remains of the Neanderthals unearthed by paleontologists seem to indicate that these primitive people entertained some kind of hope in an afterlife.

Generally speaking, such beliefs seem to have taken one of two forms, or else some combination of the two. The first, and probably the most widespread, is belief in a "soul" or spirit of some sort that escaped from the body at death, possibly to be reborn in another body, whether it be human or that of some bird or beast.

The second form of belief, less widespread yet well-known from the biblical tradition, is in a "resurrection" or raising-up of the same body that was buried—in other words, the same old shell, but hopefully renovated some and given, through God's saving power, new life.

Today, of course, such relatively primitive beliefs have fallen upon hard times. Belief in reincarnation or the "transmigration of souls" seems pretty absurd to anyone who thinks one's identity as an individual person is totally determined by our particular genetic makeup, sexual identity, or our specific location in time and space. And as the alternative picture of these same bodies rising up out of the grave seems even less plausible, for most Christians the belief in the resurrection has become more of a symbol of a vague hope than anything else. Indeed, except for those who have had some sort of personal experience of God, the life of faith, particularly when it comes to these matters, is more or less like whistling in the dark—even while the tunes increasingly make less and less sense.

Yet it seems that hope never completely dies. A century ago, the atheist Friedrich Nietzsche—famous for his proclamation that "God is dead"—himself believed that given an eternity of time, every atom of the universe would sooner or later recombine with others in exactly the same combinations that constitute our present existence to reproduce new copies of ourselves, even repetitions of our actions and our thoughts! Although most dismiss him as the mad philosopher whose ideal of the "superman" helped pave the way for Nazism, his dream of "Eternal Return" lives on today in the speculation of some cosmologists who theorize about a "multiverse" that endlessly re-creates other universes—though one hopes they do not believe that Nietzsche himself will return to haunt us once again!

Nevertheless, these speculations prove my point, I think, that even scientists are loathe to admit that the long path of evolution, winding through billions of years of painful growth as well as loss, leads ultimately to a dead end, with nothing more or better in sight. In other words, while belief in individual survival after death may seem to be on shaky ground at times, especially today when science seems to have solved just about every mystery, still, some sort of belief, or at least a vague hope, in the survival of the human spirit remains.

## Spiritual Blindness
(March 5, 2005)

The story of the man born blind that is found in John's gospel (chapter 9) illustrates that there is such a thing as "spiritual blindness" or the inability to grasp spiritual realities. Just as there are some people born into the world without the ability to see physical things, so too there seem to be other people who are unable to apprehend what is unseen. The only question is (as it is in this gospel story), is it their fault or the fault of someone else?

St. Augustine pondered this question at some length. Speaking about himself, who only became a baptized Christian in midlife, he wrote: "As usually happens, the person who has tried a bad doctor is afraid even to trust a good one. So it was with the health of my soul, which could not be healed except by believing, and refused to be healed for fear of believing falsehood" (*Confessions*, book IV, chapter 4). So it appears that the inability to believe, and thus see "spiritually," can sometimes be the result of being given the wrong spiritual "medicine" or being exposed to a religious "quack."

Still, I think it can also sometimes be our own fault as well. Take what could be described as not either physical or spiritual blindness but, instead, mental or intellectual blindness, and I think you'll see my point. For example, while I've always been keenly interested in science, I seem to suffer from an inability to grasp abstract concepts when they are expressed in mathematical terms. You might even describe me as "mathematically challenged" whenever I see a mathematical formula of any sort. Sometimes I don't even have to see a formula on paper; it's enough for me even if I hear such terms, like Stephen Hawking's use of such concepts as "imaginary numbers" in his books.

Now in this situation I can react in one of several ways. I can act like an Archie Bunker and yell "Don't confuse me with facts, my mind is made up!" Or, on the other hand, I could maybe admit that perhaps I suffer from a disability of some sort and that perhaps scientists like Hawking and others just might know what they are talking about. Or at least I might consult other experts in the field to see whether or not they agree with Hawking's ideas. In other words, I should try to keep an open mind.

By now I hope my point is more or less obvious. Religion, or more exactly belief, is a means of knowing, and like most other forms of knowing, it depends on our ability to trust people who are supposed to be "in the know." Even more to the point "theology"—a word that means the "science" of or the "knowledge of God"—is a specialty that demands more than just good intentions or the ability to read the Bible (even if one has learned to understand a smattering of Hebrew or Greek). It demands long years of study and accreditation, much the same as in any other science. Even more, it demands honesty and open-mindedness and perhaps still more, the humility to be able to admit when one has been proved wrong.

The cardinals of the Holy Inquisition, I'm afraid, did not prove themselves to be very good theologians when they refused to look through Galileo's telescope because, according to them, the Bible taught that the Sun circled the Earth. Today we still have some churchmen who claim that evolution could not have happened because the Bible doesn't say it did. Yet it seems that we also have to defer to some scientists who can find no place for God in the universe because they can't fit God into their equations or their still-elusive goal of "a theory of everything."

Augustine also had something to say about this kind of situation. He believed that when the scriptures seem to be contradicted by clear, consistent reasoning, then it is probably because we are reading the scriptures wrongly. Still, I wonder if the opposite isn't also true, that is, that sometimes the reasoning is not very clear or consistent as it might be. In any case, although Carroll O'Connor (who played the "Archie Bunker" role in the television series *All in the Family*) is himself now gone, it seems to me that the spirit of Archie Bunker and his "already made up" mind is far from dead.

---

# Confession
(December 13, 2005)

Some years ago the Swiss Protestant psychiatrist Paul Tournier wrote a little book in which he warned his Catholic friends that if their church ever foolishly gave up the practice of individual confessions as a result of Vatican II inspired reforms, then a lot of psychiatrists would get rich from the growing number of people in dire need of unburdening their souls.

Apparently there is now a cheaper way of doing so. First there is the growing popularity of "Post Secrets," an artistic project which began with anonymous homemade post cards on which one writes down one's guiltiest secret and sends it to help relieve one's conscience at least in some way. And now we have the appearance of similar blogs on the Internet. I suspect this phenomenon confirms a lot of what Tournier had predicted.

Should anyone really be surprised? Being told from a pulpit that God forgives all sins, or kneeling down and admitting that we are all sinners in general, is fine, but people have a need for someone to individually assure them that God forgives their own *particular* failings or sins. And the worse the sin is the more pressing the need. As Tournier pointed out, Protestant pastors may not sit in a confessional box to do this, but they end up doing a lot of it in their offices anyway.

As for the sacrament of Penance or "Reconciliation" (as it is now officially called), it has had a mixed past. For the first five or so centuries of Christianity it was a public ceremony where penitents were required to confess their sins (at least the ones that were already public knowledge) before the bishop and were duly assigned public penances in return. At the end of Lent, provided they had faithfully performed their assigned penance (like forty days wearing sack-cloth and eating bread and water only) or had been granted an "indulgence" to do something less rigorous, they were, as a group, then officially "absolved," that is, readmitted to communion by the bishop of the local church.

Later on, when this sort of strong medicine proved too much for the average Christian, bishops began to allow priests to hear individual confessions and assign predetermined penances (listed in books called "penitentials") in private but still often reserved the granting of the absolution to themselves. Eventually, priests were entrusted with the entire process, except in the case of certain "reserved" sins.

In recent years, there has been a tendency to return to the ancient idea of public "Penance Services"—only skipping the public confession of sins by individuals and rigorous penances that so scared off penitents in the past after Christians had ceased to be the kind of people who did not fear being thrown to the lions. No doubt these services are also a lot easier on the clergy, since preaching a rousing sermon on God's forgiveness is a whole lot easier (and ego-enhancing) than spending hours upon hours sitting in a small room listening to the same old list of all-too human failings.

Then the question raised by Tournier and the "Post Secrets" phenomenon returns to haunt us. Can such shortcuts really do the job that needs to be done? Confession, or Penance, or Reconciliation (or whatever you want to call it) is just as much a psychological necessity as a religious one, or as they called it in the early church "a second Baptism, only this time not in water but in tears." It is the sacrament of ongoing or continuing conversion, God's answer to our unfortunate need of being reborn—too often again, and yet again.

---

# Holy Indifference
(July 27, 2006)

It may be difficult for us to comprehend, but not all religion down through history has been exclusively concerned with the goal of obtaining life after death. No doubt in more primitive eras just the task of keeping enough food on the table to stay alive in this world was enough to keep one praying to the gods. Worrying about what happened afterward was pretty much an afterthought, perhaps motivated as much by a desire to see the wicked punished as it was by any additional reward for the good. Even then it took the Hebrew people well over a thousand years to progress from the revelation of the Ten Commandments to any clear idea of a future life or resurrection.

Of course, there were major exceptions. From early on in their five thousand year history, the Egyptian people seem to have been obsessed with the idea of living happily ever after. And no doubt the growing esteem for individual identity and personal worth among the classical Greek and Roman civilizations prepared the way for Christianity, with its clear promise of eternal life. Still, even then, the quest for personal fame generally took second place to the higher claims of group loyalty and national identity. It is only during the modern era that the individual person, with claims to his or her personal rights, has taken its place front and center. No wonder then that "saving one's soul" seems to have become the end all and be all of the personal religion of so many.

Yet when we look more deeply, an interesting phenomenon appears. It seems that at least sometimes those we might consider to be most spiritually mature appear to become almost indifferent to their own personal fate as long as God's will is accomplished in their life. We can see this in St. Paul who wrote that, if it were possible, he would be willing to be "condemned," providing that loss might benefit his own people (see Romans 9:2-3). We find similar avowals of what might seem to be a kind of indifference to their own fate in the lives of not a few modern-day saints as well. How do we explain this?

I think that the answer can be found in the human process of maturation. Just as small children have to be taught to distinguish right from wrong and behave accordingly through the promise of reward and the threat of punishment, the same applies to beginners in the spiritual life. When people have achieved at least some degree of maturity, they do what is right not out of fear of punishment or even hope for a reward, but simply because it is the proper thing to do, especially when they become as much concerned with the well-being of others as with their own well-being. If there is concern about an afterlife at this stage, it may have more to do with the future of humanity or of all creation than it does with the fate of any individual.

No doubt, some will object, pointing out how such indifference to one's personal future could be used as an excuse for bad behavior. Indeed it might, especially by those who are immature or selfish. There are even those, as in the case of suicide bombers, who find such beliefs to be an incentive to religious fanaticism. Yet when all is said and done, it seems to me that for those who love God above all, or who love their neighbor even more than themselves, there remains a simple faith or trust that, while it may not make them totally self-forgetful, nevertheless, when it comes to themselves, leads to a kind of "holy indifference."

## The Secret of Sanctity
(August 23, 2007)

Many years ago the French writer, Leon Bloy, wrote that "There is only one real tragedy in life, and that is not to be a saint."

Apparently I was not the only one struck by that observation, because a few years back someone who had apparently read the same passage, in turn wrote to me from sunny California, asking me what my definition of holiness is, or what it takes to become a saint. Not that I consider myself to be one, but after a great deal of thought on the subject, I believe that to become a saint, one must *see God in all things and act accordingly.*

As the years have passed, I have become more and more convinced of this. Yet as tough or demanding as the "acting accordingly" part may be, I see the really fundamental problem as being first of all in the challenge of how to go about seeing God in all things.

It may be that at certain times, for example, immediately after escaping from a serious danger or threat to your life, you are suddenly seized with the realization that someone or something is watching out for you. This may be reassuring, but I wouldn't recommend courting "near death-experiences" as a way of looking for the presence of God. Your good fortune may be just dumb luck.

On the other hand, there is the kind of "peak experience" that the psychiatrist Abraham Maslow wrote about, claiming that just about everyone has them from time to time. This may be a very gratifying thing, but wise spiritual directors have warned us that attempts to seek such esoteric or mystical experiences can be dangerous and rife with self-delusion or, at the very least, inherently self-centered. They can easily become, as one old saying on the subject puts it, "Seeking the consolations of God rather than the God of consolations."

This leads me to believe that the safest route is more or less philosophical. It is to cultivate, as much as possible, a deeper awareness of the wonder of existence, what the philosopher Jacques Maritain called "the intuition of being" or the wonder of existence in itself. It is to try to realize, as much as possible, at all times, that nothing exists except to the extent that it is grounded in God, whom philosophers have understood as the source of all that exists or, as St. Augustine put it, as "Being in itself."

For some, as for Augustine, this intuition is, as it were, a presence discovered primarily within one's own self, or as he wrote in his *Confessions*, "You were within me, but I was outside, and it was there that I searched for you" (Book 10, 27). Yet for others, it is more the other way around, that we exist in God, so much so that when St. Luke describes the Apostle Paul proclaiming "the Unknown God" in Athens, he quotes the ancient Stoic poet Epimenides, who wrote that "In Him we live and move and have our being" (Acts 17:28).

In fact, I am convinced that this sense of existing within God is so important that I am often drawn to quoting another "pagan" philosopher, this time not a Stoic, but the last of the great neo-Platonists, Plotinus (205-270 AD), who in turn had a great influence on Augustine. As Plotinus wrote, "He [God] is everywhere in entirety: at once. He *is that everywhere* and everywise. He is *not in* the everywhere, but *is* the everywhere—the giver of existence to everything in that everywhere" (*Enneads* VI, 8, 16; emphasis mine). Or again, as the medieval German mystical theologian Meister Eckhart put it, God is the very "ground" of our existence, so much that in so far as we exist at all, we are sharing in the nature of God. So too, the mystic Mechtild of Magdeburg, who wrote; "The day of my spiritual awakening was the day I saw—and knew I saw—all things in God and God in all things."

While all this may sound like pantheism to some (Eckhart was hauled before the Inquisition to explain himself) it is not a simple-minded identification of everything as being God. Instead it is the realization that without the sense of God's presence in everything and in everyone, and, in turn, our existence in God, we are unlikely to advance very far in the spiritual life or, much less, to begin with, even have an adequate idea of God.

# Part 9
# Philosophical Musings

The topics treated in this section tend to be of a more general nature. Yet, even if they are of great importance to religion, they are approached here in a more philosophical manner. Underlying this approach is the conviction that theology, as an exploration of beliefs that employs philosophical reasoning, depends largely on or is affected by the worldview or cosmology that underlies it. For this reason, in many, if not in all of these essays, I have attempted to apply evolutionary insights to addressing perennial human concerns

---

## Arguments for an Afterlife
(June 30, 2000)

Ever since humans emerged as self-conscious beings, our problem has been how to cope with death. Animals instinctively avoid death, but humans, in their reflective self-consciousness, are normally terrified by it. Generally speaking, this coping has taken two directions, depending largely on two very different views of the world.

View #1: Despite various creation stories, most ancient peoples thought the world is eternal. While it might go through cycles of decline and rebirth (like the yearly seasons on a cosmic timescale), it will basically last forever. The natural reaction to such a situation, it seems, was to imagine that something in us—a "soul" or "spirit"—would pass on to inhabit other bodies, one after another (the concept of "reincarnation" or "transmigration of souls") until finally freed from this apparently endless cycle of birth, death, and rebirth to enjoy, as pure spirits, a realm of heavenly nirvana or endless bliss.

View #2: As always, there are exceptions, and most notably among them were the ancient Hebrews, who thought not only that the universe was created at a definite point (the beginning of time) but also that it is definitively destined to end at a definite point—the very end of time. Unlike the pagans for whom personal survival in an endless universe was an obsession (just think of the Egyptians with their mummies and massive monuments), for the ancient Jews it was not the survival of the individual but the survival of their names, their family and race, and most of all, the future of creation itself that held first place. In such a context, if there was to be any survival of self after death, it could only be through a new act of creation, "a new heaven and a new earth" within which our "self" would be re-created. In fact, despite the mistranslation in most our Bibles of the Hebrew word *nephesh* (which is best rendered as "a living being"), the fact is that the Hebrew language had no clear concept of anything like a "soul" in the philosophical sense of the word *psyche*—at least when it was thought of as a kind immortal, spiritual substance of some sort. From the Hebrew standpoint, either we will be raised up (that is "resurrected") by God's life-giving Spirit as part of a whole people or we are forever doomed to eternal death.

Quite naturally, when Christianity first spread to the mostly Greek-speaking world it tried to combine these two views by reshaping the pagan ideas of the soul to fit within the biblical view, but the effort has never been very satisfactory. It has resulted in doctrinal confusion (who needs a resurrected body if you already exist as a pure spirit?) and, perhaps even worse, an individualistic ("me and Jesus") view of salvation that paradoxically has paved the way for the self-absorption of New Age "spirituality."

As it turns out, however, contemporary science, especially cosmology, shows the ancient Hebrews to have been basically correct: the universe had a definite beginning (the big bang) and will probably, even if less spectacularly, come to a definite end. Likewise, modern science cannot find any evidence for a "soul." Increasingly all the phenomena that philosophers once used to prove the existence of the soul are explained away by modern psychology and the neuroscience. It seems, then, that Christians and others who hope for a life beyond death need to turn back to these earliest Jewish ideas and perhaps refine them a bit here and there—perhaps with the aid of contemporary physics. (Is not all matter, including our bodies, but an "energy state"? But in that case, is not consciousness a particular configuration of energy?)

Even more, I think we need to go back to the spirit of Jewish thought and not worry so much about our individual selves as the future of all creation. True, it could be that the universe (as some religions have taught) is just a game of the gods, a plaything of divinity, and that the best thing we can do is try to escape from it altogether. But truly biblical religion says otherwise. It tells us that God is deadly serious about creation—serious enough to have physically entered into the game and played it for all He is worth. We can, I think, do no better than to do likewise.

---

## Ends and Means
(March 21, 2001)

A good portion of the world's problems occurs when ends or goals become confused with the means to accomplish them. As Einstein observed, "Perfection of means and confusion of goals seem, in my opinion, to characterize our age."

Yet confusion of ends and means is nothing new. It has been said of the ancient Epicureans, like today's gourmets, that instead of "eating to live," they "lived to eat." So what is so new about all this? Is it simply the perfection of our technology, ranging from microwave ovens to nuclear bombs, or is it something more?

It seems to me to be a more fundamental problem than just that. If one observes the natural world apart from humankind, there appears to exist a kind of natural balance between the ends or purposes of nature (survival) and the means of survival—food, shelter, self-defense and sex. It is only when we reach the human level of existence that we find creatures like ourselves habitually overeating, or eating or drinking things that destroy our health, overcrowding or greedily destroying our environment, or developing means of destruction that could wipe out the entire human race.

Yet I think this apparent difference is only superficial. Although the drama of evolution can be described as the "survival of the fittest," the struggle involves a lot more than mere survival. A species either finds a secure means of survival or it will not survive at all in the long run, and for most species this means the continuous invention of better or more efficient ways to survive. And generally speaking, this invention takes brains. Hence humans, with the most complex brains of all creatures, have more than merely survived; instead, we've ended up dominating the whole scene. The problem is what is to be the next act?

This is where Einstein's observation comes in—for if we have run out of goals or purposes for our existence that, more than anything else, will ensure our eventual self-destruction, not simply as individuals who have nothing more to live for but as a whole species or race. More of the same is not an adequate answer. Multiplication of means (more food, more comfort, more pleasure, more sex) spells more problems unless, in the long run, we can find an ultimate purpose or meaning for all of this.

Historically speaking, this has always been the function of religion. The great historian Arnold Toynbee went so far as to claim that no great civilization has ever come about without the organizing and motivating principle that we find in religion, nor has any civilization lasted for long once it abandoned its core beliefs. This is not to say that people haven't managed to survive the destruction of their culture or civilization in the past, but the price they paid was the stagnation of their culture or its replacement by another civilization.

Still, all that was in the past. Perhaps this is the point where we need to be reminded of another, more well-known observation by Einstein, the one where he pointed out (after the atom bomb was invented) that "Everything has changed except our thinking." Perhaps so, and after having escaped (at least so far) nuclear self-destruction, how sad or perhaps even more ridiculous if we end up self-indulgencing or pampering ourselves to death.

## The Trinity for Monotheists
(June 2, 2001)

Many years ago a story came out of France about a young French-speaking Muslim scholar from Algeria. It seems that his Islamic mentors sent him to Paris to study Christian theology so as to better refute the doctrine of the Trinity and so discourage North Africans from becoming Christians. Instead, the young scholar was so impressed with the doctrine that he himself converted to Christianity.

This story may seem unlikely to those Christians who have given up struggling with this deep mystery or those others who may have written the Holy Trinity off as theological, or even mathematical, nonsense. But the fact is that, even apart from Christian doctrine, some of the world's deepest thinkers from the very earliest times have long considered God to be three-fold or triune in nature. According to Plotinus—who had little regard for Christianity—the philosopher Plato, four centuries before Christ, had written of three "gods" or the "triplicity" of the divine: the "One" or "Supreme" who is unknowable, the "Intellect" or "Mind" through whom the universe is created, and the "Soul" who animates and guides the world. Plotinus' claim has been disputed, but others point to the Stoic philosophers who envisioned God as revealing himself in his *Logos* or "Word" and as present in the universe as its immanent "World-Soul." All this found echoes in the writings of the Jewish philosopher Philo of Alexandria and others who greatly influenced early Christian thought. And there are even echoes of this kind of thinking in the Hindu

Vedic philosophers, with their three-fold description of the Absolute (Brahman) as *Sat-Chit-Ananda*, that is, "Being, Knowledge, and Bliss."

In the *Tanach,* or Hebrew scriptures, God is pictured as simultaneously transcendent in his glory, yet revealed in the universe as his personified Wisdom, and omnipresent in it through his Spirit. So again we have evidence of a God who is both transcendent or "beyond" but at the same time immanent or "within" creation through his all-knowing Mind and life-giving Love.

Can there be any wonder, then, that Christians, in pondering the identity of Jesus, quickly came to the conclusion that he was here on earth the expression of divine Wisdom—the "Word of God made flesh"—and that the same Holy Spirit who made this possible is also that Spirit who enlightens and sanctifies us?

The only major problem with all of this really seems to be in the terminology. Plotinus wrote of three divine *hypostases* or "substances," speaking as if they were somehow separate beings in and of themselves. Although some Christian theologians borrowed the Platonists' language, the early Christians more commonly used the term *prosopon* (Greek for "face") or *persona* (the Latin for an actor's mask) to describe each of these three aspects of God. But given the shift in the meaning of "person" in its present, modern, individualistic sense, there are contemporary theologians, who like the late Karl Rahner, thought there should be a moratorium declared on the use of that word as being misleading and counterproductive. Christians do not, or are not supposed to, believe in three Gods.

In a sense, then, progressive Christians, like Rahner, tend to agree with the Unitarians and other monotheists. But they also differ with them, however, in insisting that Jesus Christ was—and still is—through the power or presence of God's Spirit, the uniquely personal embodiment of the divine *Logos* or Wisdom.

---

## Coping with Tragedy
(August 15, 2001)

In terms of the title of Rabbi Harold Kuschner's best-selling 1981 book *When Bad Things Happen to Good People*, we can't help but ask "Why?" How can a God who is all-knowing, all-loving, and all-powerful allow such things to happen—whether it be the killing of one innocent child, the deaths of a whole planeload of passengers, the destruction of thousands, even tens of thousands, by earthquakes or the extermination of six-million Jews by evil tyrants?

The rational answer is, of course, that although we humans live on a planet that is teeming with living beings, it is still within a universe that is, on the whole, not particularly friendly to life.

At present, astronomers are discovering, at the rate of several per month, hitherto unknown planets orbiting almost every nearby star they examine with their huge new telescopes. But so far they have discovered few, if any, that seem to have even the barest requisites for an environment hospitable to life. The vast majority of them are either barren chunks of rock or vaporous conglomerations of gas. And when it comes to our neighbors in our own solar system, if they once harbored life of any sort it either died long ago under a lethal brew of greenhouse gases as in the case of Venus or else were frozen into immobility as on Mars. As for life on earth, paleontologists have uncovered evidence of at least five major extinctions, the last of which, some sixty-five million years ago, wiped out the dinosaurs. Previous mass extinctions wiped out an even higher percentage of species. And cosmologists can almost guarantee that there will be a day when we, the whole human race, will be the next to go. So it seems that if, as some believers insist, we are the product of intelligent design, it would be best not to inquire too deeply into the motivations of the designer.

At best, if this designer was aiming at the emergence of creatures such as ourselves, having free will and the ability to know and love, the price to be paid is for us to have to live in a universe that is dominated by uncertainty, accidents, and chance.

In the face of all of this, the Christian answer to this problem is, at least to some extent, unique. It involves a concept of God inherited from Judaism that is quite unlike the concept of God that has otherwise so dominated human thought down through the ages—that of an aloof, transcendent supreme being who is unaffected by human joys or struggles but instead sends blessings or inflicts us with sorrows according to his own pleasures or whims. Instead, the biblical view is of a God who not only cares deeply but, even more, cares enough to identify with us to the point of becoming one of us in the person of his Son, who was himself a victim of a tragic miscarriage of justice. So complete is this union in Christ between God and our suffering humanity that the second-century bishop, St. Ignatius of Antioch, wrote in one of his letters, without further qualification, of "the passion [suffering] of our God."

Whether such a view is, in the end, a satisfactory answer to why bad things happen to good people remains largely a test of faith. For those who would like to think of God as a kind of celestial Santa Claus, such an answer is deeply disturbing, even scandalous. But for those who, like the philosopher Alfred North Whitehead, describe God as "our fellow sufferer," such faith is not impossible. Indeed, in the face of tragedy it may be the only thing we have.

---

## Tradition and Change
(February 4, 2002)

In the opening song of the long running musical and later movie *Fiddler on the Roof* the principal character, a Russian Jewish farmer named Tevye, sings about why things are the way they are. And his celebrated answer is, of course "Tradition!" Poor Tevye, it seems, is caught up in the struggle between the old ways of doing things and the fresh and brash ways signified by his daughters and their beaus, who are intent on leaving the farm and the oppression of Czarist Russia and emigrating to the brave new world of America.

This is not to suggest that the religion of Jewish peasants in the late 1800s and early 1900s in eastern Europe was entirely dominated by tradition; in fact, the Hasidic mysticism that flourished among eastern European Jews was considered quite untraditional by more highly educated Jews in western Europe and America. Even today quite a gap exists among Jews in America (as well as in Israel) over what is the "soul" of Judaism. Is it the tradition of the *Tanach* (what Christians call the Old Testament) or is the free spirit (God's "Holy Spirit") expressing itself in the lives and loves of the believers?

This would seem to suggest that we need to take a hard look at what drives religion. Henri Bergson, a Polish Jew who became one of France's leading philosophers in the past century, famous for his book *Creative Evolution*, wrote another less known book *The Two Sources of Religion and Morality*. In it he showed how religion itself evolves through an interaction or combination of "tradition" (what is handed-down from earlier generations) and "mysticism" (the source of new inspirations and new ways of understanding). According to Bergson, if you only have the first, eventually you'll end up with stagnation. But if you only have the second, you end up with chaos, and, it seems, a mess of "cults."

For balance you need is a combination of the two, a tradition that can hand down the essentials and can authoritatively decide what fits and what doesn't, but at the same time, a lively bunch of mystics and thinkers who can give the tradition new insights and ways of understanding to think about.

There is always bound to be some competition between the two. From one period of time to another you are most likely to have one or the other tendency dominate the scene. Bergson compared it to something like a flight of stairs. The periods where new inspiration occurs are like the vertical risers that bring you to a higher level, and the periods of consolidation, where the new insights are assimilated into the tradition, are like the treads that give the foot a place to rest and serve as a platform from which to move upward into the next stage. Of course each time there seems to be a change of direction, from horizontal to vertical or vice versa, there is bound to be a certain amount of hesitation or resistance. But this is what makes for a creative tension.

Christianity has also experienced this same sort of struggle throughout its history and has long felt this same tension. It was part of what tore Christianity apart at the time of the Reformation. The traditional Catholicism of medieval Europe was being challenged by fresh new insights from the Protestant Reformers. And, in turn, the Catholic "counter-reform" that took shape at the Council of Trent itself in time became a new "tradition" that was challenged by the new theology, spirituality, and other innovations of the Second Vatican Council.

(An added note: In 2007, are we now seeing, especially with the new "indult" restoring the pre-Vatican II "Tridentine Mass" as a more common option to please traditionalist Catholics, an attempt to turn back the clock? Perhaps so, but I expect the movement itself will eventually be superseded by yet another phase. And so it goes.)

---

## Sexual Evolution?
(May 24. 2002)

In the 1960s and 1970s it became commonplace to speak of the "sexual revolution." But what is happening today, with astronomical divorce rates, the breakdown of the ideal of the nuclear family, the coming-out of gay/lesbian society, and the airing of clerical sex scandals in the Catholic Church, has, I think, less to do with a revolution (there have always been rebellions of this sort) but has more to do with what might be seen as an arrested psychosexual evolution. The whole problem revolves around dealing with this biological force which has had so much to do with the origins of life and the development of the human species. The challenge now is how to use it in such a way that it does not end up destroying us.

About three millennia ago, the more spiritually advanced civilizations in the Far East, especially in India, began to believe that sexual abstinence could result in the redirection of sexual energy to more spiritual goals beyond that of biological reproduction and human companionship. This "sublimation" of the "libido" (as Freud later termed it) accounts for the appearance of Hindu "yogis" or other religious ascetics in India and, about five centuries before the birth of Jesus, the emergence of Buddhism, which began more as monastic order of celibates than as a new religion. Similar movements began in the West and Middle East, such as the Pythagoreans in Greece, the Therapeutoi in Egypt, and the Essenes among the Jews. By the third century AD, Christianity began to adopt these practices with its own monastic movement, and by the twelfth century, the Western Church made celibacy the rule for all its priests.

Not that this discipline has been perfectly kept. Sometimes it seems to have been honored more in theory than in fact. But during these thousands of years, most of the world's major religions continued to respect this ideal, even if it mainly served to remind their followers that anything—like remaining faithful to a spouse for a whole lifetime—is possible, given God's help. Instead, what we find today, with the loss of such ideals or examples, are divorce rates running close to 50 percent, even in some predominantly Christian nations as the United States or, as in Europe, such widespread use of contraception or abortion that supposedly Catholic populations are failing to reproduce themselves. Meanwhile, population growth in many developing non-Christian or non-Catholic nations continues to outstrip resources.

So the problem facing the Catholic Church is obvious. It is not just a question of the breakdown in the observance of clerical celibacy or what to do about the declining ranks of clergy. It is a much broader issue than that. Ultimately, it is the challenge of deciding how to best lead the way in a world that, one way or another, seems bent on destroying itself.

In many ways sexuality is like a powerful river flooding the world, indiscriminately spawning life wherever it flows. Held back and channeled, it can work wonders, converting barren wastes into productive land. It can even be transformed into other forms of energy serving the advance of civilization and, with it, the further evolution of the human spirit. Yet unless this is done with great caution and respect for the raw power this flood contains, things can go terribly wrong. And when that happens, instead of bringing us closer to a transcendent or heavenly goal, all hell can break lose.

## The Five Loves
(August 29, 2002)

It has been said that the Inuit have a dozen or so words for snow, depending on consistency, granularity, or the like. This is not just some kind of literary or rhetorical conceit. Rather, knowing just how one kind of snow differs from another, and being able to effectively communicate that difference, is vital information for those who live in the arctic. In that harsh environment, misjudge what is happening outside, and you might soon be dead.

Something of the same sort of vital information is necessary for those who enter upon marriage. Misjudge what is meant by the term love in the context or environment of marriage and one could soon find oneself in big trouble. That we have only one word—"love"—to cover so many varieties of loving maybe shows that we are sadly lacking in experience or something or other. The ancient Greeks knew better. C. S. Lewis, the novelist, spiritual writer, and Oxford don, once outlined, in his insightful book *The Four Loves*, the vital differences the ancient Greeks so well understood and described with their more precise vocabulary.

First, there is *storge*, the kind of natural or familial love that binds husband and wife or parent and child together. Storge is also the attraction we have for things, activities, or persons who simply please us for the sense of fulfillment they give.

Second, there is *eros*, the word we usually associate with sexuality but which originally had a much broader meaning, applying to anything that is strongly self-satisfying. Where people may be drawn together through a mutual interest (by a storge for travel, or art, or skiing, or sailing) it is eros that propels them into an intimate relationship, into a passion that bears fruit in family, and, we hope, bonds them together for life.

Next, or maybe alongside eros, there is *philos* or friendship, which is less passionate than eros, but ideally, just as long-lasting. And if it is to be long-lasting, it has to be generally more disinterested, and less self-serving than eros. Blessed and long-lasting is the marriage in which one's spouse is truly one's very best friend.

Finally, there is *agape*, the kind of self-sacrificing love that Paul speaks of in his famous thirteenth chapter of his First Epistle to the Corinthians. It is also the same kind of love described in John's Gospel, where Jesus tells us that there is no greater love shown than when a man (or woman) lays down his or her life for his or her friend. In other words, it is the kind of love that alone can guarantee that a marriage will last, through better or worse, in sickness and in health, through hell or high water, until death do them part.

Impossible? Yes, it probably is, so I think we have to invoke, a fifth kind of love, which is *charis*, a word which in Greek originally meant a "gift," but which is now usually translated to mean "grace" or sometimes more weakly spoken of as "charity." But it is something much more vitally necessary than is conveyed by these translations. The necessity of charis is rooted in the realization that agape, self-sacrificing, totally self-disinterested love is impossible without God's help. In other words, that such love is a gift, a "charism"—the result, St. John tells us, of God first loving us, thus is the loving, "saving grace," that alone enables our poor human efforts to bear everlasting fruit. Without it we can accomplish nothing that will last. Neither storge (attraction) nor eros (passion) nor philos (friendship) can last except through God's help, and as for agape (true self-sacrificing love) without God's charis, it is altogether impossible.

---

## The Quest for Meaning
(June 11, 2005)

It seems to me that, philosophically speaking, there are basically two views of life's meaning. One is that the meaning or purpose of life, indeed, of the universe itself, is something outside of or greater than ourselves, even fixed from the beginning of time and remaining constant, regardless whether or not we agree to go along with it. This is essentially what constitutes a religious attitude toward life, even if one avoids belonging to any particular church or organized religion.

The other view is that the universe, and consequently our life in it, is essentially meaningless except for whatever meaning or purpose we ourselves choose to put into it. And although it is evident that at least some can pursue their own purposes with an almost religious fervor, it appears that this second attitude is essentially irreligious. So which attitude or view is best?

Intellectually, the latter seems to have an advantage in today's world with its bias toward scientific proof compared to popular religion's reliance on gut feelings and myths and legends dating from humanity's childhood. Likewise, in recent times, there a great deal of respect, even a cult, if we may use that word, has grown up around the idea of the self-determined, autonomous individuals who decides entirely for themselves the meaning of their lives in the fashion extolled by Jean-Paul Sartre and other modern existentialist philosophers.

Then of course, we also have those who never tire of pointing out all the persecutions, inquisitions, and other horrors inflicted upon humanity by religious fanatics. No doubt, religion has produced more than its share of scoundrels. Yet in most recent times, the greatest criminals and butchers of humanity have been men notable for their scorn for religion, even while sometimes cynically using it or imitating it to forward their murderous designs. Compared to Stalin, Hitler, Mao, or Pol Pot, Osama bin Laden seems like a curious throwback.

Psychologically, however, is where religion seems to most shine. Although religion seems to sometimes have produced its own forms of emotional disturbances, by far the largest share of neurosis (at least according to the late psychiatrist Viktor Frankl) can be classed as "existential"—a certain interior hollowness or lack of interior peace traceable to not knowing why or for what one exists. In fact, it seems that the greatest strength of religion, which Frankl described as "the quest for meaning," is that it is, at least for most people, best able to fulfill that need. Indeed, in giving this sense of meaning, faith (which Frankl described as being "trust in meaning") also brings that sense of fulfillment or happiness that again, according to Frankl, can only come from living our lives for something greater than ourselves.

---

## Instinct and Reason
(January 14, 2006)

It is often said that religion, Christianity in particular, has taken a repressive attitude toward sex—which is undoubtedly true. Early in its history, Christianity allied itself with the remnants of ancient Platonic idealism which, in tandem with a biblical patriarchalism, produced an enthusiasm for monastic life and celibacy and a negative attitude toward marriage and/or everything having to do with the body.

However, as true as this may be in some respects, this view overlooks, I think, the much more important role played by the evolutionary emergence of rationality. What marks the human species as distinct from all other forms of life is not that we walk upright on two legs (although, in freeing our front legs to become arms and our front feet to become hands may also have had something to do with it) but that we can reason. We are, as Aristotle observed, "rational animals." Well, at least we are most of the time.

The problem is that our instinctual drives have not disappeared entirely. In fact, to some degree, once reason began to assert itself during the course of evolution, it seems that the instincts became strangely unhinged. The result was that where the rhythms of nature tend to control instinct in many species of animals (we need only think how most wild animals confine their reproductive activities to distinct seasons), with humans (as often with domesticated animals) sexual drives tend to assert themselves whenever the opportunity presents itself, even if to the detriment of the whole species.

So it seems that what the major religions with their moral codes have really been attempting to do has been to try to promote rational behavior. This can be seen especially in Christian history, where the first alliance of theology with philosophy came about not so much with neo-Platonic idealism but with the sober ethics of Stoic philosophy. While both schools of thought argued for higher ethical conduct, Stoicism based its arguments not on an appeal to an ideal world beyond but, instead, on experience gained from living in this one. Hence Christianity's (and Catholicism's in particular) long alliance with the tradition of "natural law" reasoning.

The problem is, however, that for such an approach to be effective it has to be grounded in a realistic understanding of nature. As much as we would like to believe we are capable of always acting rationally, any attempt to understand human nature and behavior that ignores our evolutionary inheritance is bound to be defective. We need only observe the ineffectiveness of campaigns to control the spread of AIDS that focus solely on abstinence from sex before marriage and fidelity in marriage, which are fine, highly rational ideals but fail utterly to cope with the danger when irrational drives take over.

If there is a lesson in all this, it is that ethics—which is morality based on reason—is ineffective if it ignores the vital role played by the instinctual and the irrational. We may be indeed, as Aristotle said, "rational animals," but we are no longer being realistic if we forget that for all our rationality we are fundamentally still animals.

## Oneness, or a Theory of Everything
(February 4, 2006)

Philosophers have long pondered the problem of the One and the Many, wondering if there is a single principle or essential unity that permeates everything. But when all is said and done, it really seems that the search for unity or oneness beneath the incredible complexity of the universe is ultimately a search for God.

This can be seen not only in religions where monotheism (belief in a single God) replaced polytheism (a belief in many gods) but also where monism (that God is everything) has replaced pantheism (that everything is God). It can be see in efforts to bring the world's religions together and within Christianity where ecumenism—the effort to overcome sectarian rivalry—seeks to fulfill the prayer of Jesus that "all may be one." Meanwhile, a vaguely mystical "spirituality" attempts to replace religion entirely for those who have lost patience with all the rest.

This longing for or movement toward oneness can be seen in the various sciences as well. Physics, that most fundamental of the natural sciences, seeks what the experimental physicist Leon Lederman has called "the God Particle," while his more mathematically-inclined colleagues, following Einstein—who spoke about wanting to see the Universe "as God sees it"—seek to unite the force of gravity with other three basic forces (the weak and strong atomic forces and electromagnetism) within a overarching "theory of everything."

We have seen this drive at work with Darwin, who sought to explain through a single theory all the phenomena that might account for the diversity of life, with its tens of thousands of species, and with the neo-Darwinists, who attempt to explain not just biological evolution, but also all varieties of human behavior in terms of evolution.

Likewise, in biological research today, the immense complexity of the human genome, indeed of all life, can be reduced to the endless recombination of just four basic components, the nucleotides adenine, guanine, cytosine, and thymine. Through such research, the practice of medicine may some day be able to finally arrive at a single, comprehensive approach to preventing or curing a major portion of the world's diseases, just as this new knowledge has enabled agricultural science to greatly advance the kind of genetic "engineering" that was accomplished over past millennia by more hit or miss methods that slowly advanced human life beyond the Stone Age.

So too in the social sciences, like sociology and psychology, and even history and economics. Here one theory after another attempts to reduce the complexity of human behavior into predictable patterns that might not only explain past behavior but also enable us to avoid future man-made disasters. Even in politics, the great challenge remains of how to manage human diversity in such a way that we do not end up destroying everything that we have accomplished up until now.

No doubt many are suspicious of any tendency to seek simple answers to complex problems. Many may see this as an inborn tendency toward mental laziness, and in some instances, this may be the case. But finding simple answers that really work is never easy, for, at its deepest level, like the religious-philosophical impulse that fuels it, it is an attempt to move beyond the bewildering world of superficial appearances—what the Greeks called the *kosmos*—into a more comprehensive vision of the whole system that we call the Universe.

---

## Time, Memory, and Meaning
(August 12, 2007)

Can anything have meaning unless it somehow lasts forever? How can something that only lasts a moment have any lasting significance?

Certainly, one of the great paradoxes of existence is that what is most permanent (for example, rocks) in themselves hold little or no meaning for us, while that which is most fleeting, be it a thought, a word, or even a glance, can be most meaningful of all. So we try to defeat this paradox by writing books, recording voices on tapes or plastic disks, or capturing images on film. Or, when all else fails, names and dates are chiseled on those rocks or stones. And yet we know that sooner or later even these records will be erased by time. What then?

All this suggests that memory is the only guarantor of meaning. Lose one's memories and one has, at least for all practical purposes, lost all meaning. A culture or civilization that has lost its collective memory is like a reservoir that has gone dry. So might it not be said that for the person who has lost all memories of the past life becomes meaningless, a round of activity devoid of any apparent continuity, coming from nowhere, promising nothing?

Yet, like any other kind of thoughts, memories are hardly more than sequences of impressions stored, apparently randomly, among the synapses of the brain. And as such, they can be rearranged, reconfigured, even recreated to recall what may have never happened—perhaps even previous lifetimes that were never lived! Indeed, someone once asked the Dalai Lama if he remembered his previous lives, and his answer was that when he was young he thought he did, but now, in later years, he tends to doubt it.

Nevertheless, or at least it seems to me, memory may be the key to immortality, indeed the secret behind existence itself. St. Augustine, in his famous treatise on God as a trinity, said as much when he compared the relationship between Father, Son, and Spirit to the faculties of the mind. The Son or "Word" (*Logos*) of course exemplifies, even embodies, the reason or rationality of God manifest in the created world. The Spirit is, as it were, the manifestation of the divine will, the vehicle of God's love. Yet, when it comes describing the Father, Augustine turns to God's memory as the source or ground of all other existing things, indeed, as "Being in itself."

If this is so, then perhaps the only chance any of us have of becoming immortal, or of our lives having any lasting meaning, comes from the fact that whatever else in this world is eventually forgotten, we shall, live on in the ever-living memory that lies at the heart of that act of eternal, infinite being which is God.

---

## Spinning Our Own Cocoons
(December 14, 2007)

Biologically speaking, a cocoon (from the French *cocon*, meaning a "shell") is a structure built by some species of insects to protect themselves as they go through the pupa stage, while transforming from a larva to an adult. Yet metaphorically speaking, might we not say that humans build similar shells or cocoons around themselves? Unfortunately, however, these human cocoons often result in no further development at all.

Certainly we often see this happening on the psychological level and even sometimes in the physical or material infrastructure of our lives. Gated communities and segregated neighborhoods are one such example, especially in American life. But another, more pervasive, symptom is the American disdain toward learning another language other than English or what sometimes seems to be a deliberately cultivated or willful ignorance of or lack of care for what the rest of humanity may feel or think. This attitude, in turn, has led to a disastrous decline of America's prestige in the world.

Sadly, such an attitude also all too often carries over into our spiritual lives. In fact, we might say that without an expanded awareness of the world around us and a real care and concern over what is happening to others, we are doomed to remain spiritual dwarves, trapped in our own little world of our own making, unable and often unwilling to encounter God in all God's fullness or in his immensity that enfolds the whole universe.

For example, as an amateur astronomer, I'm struck by the irony that much of the technology that has enabled us to see far beyond the confines of our comparatively tiny planet has, at the same time, for most people closed off the view once enjoyed by our ancestors before our technology began to flood the night sky in a sea of artificial light. We have, in effect, spun yet another cocoon around ourselves, one which results in an even greater disconnect between the ways we consciously live our daily lives as opposed to the actual state of the world in which we live. Among the results is the ecological crisis that we have unwittingly brought upon ourselves.

Unfortunately, I see the same thing happening in our spiritual vision. In fact, as a theologian I am particularly struck or dismayed by the apparent unwillingness—or is it some kind of congenital inability?—of my colleagues to think beyond the mental maps inherited from the past, much as if the greater universe revealed by contemporary science or even centuries ago by Copernicus should have no bearing at all on our understanding of the beliefs that shape our faith. In this they seem to me to be like the churchmen who once refused to look through Galileo's telescope, or like the creationists who today still insist that evolution is "only a theory," or even like those—who I must admit have included myself— who refuse to admit that a greater universe, beyond that which we now know, could possibly exist.

How to explain this? Perhaps it has to do with the basic function of cocoons or whatever other form of protective shell that nature has devised. When an organism is in a stage of transition, it remains particularly vulnerable, in danger of being destroyed entirely by the encroachments of the outside world. Yet the purpose of this cocoon is to serve as a kind of womb, but it is only to be used as long as is necessary for a new stage of life to emerge. Otherwise the cocoon, whether it is physical, mental, or spiritual, instead becomes a kind of tomb.

# Part 10
# The Environment

Until recently, it almost seemed that religious people generally suffered from a kind of pervasive indifference to environmental issues, while those who were really into "deep ecology" seemed to have almost made their concern into an alternate form of religion. However, the situation seems to be rapidly changing.

The series of essays that follow begin with three that were written for the *North Woods Call*, a bimonthly publication geared to conservationists, sportsmen, and to nature-lovers in Michigan. The remainder of the essays in this section were written for a more general readership as ecological topics gradually began to capture the public's attention, particularly with the advent of more obvious signs of global warming, which is already seeming to affect the seasonal weather patterns of Northern Michigan. However, the emphasis here is on placed on the theological and ethical premises and implications.

## Fishing, Hunting, and the Appreciation of Life
(January 9, 1989)

Recently an interesting item in a local *Trout Unlimited* newsletter caught my eye. It was part of a report of a meeting of fisheries biologists and social scientists from Michigan, Minnesota, and Wisconsin. The report listed reasons that anglers gave for their fishing (besides catching trout). In fact, reasons that ranked ahead of actually catching fish were: appreciating nature, using skills, seeing trout feeding, being outdoors, and appreciating solitude (in that order). It also appears that as the angler's experience increases, the greatest satisfaction is achieved in passing these skills and attitudes on to others.

For many trout fisherman steeped in the tradition of Isaac Walton and the tales of Ernest Hemingway and Robert Travers, this is no news at all. Yet for anyone interested in understanding why anyone takes up any outdoor sport such as hunting or fishing, it does strike more than just a responsive cord. It goes to the very heart of our self-understanding as persons engaged in the process of living life.

For any of us who have lived long enough and reflected at all on why we spend a spring evening on a trout stream battling swarms of mosquitoes or black flies, or why we spend hours freezing ourselves in a deer blind in the middle of November, and still continue to do so after decades of such self-inflicted torture, we are probably well aware of a change in our reasons for putting ourselves through such wear and tear and abuse. When we were kids we went out and caught as many fish as we could, and as an adolescent hunter any deer (or any with antlers on) would do. Not for long though! Soon we were gunning for the largest rack or angling for the biggest fish as if our very life depended on it.

In some ways it did. The more fragile our self-esteem, the more we were driven to excel. At the same time, the trophies, antlered or finned, represented more of a challenge as well, separating real sport from mere "meat-hunting"—so much so that eventually we almost began to feel a pang of regret to see that trophy killed even while we were elated to have been clever enough to have outwitted it.

Sooner or later, once this true "sporting" ethic has taken firm hold of us, then not even the trophy status means much unless the method itself becomes a challenge in itself. When a man moves into this phase, a medium-size trout, taken cleanly on a dry fly (preferably tied on a barbless hook on the end of a 6x tippet) weighs in more in the satisfaction of one's mind than a "lunker" dragged out of its lair with a worm impaled on a triple hook at the end of a 20 lb. line. Likewise even a "spikehorn" buck lured into range, arrowed with a careful shot, and perhaps trailed for hundreds of yards represents more of a personal triumph then any number of six-pointers blasted by a repeating rifle over a pile of sugar beets. For the same kind of satisfaction I know persons who long ago traded their last cartridge rifle for a muzzle-loader—this long before the special black-powder season had every Tom, Dick, and Harry buying factory-made thunder-sticks so they could find another excuse to get another eight to ten days away from wife and kids.

At this point, what comes next—just bigger racks or more and bigger trout? I don't know if the fish biologists study the likes of Erik Erikson, Jane Loevinger, and other such professional psychologists. But the social scientists who attended the meeting reported above should be paying attention to what they have to say.

According to Erikson, the granddaddy of developmental psychologists, the final stages of maturity are marked by the concern for "generativity" and "final integration." The first of these two final stages (usually beginning in middle age) is not about having more children (although I know more than one fellow who in the midst of his mid-life crisis seemed to think that was what it was all about) but is more concerned with the future that is being handed on to the next generation and those yet to come.

I suppose this is where the "mentor" role comes in. Yet I don't think being a "mentor" means that one has to necessarily open a trout-fishing school or teach kids how to shoot. It might also mean that we become more and more concerned with wildlife habitat and conservation in general. Or it may only mean that we take our greatest pleasure from teaching ourselves to observe and understand and live in harmony with the ways of nature. It may even lead us back, paradoxically, to merely "meat-hunting," but this time only strictly for what we need. That's nature's way isn't it? Cougars don't pick bigger bucks or otters bigger trout to satisfy their ego-needs. They only need to fill their stomach.

All of which points to a stage beyond. Perhaps few ever reach it, even if they live to be ninety or a hundred. "Final integration" may sound like a euphemism for being six-feet under, but it is much more than that. It means living in a state of complete harmony and oneness with reality. What this entails, I suppose, depends on one's ultimate philosophy of life. For a small number their view of life may include a Buddhist or Jain-like "compassion for all sentient (feeling) beings" that precludes their ever hooking another fish or pulling a trigger again. Theirs is a totally "seamless garment" view of life that virtually identifies all life, no matter how humble, as a spark of the divine. Others are less concerned about what taking a life does to the animal or fish than what it does to the person who performs the act. Does it degrade us to the status of killer, or are we elevating ourselves to the status of "gods" who appropriate to ourselves the power of life and death?

These are heavy questions—the kind that wise old men and philosophers ponder—perhaps made more poignant by the knowledge that our own lives have about run their course.

I have not yet decided where I stand in relation to the above. I look at reality and see that all living things must die and that in the order of nature most things, be it a grain of wheat or a fatted calf, die that others may live. Yet I also know that if my own "final integration" is to come about, I have to most of all "die to self" or to that selfishness that makes me imagine that I'm the center of my own little universe.

How I go about this, I suppose, is a matter of how I think the Almighty intended this universe to be. So whether I continue to hunt or fish is in itself perhaps beside the point. What counts is the spirit, the reasons or motivations that impel me one way or the other and, more important still, my concern and care for the well-being of others besides my own self.

## Of Mounds and Men
(September 2, 1989)

In June of 1989 I spent the better part of an afternoon wandering through a major part of the Cahokia Mounds just outside East St. Louis, Illinois. Misnamed after the Cahokia band of Illini Indians who occupied the area in more recent times, this six and a half square mile park, which has been named a "World Heritage Site" by UNESCO, was the location of the largest concentration of American aborigines north of central Mexico. Archaeologists estimate that 20 to 40 thousand people of the Mississippian culture—perhaps even double that number when the large number of outlying villages scattered through the 175 square mile river bottoms around the greater St. Louis area is counted—flourished there between 900 and 1400 AD.

The park area contains more than sixty mounds of many sizes and at least three distinct shapes. Flat-topped ones, with either round or rectangular bases, served, it seems, as artificial hills on which ceremonial and public buildings and the residences of very important people. Cone-shaped mounds prove to have been mostly burial sites. And oblong or ridge-shaped mounds served a variety of purposes, including some for burials and others as directional markers. The most prominent is a flat-topped rectangular hill about a hundred feet high and fourteen acres at its base, which was the site of a series of large temples to the sun. Evidence indicates that these people built in logs and thatch and periodically burned the old buildings, kept enlarging the mounds, and built bigger buildings to replace the earlier ones.

A ten-foot-high wooden stockade with a parameter of about two miles enclosed the central part of the town, with frequent guard houses and observation platforms suggesting either an inner defense wall or a way of separating the privileged from the underclass who lived in the "suburbs." Three such walls were built, with the later ones showing signs of a growing shortage of large timber.

To the west archeologists have discovered the remains of a primitive solar observatory that enabled the priests to accurately time their religious ceremonies and planting seasons for their basically agricultural way of life. Extensive hunting on the site probably wiped out most game for many miles around.

One of the ridge-shaped mounds, excavated a few years ago, revealed the burial place of an important chief who was accompanied in death by four men (minus heads and hands) and fifty-two young women neatly laid out side by side. Ornaments of shells, mica discs from the Great Smokey Mountains, and Lake Superior copper reveal that they either controlled or traded with a vast area.

No one knows exactly who these people were or what language they spoke. Their culture appears to have been similar to the Natchez and other lower Mississippian people encountered by DeSoto, LaSalle, and other early European explorers, but by the time the French settled the area these particular people were long gone. Again, no one knows why—war? disease? famine? fuel shortage? sheer overcrowding? There seems to be no clear evidence of what happened except hints provided by an abundance of overfilled garbage pits.

A mile or two to the west, on the other side of combined Interstates 55 and 70, is another huge mound, this one of present-day garbage trucked out from St. Louis and a few miles farther on, is a new urban disaster area. Bankrupt and unable to pay its own firemen and police, with a forty to sixty percent unemployment rate, and with sewers overflowing into pot-holed streets, East St. Louis seems on the verge of becoming another lost city—the forerunner of another dead civilization?

The aboriginal Mississippian culture lasted five hundred or so years before it seemingly self-destructed, if by nothing else, apparently polluting itself to death. Given our own rate of fuel consumption, water, and soil and air pollution, not to mention the self-destructive potentials of nuclear arms, how long can we expect our present modern civilization to last? Despite their worship of the sun, these ancients violated the limitations of both nature and their own technology. Can modern worshipers of technology and destroyers of nature do any better? Our modern American civilization has been around a scant three hundred years. At the rate that we are destroying our own environment, I wonder if we can spare another two hundred years to find out?

## God and Nature
(November 20, 1996)

> We should understand well that all things are the work of the Great Spirit. We should know that He is within all things: the trees, the grasses, the rivers, the mountains, and all the four-legged animals, and the winged peoples; and even more important we should understand that He is also above all these things and peoples. When we do understand all this deeply in our hearts, then we will fear, and love, and know the Great Spirit, and then we will be and act and live as He intends. (From John G. Neihardt, *Black Elk Speaks*)

I first came across this often-cited quotation from the famed Lakota (Oglala Sioux) elder, Black Elk, among a whole stack of quotations, old and new, compiled a few years ago by one of the groups opposed to all hunting and fishing here in the United States. Apparently these folks believe that if we all followed the advice of Black Elk, we'd all rise up and throw away our guns and fishing tackle. But I hardly think that is the case.

First, think about it. Black Elk was a Lakota—a member of one of those nomadic tribes on the western plains that most depended on the hunt for their existence. You can't raise much corn or squash or beans when you spend all your days following the buffalo migrations. For them, the hunt was everything. With this source of food, the Lakota became the most powerful tribe on the plains. Without it, as the invading whites knew well, they'd all be reduced to near starvation—which is exactly the reason the whites deliberately wiped out all the vast herds of bison. It is impossible to imagine someone like Black Elk as a vegetarian, at least voluntarily so.

Even more to the point, read what he said. Read it very carefully. He makes two assertions about the Great Spirit (*Wakan Tanka* in Lakota). First: "He" is in all things. Second: He is above all things. In other words, to put it in more philosophical and theological terms, God is both immanent and transcendent. Lose this double perspective, and all kinds of things go wrong, both with our view of the Almighty and with our view of nature, even worse, with the conduct of our lives. And this includes the way we relate to the animal world.

The reason for this is that when one view of this ultimate reality excludes the other, we are apt to fall into either one of two extremes. On the one hand, if we imagine God as completely immanent or contained within all things, we end up in kind of pantheism that can't distinguish the divine or the sacred from creation—the kind of mentality that holds it to be a sin to kill any animal for any reason whatsoever. Or else, on the other hand, we will end up with an overly transcendent view of God that locates God in some far-off heaven—a kind of divine watchmaker, leaving ourselves free to promote ourselves as "masters of the universe" with a "manifest destiny" to subdue nature and whomever or whatever—especially all animals or "backward peoples" that get in our way. Obviously, it is that latter view that predominated in American society from the beginning, and which still dominates the thinking of those who rant and rail over those they scorn as "environmentalists."

However, I think it is particularly significant that even Black Elk saw that, no matter how essential it is to begin with a sense of God's presence within all things, in the end it is more important that we do see God as ultimately transcendent—that is, that "He is above all things."

Why? For one, (as the medieval philosophers were quick to point out) only a God who is beyond or above all created beings can be, at the same time, present within all of them. Transcendence and immanence are not so much opposed as complimentary.

In addition, a God who is simply identified with nature is really no explanation for the universe, which as Black Elk must have sensed, as the world of the Lakota came apart—and as science now tells us—had a definite beginning and most likely will come to a definite end. As modern cosmologists tell us, the origin (and the likely destiny) of the universe can only be imagined in a "singularity" that transcends both space and time.

However, more immediate to our concerns, a view that holds all forms of life as equally sacred, while it may seem to benefit the environment, does not make much sense in the long run. Black Elk realized, as did all the ancients—and certainly much more than nonhunters buying their food wrapped in plastic bags in a supermarket—that all forms of existence, and especially all forms of life, exist in a great hierarchy or "chain of being" in which one form of life exceeds and yet depends upon another, much as a predator upon the prey. The law of nature is pretty much eat or be eaten, and for the most part, it is the dumbest critters that get eaten the most. In other words, the great "chain of being" is reflected, to a large extent, in the food chain. Nor are we humans (even those who choose to be vegetarians) exempt from our role in all of this.

Yet, for all that, we humans are different. Animals may instinctively know these things. Still, only we humans "know that we know"—that is, can be fully aware of our own awareness and reflect upon it. For it is only when we finally "understand all this deeply in our hearts" that we will come to "fear and love and know the Great Spirit" and only then will we have reached the point were we will "be [exist] and act and live as He intends."

Something to think about, surely, as we sit and contemplate the world from a deer blind, or as we stand, carving knife in hand, over our Thanksgiving turkey.

---

## Environmental Concern as a Moral Imperative
### (May 27, 2003)

In recent years, many Christian churches have begun to turn their attention to environmental issues. Some, particularly those Americans who like to think of their religion as an exclusively "me and God" relationship, geared mostly to what may happen to us when we die, have become upset with this development. They somehow fail to see the connection between religion and respect, right here and now, for the environment.

On the other hand, others, many self-described "deep environmentalists" would fault biblical religion for fostering a careless, dominating attitude over nature. These critics frequently cite the passage in Genesis (1:28) where humans are told they are to "subdue" the earth and its creatures. This somewhat negative impression is sometimes even furthered by some Christian groups whose predictions of an immanent end to the world seem to have provoked, even if not intentionally, a kind of "eat, drink and be merry" attitude that would open the door to unrestrained exploitation of our natural resources.

However, for those brought up in the tradition of seeing creation as God's own good gift to be shared and cultivated as a common heritage for the benefit of all humanity, it is hard to see how one can miss the connection between morality and environmentalism, even if it is motivated by the future benefit of the human race. Scientists tell us that with luck and careful planning the earth could still be the home of humankind for many tens, perhaps even hundreds, of thousands of years to come. So if we succeed in making our planet incapable of human habitation in the next hundred or so years, won't we have to answer to God for this? Just as in the past the biblical prophets denounced those who robbed workers of just wages for the sake of their own profit, so too today must not religious leaders denounce those who continue to poison the air, water, and land solely for the sake of economic gain?

The situation has become increasingly critical. The world's human population has reached six billion and will probably reach nine billion by 2050, after which current predictions are for a leveling off if not a slow decline. Already, in many of the less-developed areas of the world, drinkable water is in very short supply and pollution on a massive scale continues to contaminate what little fresh water may be left. And what are we to say about our own more technologically developed part of the world, where the deep wells of corporate agriculture are rapidly depleting underground aquifers and acid rain has begun to kill off oxygen-producing forests? Eventually, throughout the whole world, major climate change, heightened by the accumulated effects of global warming, could necessitate major migrations of the human population.

This last point, with the dislocation and upheavals of society it could occasion, is too often overlooked. In his 1990 New Year's (World Peace Day) Message, Pope John Paul II not only pointed out the dangers of irresponsible industrial and technological development, condemning the pursuit of profit at the expense of human life and well-being, but also underlined the threat to world peace that this poses because of the fundamental injustices that are often the result of environmental degradation. As the pope put it, "If man is not at peace with God, the earth itself cannot be at peace."

The pope then called for not only individual renunciation of sinful and selfishly wasteful lifestyles) but also more international cooperation to address environmental issues and much more concern on the part of the developed nations to help the rest of the world. Yet in our part of the world, the part that claims to have the most influence, this call has still gone largely unheeded.

No doubt the "deep environmentalists" will see all this as a move by the Church to co-opt environmentalism for its own purposes, while those opposed to religion having anything to say about economic growth and justice will be equally unhappy with any of the churches that seem to be jumping on the environmental band-wagon. Yet, for those who are truly concerned with their relationship to the Creator, as well as the peace of the world, the message should be clear. If we cannot live in peace with (as well as on) the earth, how can we expect to be at peace with God?

## Christians and Global Warming
(October 17, 2006)

A recent airing of a Bill Moyers special on PBS titled "Is God Green?" focused on the growing left turn of the Christian Right toward environmental concern. It seems that evangelical Christians in the United States are finally beginning to come to grips with what most environmental scientists have been saying all along—much to the dismay of other conservatives who continue to live more or less in a state of denial, at least when it comes to assuming any responsibility for the predicament in which we find ourselves.

Not that anyone who examines the evidence has any doubt that the earth's climate is undergoing a marked warming trend. Mountain glaciers and Arctic and Antarctic ice shelves are melting at an accelerated rate. Many more southern species of wildlife are migrating northward. And recently, record summer heat waves causing thousands of deaths have hit Europe and parts of North America, while tropical storms of increased intensity are causing unprecedented havoc.

While scientists readily concede that the earth's climate has gone through major changes, many of them of an apparently cyclical nature, in eons past, the question not yet fully determined is how much human activity has accelerated whatever is going on now. Much of the evidence remains circumstantial, such as the marked buildup of greenhouse gases in the atmosphere that coincides with industrial activity and population growth. However, the evidence for many other forms of environmental destruction that has increasingly made parts of the earth uninhabitable is much more direct. Polluted rivers, depleted aquifers, loss of topsoil, devastation of oxygen-producing forests—all these are environmental disasters for which humans will have to answer not just to succeeding generations but also, according to Christian belief, to God.

Not that any of this is completely new. Some twenty-six centuries ago the prophet Jeremiah lamented,

> How long must the earth mourn, the green of the whole countryside wither? For the wickedness of those who dwell in it beasts and birds disappear, because they say, "God does not see our ways."
> (Jeremiah 12:4)

Now it seems that believers, who for a long time had convinced themselves that God had given them a carte blanche to "dominate" or "subdue" the earth (depending on how you translate Genesis 1:28) have suddenly realized that as stewards of God's creation they will also be called to account for what they have done to it.

Perhaps for the more liberal, socially conscious churches none of this is new. Still, for the evangelical wing of American churchgoers, who prided themselves on their political conservatism, it seems almost like a new revelation that one can hardly be consistently conservative without being, environmentally speaking, a conservationist. If so, we can only hope most other Americans will see the light.

## Population and Pollution
(February 17, 2007)

Now that the public has finally woken up to the danger that global warming and other associated forms of environmental disaster pose to our planet, very serious ethical choices face us as well. Foremost is the question of population control. For if we are already confronted with what amounts to an environmental Armageddon with some six-billion or more people on the face of the earth today, what happens when the population reaches, as experts predict, at least nine billion by the mid-point of this century?

True, some of these same experts claim that once we reach the nine-billion mark things will stabilize. Yet there seems to be a "catch 22" lurking in that prediction. The prediction is based largely on the observation that when countries become "developed" through industrialization population growth is almost inevitably decreased or, as is the case with Europe, almost comes to a total halt. However, the flip side is that when this industrial development happens, the amount of pollution produced by this same population grows by leaps and bounds.

The major example of this problem at present is the United States. With only about 5 percent or one twentieth of the world's population, we are responsible for 20 percent or one-fifth of the world's pollution and global warming effects. So what happens when China, with about one-fifth of the world's people, becomes as industrially developed as the United States? It hardly takes a rocket scientist to figure out that when that happens the amount of pollution and global warming could practically double within a decade or so, unless drastic new anti-pollution measures are taken.

So what to do? China has long taken draconian measures—such as enforcing a one child per family rule, even by abortion if necessary—to stabilize it's population growth, and seems to have largely succeeded, even to the point where in some areas it is now offering family subsidies to those couples who produce an additional, especially girl, child. India, with its intensive birth control promotion, including sterilization, has been less successful in curbing its growth. By the end of the century, its population is expected to surpass China's, even though its industrialization is advancing full tilt.

It appears then that the only sane remedy—one that includes a limit on population growth—has to be one that also emphasizes drastic measures to cut back the amount of pollution. It also has to be one that begins with those populations that are consuming the highest amounts of energy, whether measured proportionately—such as is case with the United States—or measured in absolute terms, as in the case of China, whose energy consumption will soon equal that of the United States. High-tech fixes, like producing large amounts of ethanol to replace petroleum-based fuels (gasoline, diesel, and fuel oil) are not enough, and, in fact, in some ways could make the situation worse. Replacing electricity generated by fossil-fuels with that produced by solar, hydroelectric, and wind-powered generators may help some. New, safer nuclear-powered electrical generating plants, such as those developed by France, could also greatly help.

However, when push comes to shove, nothing can replace the necessity of adopting a simpler, less energy-consuming lifestyle. Here, on this count, the so-called developing nations still have an advantage. This is the kind of life most of their people have been living all along.

What remains, especially for those of us who have lived so lavishly at the expense of the environment for so long, is to share our truly worthwhile life-enhancing developments, such as our nutritional, medical, and other social advances, with less fortunate peoples, while ridding ourselves of the wasteful and pollution-producing habits that are rapidly destroying our environment.

It is this challenge, perhaps more than any other, that forms the moral/ethical imperative of the remainder of this new century. Many of the other problems, like war, disease, and famine, are directly or indirectly connected with environmental degradation. Some of them may be temporarily "fixed" by various short-term measures. Nevertheless if we fail to secure the long-term future of planet Earth as a suitable home for life, we will have lost it all.

## Facing the Future
(July 17, 2007)

Suppose that you are forty-five years old, a smoker, a bit overweight, and are suffering from what seems like a minor complaint, like shortness of breath, and decided that maybe you'd better see a doctor, especially since you seem to be running a bit of a temperature. And suppose that after taking a family history—which perhaps included a parent or grandparent who lived to be 95—and after checking you out, the doctor were to say to you that it is entirely up to you, and that if you lost some weight and quit smoking and started exercising more, you too might live into your 90s, but that short of taking such simple measures, your chances are slim of even making it through your 60s. What would you choose to do—heed the doctor's advice, or simply ignore it and go on living the way you have been?

It seems that lots of people do the latter. Given a choice between a long life that demands some sacrifice and self-discipline, and a short life that doesn't, they'll choose to just keep doing what they've always done, heedless of the consequences to themselves, as well as perhaps to their family.

Next, let's take this "supposing" one step farther. Suppose the doctor says that as a result of your bad habits, not only you but also your children, and even your grandchildren and your descendants all down the line will have shortened lives and whose health will be even more threatened?

"Impossible!" you say; "Who ever heard of such a thing?" Well, perhaps it sounds like a strange medical scenario, but the comparison in some ways fits when it comes to our present treatment of the environment. The earth is running a temperature (global warming), it is short of breath (air pollution), and is overweight and flabby in places (especially when it comes to the developed countries). And while the overall condition of the planet may not affect the immediate sense of well-being among those countries that are comparatively well-off and prosperous, the fact is that is precisely the population of these same countries that are going to have to make the biggest changes in their life-style if the whole world is going to somehow escape the dire long term consequences.

Of course, while we can always be sure, unfortunately, that there will always be some people who will shrug and say "So what?" or even point out that the Earth, just like ourselves, will eventually die, so why not in the meantime continue to just "eat, drink, and be merry?" Or why give a damn about the future?

Nevertheless, it seems to me that sooner or later such people (and nations) have to be held to account, if not before God—surely the Creator should be more than just passively concerned—then certainly before the tribunal of world opinion. Just as in civil society we end up having to quarantine those whose disease threatens the health of the rest, perhaps we will have to figure out some way of isolating those people or even whole countries that fail to act in the world's public interest. How to do this is another matter. Still, rationing the flow of oil to those countries that waste it might be a good beginning.

---

# Environmental Escapism
(July 28, 2007)

According to Dr. Quentin Chiotti, a Canadian environmental scientist, when it comes to facing up to the environmental crisis facing the world, there seems to be a number of degrees (he speaks of four) or stages of denial at work among the general public.

The first stage is a denial that there is any crisis to begin with—this despite the overwhelming evidence presented not just by science, but even by commonsense everyday observation (like keeping tabs on what kinds of bugs are invading your backyard or how many days a nearby lake or stream is frozen over).

The second stage or degree of denial is that even if one admits there might be a problem, one denies that humans are in any way responsible or contributing to it. At this level we find ourselves reminded that the earth has passed through many cycles of climate change before, and that all the evidence that human activity has added much to it is only circumstantial or is merely a "statistical coincidence."

The third degree occurs when it is acknowledged that humanity has probably mucked things up, but then denies that anything effective can be done to alleviate or at least mitigate the problem. In other words, after admitting the problem, deciding to capitulate to pessimism.

The fourth stage happens when whatever effective measures might be taken are seen as costing too much—this despite the predictions by economists that attempts to fix the problems later on instead of now will be immensely more costly.

I think, however, that there is a fifth and final stage in the denial process. It is reached when, however costly it might be, people refuse to take on the ethical or moral responsibility to do what has to be done to try to insure the future well-being of humanity.

It is hard to say exactly what motivates this denial process at each and every stage, although it is probably safe to say that it begins with ignorance—perhaps of the willful type—and progresses, as awareness increases, especially when we get to the fifth stage, to outright selfishness.

No doubt various vested interests, both economic and political (and when have they not been closely intertwined, especially in our capitalistic society?) have deliberately promoted the first stages of this process. In fact, vast amounts of money have been spent to deliberately mislead the public.

The question is then, can these same economic-political interests be persuaded to plan far ahead enough, even if only for their own well-being, to change course and begin to promote a more environmentally sustainable future?

Fortunately, there has been some signs as of late, that some of the really big corporations—those whose annual earnings in many cases surpass the GNP of even some of the smaller nations—have begun to look ahead and have become alarmed enough to start to seriously rethink their plans for their future. The question is, however, whether these leaders in the economic world and their political allies can change the climate of public opinion enough to persuade consumers that there is a viable alternative to what could otherwise turn into a doomsday scenario?

This last point, I think, is particularly important. Scientists, philosophers, and even religious leaders may argue and even preach to the public about what needs to be done. It is my guess that unless a real political will for change can be generated, the world will either slowly succumb to business as usual or else, when people finally realize what is happening, plunge themselves into a mood of stoic despair, deciding that in the face of certain death, they just might as well abandon all efforts to save themselves.

## The Earth and Humanity: Further Thoughts
(August 8, 2007)

When all is said and done (and I'm already wondering if I haven't already said as much as I can on the subject) I'm wondering if the biggest obstacle to any concerted effort to save the planet from the effects of global warming, or from any other threat to the long-term survival of the human race, remains the seeming insignificance, at least when measured on a cosmic timescale, of humanity's existence.

Consider, to begin with, the age of the Earth compared to that of the Universe. The latest estimates seem to hover around the figure of 13.7 billion years from the initial "big bang" to the present. Our sun, only one among billions upon billions of similar stars, is believed to have begun its life approximately five billion years ago, with its planets, including Earth, having been formed about 4.5 billion years ago. In other words, our home in this vast Universe might be seen merely as an "afterthought" in the Creator's mind, something that God cooked up to alleviate boredom after apparently eight or so billion years of watching celestial fireworks. (Actually, astrophysicists tell us the earlier generations of stars were too poor in elements to provide the more complex building blocks needed to generate life. What were needed were later generations of stars containing more complex elements such as carbon, and other "heavy metals.")

Second, we need to consider that it took nearly three billion years of evolution just to move beyond the stage of simple single-celled organisms. Creatures like the now long-deceased dinosaurs, the first birds, and even the apparently insignificant proto-mammals only showed up at the beginning of the Tertiary period, starting about 80 million years ago after most of the dinosaurs were wiped out, making the existence of mammals much safer. So too, the first primates, from which we are descended, only appeared a several million years ago.

Finally, we have to consider that the first hominids date back to less than a few hundred thousand years ago—or in terms of the often-used clock face scale, just a minute or so before noontime. Again, God seems to as have been in no hurry.

However, this suggests another simile, because with the sun believed to be halfway through its estimated ten-billion-year life span, we might say humanity is faced with a "High Noon" shoot-out situation, where one false move will result in its sudden demise. Either we get it right now, or for us there will soon be no future.

That is not to say that there might not be other similar situations elsewhere in the universe. In fact, from a theological perspective, assuming that the Creator knows what he is about and intended intelligent life to occur elsewhere as well, I'm convinced that we humans are hardly God's only successful experiment up until now. However, if that is the case, then I'm also inclined to think it is all the more possible that divine providence is not going to intervene to save us from ourselves if we ignore all the warnings and do ourselves in. God would not be so stupid, I think, as to have put "all the eggs in one basket." In other words, we humans, despite God's love for us, may not be quite as special as we like to think we are.

Viewed in terms of this cosmic perspective with its vast time scale, we might even say that cosmology frames the ultimate limits of ecology. Until we understand this, we have not seen, as the old saying goes, "the forest for the trees." I say this not to belittle the importance of our environmental concerns. Instead, I say this as a reminder that how long humanity survives is going to be left largely up to us. If, as Teilhard de Chardin said, God "made man to make himself," then it is equally possible that we have reached the point in evolution where we may be soon responsible for our own unmaking.

# A Final Word

Over the past few years, I have tried to pare down my own thoughts about ultimate realities to just a few simple, and what I consider inescapable, truths of universal significance. As I see them, these truths are basically *three*, corresponding to physical, psychological, and spiritual facts or laws but exemplified in a specifically religious corollary.

The first of these truths or facts has to do with the fundamental structure of the physical or material world and the nature of our existence within it. It is that *everything in this world, and, most likely, also the universe itself, is impermanent.* In addition—as if this is not sobering enough—since whatever permanence exists in the physical seem to be in an inverse proportion to its complexity, it would seem that humans, as the most complex of creatures, are among the least permanent of all.

While our first perception of life is in the process of living—as it should be, lest we lose heart—still the fact remains that in the end nothing in life is destined to last. This realization of the fundamental impermanence of everything in this world, especially of human life, has long been the foundation of philosophical and religious consciousness. The ancient religions of Asia (Hinduism and Buddhism in particular) have long cultivated this awareness as the doorway to the path of spiritual advancement, contrasting the illusion of the permanence of earthly things to the permanence of the spiritual world. Yet knowing what we now know of human origins, and of the relationship between the complexity of the human organism and the phenomenon of human consciousness, it has become ever more difficult to believe in the existence of a permanent human "soul" that can exist (or even preexist) apart from the body or return in another body to live again.

Much the same can be said regarding the other end of the spectrum, the universe itself. While some cosmologists once believed in the possibility of the universe reconstituting itself, and while some theoreticians may still dream of a "multiverse" or other "universes," empirical science knows of no other universe than our own. After the better part of a century of probing the far reaches of space, astronomers have come to the conclusion that the universe is in the process of infinitely expanding to the point where it will eventually become cold and dark, without life. Ancient dreams of a recycling or reciprocating universe (long a feature of Asian cosmology and revived in Nietzsche's theory of eternal recurrence) have been all but relegated to the realm of science fiction and mathematical flights of fancy.

Yet, even if there could be other "universes," or other branches of this universe that we may be forever incapable of contacting, would this solve the problem presented by the impermanence of our own life? On the contrary, it seems nothing we accomplish in this world can possibly escape the limits of time.

All this leads to the second major truth which is that, *psychologically* speaking, humanity has seldom been able to live contentedly with this impermanence. *One way or another, whether consciously or not, most of us seek to become immortal.*

The evidence for this statement is clear enough. As social scientist Ernest Becker (in his 1973 Pulitzer Prize-winning book, *The Denial of Death*) made clear to the discomfort of many, family, fame, and fortune are all, at their root, attempts to immortalize our own self. No one should find this fact surprising. Just as biological evolution would have ceased without the drive to reproduce ourselves, so too, without the psychological allure of making a name for ourselves, cultural evolution, indeed civilization itself, would also have come to a halt. Yet, as Becker pointed out, this same desire to perpetuate ourselves has also, time after time, especially when expressed through wars and conquests, led civilizations to the brink of disaster. This desire to cheat death, when magnified through self-aggrandizement, inevitably leads to the diminishment and, all too often, the destruction of others.

Thus it seems that, sooner or later, the advance of civilization, even the continuance of evolution itself, demands that somehow or in some way a further transition must take place. Such a transition would involve a crossing of a threshold of some sort, one that might move us from the realm of the mind, with its dependence on its physiological matrix, to the realm of the immaterial, to a realm beyond the confines of space and time. This has long been, of course, the realm of spirituality and the goal of religion, which, once it is freed from its everyday concern for physical survival, turns its attention to escaping, one way or another (reincarnation, resurrection, or a life of pure spiritual existence) the seeming finality of death and securing the promise of eternal life.

However, this promise comes at a steep price. It leads us directly to the *third* major truth, which involves a great or fundamental paradox. It is that *if the human self is to somehow survive death it can only be by way of transcending this same self.* This self-transcendence must be a movement from egocentric attachment to our own plans, our own security needs, indeed our very self, to a complete openness to the world beyond.

Here, of course, we run into a barrier of skepticism and doubt. No one, it seems, has ever come up with convincing scientific proof of the actual existence of such a spiritual world. This is hardly surprising, since such scientific proofs would necessarily remain on the level of the phenomenal world. Instead, what we do have, in terms of logical inference, is the truth that in order to achieve a goal or end that transcends our present physical boundaries we must likewise transcend our own all too often self-concerned psychological and even intellectual limits. Call it whatever you wish, such as Viktor Frankl's "paradoxical intent" or the spiritual law of "self-transcendence;" what it all comes down to is the "leap" of faith, the willingness to let go of our demand for absolute certainty that masks our insatiable desire for security and self-justification. This self-transcendence means, when translated into the language of spirituality, nothing less than dying to our own egocentricity, or, when phrased in overtly religious terms, a re-centering of ourselves on God.

Such a faith must not be confused with various beliefs that, although they may reassure us, ultimately may stand in the way of faith. Faith, in its most fundamental and purest sense is an absolute *trust* in what is altogether beyond us, a letting go of all our imagined certainties to place ourselves completely at the disposal of what lies totally beyond our ken.

This basic truth is, of course, "the great paradox," the great discovery of the Buddha, the great secret of the mystics, and the heart of the "Paschal Mystery" enacted by Christ. If the parable of the grain of wheat, which once sown "dies" to spring forth in new life, means anything at all, it is a promise that only in living for something—or Someone—greater than ourselves that we will find happiness and release from our fears.

Thus, it is my conviction (what I might call my "Christian corollary") that these three fundamental facts or laws, while accessible to anyone who studies the patterns of nature, nevertheless find their fullest expression in Christianity, with its central doctrines of Creation, Incarnation, and Redemption. If we are to escape from a return to the utter nothingness from which the universe came to be, it is only through the grace or gift of the Creator who somehow entered into the process of our own living and dying and through this process brought us the possibility of a new life beyond the confines of space and time.

# Index of Proper Names

**-A-**
Abraham, 116
Abu Ghraib, 38, 116-18
Acton, Lord, 50
Adam (and Eve), 23, 64-64;
 Second, 70, 90, 106
Afghanistan, 43, 115, 116, 122-23
Africa, 51-52, 77, 105, 108, 114,
 139; African Union, 39-40
Alabama, 52-53
Albanians, 29-30
Algeria, 114, 154
Allegiance, Pledge of, 48
Alpher, Ralph, 18
al Qaeda, 37, 43, 114, 121
America, Americans, 20, 31-32,
 34-44, 48-52, 56-57, 60-62, 93,
 104-5, 111-12, 114, 116-19,
 124-25, 129-30, 157, 166, 172-
 173, 176, 179-80
Annan, Kofi, 51
Annapolis Initiative, 126-27
Antarctic, 178
Anthony, St., 134
Aquinas, Thomas, St., 89, 136
Arctic, 178
Arafat, Yasser, 42
Argentina, 117
Aristotle, 14, 89-90, 92, 126, 129,
 133, 163-64
Arius, 16
Armageddon, 41, 84, 179
Armenia, Armenians, 114
Ashoka, King, 88
Ataturk, Gamel, 32
Athanasius, St., 134
Athens, Athenians, 59
Augustine, St., 21, 27, 35-36, 63-
 65, 78-79, 89, 98, 106, 137,
 144-46, 149-50, 166
Austria, 60
Aziz, Terak, 114

**-B-**
Baathists, 41, 118
Babylonian Empire, 113
Baghdad, 116, 118
Balkans, 29-30
Barth, Karl, xiii
Becker, Ernest, 188
Begin, Menachim, 42
Bellah, Robert, 129
Benedict, St., 138
Benedict XVI, Pope, 25, 105, 107-
 109, 125-26
Bergson, Henri, 157-58
Bible, 16, 20-22, 30, 34, 40, 88,
 113, 116, 133, 139; -belt, 56-
 57; canon of, 72-74, 99-100;
 interpretation of, 71-73,100,
 102-03, 112, 129, 145
bin Laden, Osama, 34-35, 40, 43,
 114, 165
Black Elk, 174-75
Bloy, Leon, 149
Britain, British, 124
Bruno, Giordano, 22-23
Buddha, Buddhism, 2, 68, 83, 130,
 171, 187; and Christianity 87-
 88; Hinayana or Theraveda 88-
 89; Mahayana, 88-89
Burundi, 51
Bush, George W., 33, 35, 57, 119
Bush, George H.W., 117-18
Byzantine Empire, 125

**-C-**
Cahokia, 172
Calcutta, 54
Calvinism, 22
Cameron, James, 86
Camp David, 111,125
Campanella, Thomas of, 22-23
Canaan, Canaanites, 30
Canada, 61-62
Carter, Jimmy, 91

Catholics, Catholicism, ix, xv, 6, 9, 25, 27-28, 36, 44, 49-50, 52, 55, 71, 77, 95-97, 158-59, 163; in Africa, 105; in Asia, 105; beliefs and disbeliefs, 104-5; European, 105; Latin American, 105, 108; meaning of term "Catholic" 101
CDF (Congregation for the Doctrine of the Faith), 107
Ceylon (Sri Lanka), 88
Chaisson, Eric, 11
Chalcedon, Council of, 70
Chaldea, Chaldean, 118
Chesterton, G. K., 13, 76
Chile, 117
Christianity, Christians, 8, 12, 16, 19, 28, 29, 33-37, 40-41, 44, 52, 116, 126, 176; churches, 91-110; Eastern, 48, 63-64, 68, 77, 95, 101, 106; Egyptian, 32, 79, 114; essential 8, 80-81; European, 105; divisions within, 71, 102-3; Iraqi, 114, 118-19; Jesus and, 63-90; origins of, 122-23; Palestinian, 115 (*see also* Catholic, Orthodox, Protestant)
Chalcedon, Council of, 16, 85
Charlemagne, Emperor, 101
China, 39, 42, 46, 118, 179-80
Chiotti, Quentin, 182
Christ (of Faith), 63, 77, 82-83; divinity of, 74; as Second Adam, 70, 90, 106
Confucius, 38
Constantine, Emperor, 35, 74, 88, 101, 140, 142
Constitution, of U.S.A., 122
Copernicus, 22, 167
Copts, 114
Corps of Engineers, Army, 54
Coyne, George V., 23-24

Creation Science, 20-21, 57, 113, 127
Crusades, 113, 127, 135
Cusa, Nicholas of, 22-23
Cyril of Jerusalem, St., 1, 101

-D-
Dalai Lama, 166
Daniel, Prophet, Book of, 93
Darfur, 39-40
Darwin, Charles, Darwinism, 24-26, 28, 164
Dawkins, Richard, 11
*DaVinci Code* (novel), 12, 75
Dead Sea Scrolls, 93, 133, 141
Denmark, Danes, 119
Dennett, Daniel, 11
DeSoto, Hernando, 173
Doerfinger, Richard, 58
Dresden, 35

-E-
East St. Louis, Ill., 172-73
East Timor, 115
Eckhardt, Johann, 89, 150
Eddington, Arthur, 18
Edwards, Jonathan, 67
Ehrman, Bart D., 75
Egypt, Egyptians, 41, 79, 111, 114, 134, 141, 148, 151
Einstein, Albert, 18, 24, 153-54, 164
Elijah, Prophet, 142
El Salvador, 117
Engels, Friedrich, 26
Enlightenment, the, 71
Ephraim the Syrian, St., 85
Epicureans, 153
Epimenides, 150
Epiphany, 64-65
Episcopal Church, 91
Erikson, Erik, 5, 170
Essenes, 159
Eucharist, 67, 87

Europe, 104-5
Evangelicals, -ism, 75, 77, 142, 178
Existentialists, 162

**-F-**
Fatah, 127
Fowler, James W., 1
France, French, 60, 114, 141, 173, 180
Freud, Sigmund, 26, 159
Friedmann, Aleksandr, 18
Frankl, Viktor, 1-2, 4, 112, 162, 189

**-G-**
Galileo, 20, 22, 126, 145, 167
Gamow, George, 18
Gandhi, Mohandas, 74, 137-38
Gautama, Siddartha (see Buddha)
Gaza, 124-25, 127
Guatemala, 117
Genesis, Book of, 20, 106, 176, 178
Geneva Conventions, 36, 117
Gingerich, Owen, 23-24
Global Health Fund, 51
Gnostics, Gnosticism 12-13, 79-80, 102
God, belief in, 2; concepts of, 3, 4, 6, 10-11, 15, 16, 26, 66-67; as Creator, 48, 87-88; existence of, 6, 9-10, 27-28; as first cause, 82; goodness of, 4; immanence of 89-90, 149-50, 174-75; suffering of, 156; transcendence of, 88-89, 174-75; trust in, 2-5, 15
Greece, Greeks, 53, 126, 152, 160, 165; Orthodox Church, 93; Greek (Melchite) Catholics, 118
Gregory the Great, Pope, 99

**-H-**
Hadith, 121
Hamas, 125, 127
Harris, John, 58
Harris, Sam, 10-11
Hasan and Hussein, 121
Hasids, Hasidism, 157
Hawking, Stephen, 145
Hebrews, 66, 148, 151-52, 155 (*see also* Jews)
Hegel, Georg W. F., 89
Hemmingway, Ernest, 169
Henry VIII, King, 60
Herzl, Theodore, 123
Hezbollah, 41-42, 125
Hinduism, 74, 88, 122, 136, 154-155, 187
Hirohito, Emperor, 42
Hiroshima, 36, 42
Hitchens, Christopher, 10-11
Hitler, Adolph, 32, 162
Holocaust, 113, 156
Holy Land, 30, 112-13
Holy Spirit, 70, 72, 103-4, 137, 166,
Hoyle, Fred, 18
Hubble, Edwin, 18
Hussein, Saddam, 35, 37, 38, 39, 59, 118-19

**-I-**
Ignatius of Antioch, St., 156
Independence, Declaration of, 48, 61
Indonesia, 41, 114
India, 54, 136, 159, 180
Inquisition, 22, 145, 150
International Criminal Court, 39-40, 42, 117
Inuit, 160
Iraq, 35-36, 41, 43, 114, 116, 118, 121-22
Iran, 39, 41, 119, 121
Ireland, 136, 138

Irenaeus, St., 79, 101
Isaiah, Prophet, 93
Islam, 32, 53, 66, 108, 111-28
Israel, Israelis, 32, 37-38, 42-43, 111, 113, 123-25

-J-
Jacobovici, Shimcha, 86
Jains, 74, 171
James, Apostle, 2, 68-69, 86
Japan, 36, 112, 117
Jeremiah, Prophet, 93, 178
Jesus, 63-90, consciousness of, 70, 78, 84-85; as Christ (Messiah), 63, 69, 74, 77, 82-83, 85, 89-90; death of, 66-67; ethics of, 3, 38, 130; faith of, 74, 78-79, 85; of History, 63, 81, 92, 95 103, 133; in Islam, 121; origins of, 68; resurrection of, 8-9; Seminar, 77; as Second Adam (see Adam); as Son of God, 79; as Word of God, 78; various views of, 142
Jerusalem, 86; Destruction of 83, 123, 125
Jews, Judaism, 30, 53, 66, 88, 92, 109, 113, 116, 121-23, 140-41, 157
Judeo-Christian tradition, 40, 53
John, the Apostle: Gospel of, 69-70, 81, 103, 108, 126, 144; Epistles of 98, 161
John the Baptist, 76, 138
John XXIII, Pope, 99
John Paul II, Pope, 25, 28, 36, 58, 75, 99-100, 107, 177
Johnson, Samuel, 48
Jordan, Kingdom of, 32
Joseph, St., 68
Joshua, Book of, 29-30, 113
Judas, Iscariot, Gospel of, 79-80
Judges, Book of, 113
Judgment, Last, 136

Jung, Carl, 93, 134

-K-
Kant, Immanuel, 38
Kaplan, Robert, 35-36
Karzai, Mahmud, 122
Knox, Ronald, 93
Kohlberg, Lawrence, 4
Koran, *see* Qur'an
Korea, North, 39
Kosovo, 29-31
Kurds, Kurdistan, 42, 118
Kuschner, Harold, 17, 155

-L-
LaHaye, Tim, 92-93
Lakota (Sioux) 174
LaSalle, Robert Cavelier de-, 173
Latin America, 108
Lavada, William, 107
Lebanon, 32, 34, 41-43, 111, 114, 123-25
Lederman, Leon, 164
Lemaître, Georges, 17-19
LeMay, Curtis, 42
Lenin, Vladimir, 135
Leo the Great, Pope, 99
Leo XIII, Pope, 45
Lewis, C. S., 8-9, 20, 80-81, 160-161
Loevinger, Jane, 170
Luke, Gospel of, 68, 75, 137; Acts of the Apostles, 150
Luther, Martin, 22, 49, 67, 71-72

-M-
McVeigh, Timothy, 45
Mao, Zedong, 162
Maritain, Jacques, 30, 149
Maritain, Raïssa, 30
Mark, Gospel of, 68, 70, 72, 103
Marshall Plan, 30-31
Mary, Mother of Jesus, 68; as "Mother of God," 104, 120;

as "ever virgin," 68
Maryland, 52
Mary I (Tudor), Queen, 60
Marx, Karl, Marxism, 135
Marzen, Mahmoud, 126-27
Maslow, Abraham, 149
Masons, Masonry, 48-49
Matthew, Gospel of, 68, 72, 75, 81, 95, 125
Mechtild of Magdeburg, 150
Meir, Golda, 42
Messalians, 134
Messiah, messianism, 122-23
Merton, Thomas, ix, xi-xiii, 89
Metz, Johann Baptist, 76
Michigan, 60, 141, 169
Miller, Jonathan, 11
Mississippi River, 54
Mississippian culture, 173-74
Mohammed, 83, 115, 119, 121, 128
Montanists. 93
Moore, Roy, Judge, 52-53
Moses, 83, 142
Moyers, Bill, 35, 178
Muslims, 31-32, 34, 40-41, 44, 60, 111-28

-N-
Nagasaki, 36, 42
Nag Hammadi, 142
National Council of Churches, 116
Nazis, Nazism, 2, 11, 113, 117, 144
Nazrallah, Hassan, 41-42
Neanderthals, 143
Nestorianism, 70
Newman, John Henry (Cardinal), 2, 4, 108-10
New Orleans, 54-55
Nicea, Council of, 16, 74, 85; Nicean Creed, 91, 142
Nicholas of Myra, St., 137
Nietzsche, Friedrich, 131, 144, 187
North Korea, 39

-O-
O'Connor, Carroll, 146
Olmert, Ehud 42, 126
Ontario, 62
Origen, 12, 23
Orthodoxy, Eastern, 77
   (*see also* Christianity, Eastern)
Oslo Accord, 125
Ottoman Empire, 29, 124-25

-P-
Pacholcyzk, Tadeusz, 58
Pakistan, 35, 114, 124
Palestine, Palestinians, 32, 42, 111, 124, 127, 134
Pascal, Blaise, 9-10, 89
Paul, the Apostle, 9, 16, 59, 64, 66-67, 70, 72, 81, 87, 95, 98, 106, 148, 160
Paul VI, Pope, 99
Paul, Gregory S., 56
Pennsylvania, 52
Pentecostalism, 93
Persia, 125-26 (*see also* Iran)
Peter, St., 59, 78, 100; Second Epistle of, 64, 83, 90
Pharisees, 132
Philo of Alexandria, 154
Piaget, Jean, 5
Pius XII, Pope, 18, 31, 109
Plotinus, 150, 154
Plato, Platonists, 133, 154-55, 162-63
Pohle, Joseph, 22
Post Secrets, 146-47
Protestants, Protestantism, 71, 88, 97, 102-3, 109, 158; Iraqi, 118
Puritans, 52
Pythagoreans, 159

-Q-
Qur'an, 112, 116, 123, 125, 135

## -R-

Rahner, Karl, 155
Ratzinger, Josef (Cardinal) 75, 107 (*see also* Benedict XVI, Pope)
Reformation, 71, 88, 101, 103-4, 109, 126, 158
Regensburg, 125-26
Renaissance, 103
Revelation, Book of, 83-84, 93-94, 133, 135
Rhode Island, 53, 60
Robinson, Geoffrey, 12
Rome, Romans, 49-50, 59, 140; Empire, 113, 120, 123 (*see also* Vatican)
Roman Catholic Church, 94, 100-101
Rousseau, Jean Jacques, 6-7
Rubin, Theodore, 14
Ruanda, 51
Russia, 61, 157

## -S-

Sabbath, 140-41
Sadat, Anwar, 111
Saudi Arabia, 114
Samarra, 121
Santayana, George, 31, 47
Sartre, Jean-Paul, 162
Satan, 133-34
Saudi Arabia, 41
School of the Americas, 117
Schönborn, Christof, 27-28
Schweitzer, Albert, 76-77, 84
Scriptures, canon of, 72; canonical interpretation of, 75, 102
Second Vatican Council, xii, 9
September 11, 2001, 31-32, 36-37, 40, 43-44, 47, 115
Serbia, Serbs, 29-30
Servetius, Michael, 22
Sgreccia, Elio, 58
Sharia, 53, 119
Shia, Shiites, 40-41, 43-44, 121-22
Sipe, Richard, 96
Smith, Wilfred Cantwell, 1
Socrates, 60, 83, 142
Solidarity, 37, 99
Somalia, 51
Southern Baptists, 91
Soviet Union, 61, 141
Spain, 113
Stalin, Joseph, 162
Stephen, Pope, 101
Stoics, Stoicism, 154, 163
Sudan, 39-40
Sunnis, 40-41, 43-44, 121-22
Syria, Syrians, 32, 41; Christian, 118, 134

## -T-

Taliban, 40, 43, 66
Tanach, 155
*Tao*, 4
Teilhard de Chardin, Pierre, 17, 19, 28, 185
Ten Commandments, 34, 52-53
Texas, 46
Therapeutoi, 159
Tillich, Paul, 1, 4, 91
Tokyo, 42
Tolstoy, Leo, 74
Tournier, Paul, 146-47
Toynbee, Arnold, 31, 153-54
Travers, Robert, 169
Trent, Council of, 158
Trinity, 4, 20, 154-55, 166
Turks, Turkey, 29, 31-32, 113-114, 124

## -U-

United Arab Republic, 124
United Nations, 33, 37-38, 39, 61, 124; Declaration of Human Rights, 60, 117
United States (U.S.A.) 32, 38, 42-43, 51; Air Force, 118; Army

Corps of Engineers, 54; religion in, 57, 117; (*see also* America, Americans)
Unitarian-Universalists, 142, 155

**-V-**
Vatican, 63, 97, 99, 119;
    Biblical Commission, 58;
    Vatican I (Council) 100-101;
    Vatican II (Council), xiii, 8, 48, 99, 107-8, 109, 158
Vaurouillon, William of, 22
Versailles, Treaty of, 31
Vincent of Lerins, St., 109
Voltaire, 82-83

**-W-**
Waco, 45, 93, 112
Wahabism, 41, 121, 141
Walton, Isaac, 169
Whitehead, A. N., 89, 138, 157
Wiesel, Elie, 4
Williams, Roger, 53
Wilson, Flip, 134
Wisconsin, 60
Wisdom, Book of, 4
World Council of Churches, 33
World War I, 31; II, 31, 33, 43, 112, 117; III, 40-41

**-X-Y-Z-**
Zawahiri, 40-41
Zionists, Zionism, 123-24

# About the Author

**Richard William Kropf** was born in Milwaukee, Wisconsin, in 1932. He graduated from Sacred Hear Seminary, Detroit, with a Bachelor in Liberal Arts, in 1954 and from St. John's Provincial Seminary, Plymouth, Michigan, in 1958 with a Bachelor degree in Theology awarded by the Catholic University of America. After ordination to the priesthood in 1958, he worked as a parish priest in the Diocese of Lansing, Michigan until 1968. He went on to earn masters and doctoral degrees in philosophical and systematic theology from the University of Ottawa in 1971 and 1973 and, after research in France, was awarded a doctorate in sacred theology by the Université St-Paul after the publication, in 1980, of his dissertation *Teilhard, Scripture and Revelation: A Study of Teilhard de Chardin's Reinterpretation of Pauline Themes.*

Following a decade of teaching courses in philosophy, religious studies, the psychology of religion, and theology in various colleges and seminaries in Michigan, and after further study in the Holy Land followed by travels in Egypt and Greece, Kropf sought official Church permission to live in solitude as a hermit or anchorite, taking permanent vows in this state in 1984 in conformity with Canon 603 of 1983 Code of Canon Law.

Kropf is also the author of *Evil and Evolution: A Theodicy* (1984, 2004), *Faith, Security and Risk: The Dynamics of Spiritual Growth* (1990, 2005), *The Faith of Jesus: The Jesus of History and the Stages of Faith* (2006), and most recently, *Logical Faith: Introducing a Scientific View of Spirituality and Religion*, a cooperative project with a fellow advocate of Teilhard's groundbreaking ideas, the mathematician and physicist Joseph Provenzano.

Kropf's other interests include astronomy and wildlife photography. He maintains a Web site at www.stellamar.net.